VATICAN ▲ 202

CASTE

✪
VILLA
BORGHESE

MUSEO E GALLERIA
BORGHESE

LUDOVISI

PORTA
PIA

TRINITÀ
I

BIBLIOTECA
NAZIONALE

PALAZZO
BARBERINI

S. MARIA
D. ANGELI

Piazza del
Cinquecento

CITTÀ UNIVERSITARIA

TREVI

GIARDINI DEL
QUIRINALE

STAZIONE
TERMINI

AZZO DEL
UIRINALE

QUIRINALE

TIBURTINO

VIMINALE

Piazza
Vittorio Em. II

PARCO
TRAIANO

Piazza di Pta
Maggiore

FORUM
✪

COLISEUM
✪

PALATINO

Piazza
S. Giovanni
in Laterano

S. GIOVANNI
IN LATERANO

OBELISCO
DI AXUM

CELIO

TRINITA DEI MONTI ▲ 314

TRASTEVERE ▲ 351

VILLA BORGHESE ▲ 369

CAMPO DEI FIORI
One of the most
colorful markets in
the Eternal City.
PIAZZA NAVONA
The epitome of
Roman Baroque,
showcase of the
work of rivals Bernini
and Borromini.

FONTANA DI TREVI
Your return to Rome
will be guaranteed if,
with your back to the
fountain, you toss a
coin into the water.
TRINITÀ DEI MONTI
A meeting place full
of local color, a
stone's throw from

the Via Condotti, the
artery of shopping.
TRASTEVERE
Now a center of
nightlife, the
quarter's old working
class spirit lives on in
its many small shady
piazzas and narrow
winding streets.

VILLA BORGHESE
In Rome's largest
public park, the
Galeria Borghese,
where the collections
of Cardinal Scipione,
Borghese are shown,
and the Villa Giulia,
housing the Etruscan
Museum.

● Encyclopedia section

■ **NATURE** The natural heritage: species and habitats characteristic to the area covered by the guide, annotated and illustrated by naturalist authors and artists.

HISTORY, LANGUAGE AND RELIGION The impact of international historical events on local history, from the arrival of the first inhabitants, with key dates appearing in a timeline above the text.

ARTS AND TRADITIONS Customs and traditions and their continuing role in contemporary life.

ARCHITECTURE The architectural heritage, focusing on style and topology, a look at rural and urban buildings, major civil, religious and military monuments.

AS SEEN BY PAINTERS A selection of paintings of the city or country by different artists and schools, arranged chronologically or thematically.

AS SEEN BY WRITERS An anthology of texts focusing on the city or country, taken from works of all periods and countries, arranged thematically.

▲ Itineraries

Each itinerary begins with a map of the area to be explored.

❖ **SPECIAL INTEREST** These sites are not to be missed. They are highlighted in gray boxes in the margins.

★ **EDITOR'S CHOICE** Sites singled out by the editor for special attention.

INSETS On richly illustrated double pages, these insets turn the spotlight on subjects deserving more in-depth treatment.

◆ Practical information

All the travel information you will need before you go and when you get there.

USEFUL ADDRESSES A selection of the best hotels and restaurants compiled by an expert.

PLACES TO VISIT A handy table of addresses and opening hours.

APPENDICES Bibliography, list of illustrations and general index.

MAP SECTION Maps of all the areas covered by the guide, followed by an index; these maps are marked out with letters and figures making it easy for the reader to pinpoint a town, region or site.

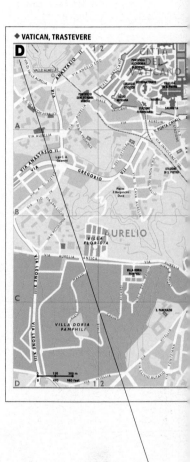

◆ VATICAN, TRASTEVERE

◆ VATICAN, TRAS

Each map in the map section is designated by a letter. In the itineraries, all the sites of interest are given a map reference (for example: **F** B2).

The mini-map pinpoints the itinerary within the wider area covered by the guide.

The itinerary map shows the main sites, the editor's choices and the places of special interest.

✪ This symbol indicates places of special interest.

▲ TRASTEVERE

From early times Trastevere (which means "across the Tiber") was primarily a working-class quarter. In the 2nd and 3rd centuries it was the main center for communities belonging to oriental religions ● 252. The early presence of Christians in this area led to the foundation of three titular churches in the 4th century: Santa Maria in Trastevere, San Crisogono and Santa Cecilia. After the period of decline following the great invasions and repeated sacking of the city ● 30, the population was concentrated around these buildings.
EXPANSION. From the 10th and 11th centuries, like the rest of the city, the neighborhood experienced rapid expansion, marked by the development of the new river port known as Ripagrande or the Ripa Romea. Then in the middle of the 13th century Trastevere was integrated into the administrative system of the city of Rome, which brought the number of Rome's districts or rioni up to thirteen. A few noble families

⏱ One day
◆ PL03-B4-C3-C4-D3-D4
E C1-K1

1. ISOLA TIBERINA
2. PALAZZO AND TOUR ANGUILLARA
3. CHURCH OF SAN CRISOGONO
4. BASILICA OF SANTA CECILIA
5. CHURCH OF THE MADONNA DELL'ORTO
6. OSPEDALE SAN MICHELE
7. PORTA PORTESE
8. CHURCH OF SAN FRANCESCO A RIPA
9. SYRIAN SANCTUARY OF THE JANICULUM
10. EXCUBITORIUM
11. BASILICA OF SANTA MARIA IN TRASTEVERE
12. CHURCH OF SAN PIETRO IN MONTORIO
13. ACQUA PAOLA
14. JANICULE
15. CHURCH OF SANTA MARIA DEI SETTE DOLORI
16. CHURCH OF SANTA MARIA DELLA SCALA
17. PORTA SETTIMIANA
18. PIAZZA TRILUSSA
19. PONTE SISTO
20. PALAZZO CORSINI
21. FARNESINA
22. MONASTERY OF SANT'ONOFRIO

(including the Stefaneschi, Papareschi and Alberteschi) lived in the area, but of their homes only those belonging to the Anguillara and the Mattei have survived from that period (both heavily restored). When the papacy returned from Avignon, for a little while Trastevere became the seat of the Studium Urbis university. At that time, there were only two points of communication with the left bank of the Tiber: the Isola Tiberina (Tiber island) and from 1475 the Ponte Sisto, which was intended to give pilgrims access to St Peter's.
ACCESS ROUTES. Until the 14th century no great town planning initiatives affected this district, its population being concentrated close to the Tiber. Numerous churches were built or renovated during the 16th century, but very few palazzi were constructed. In this period the Via della Lungara took shape, running parallel to the Tiber to provide an easier link with the Borgo (the rione of St Peter's ▲ 212). But it was not until the 19th century that the main avenues were built: the Viale di Trastevere running through the middle of the district, and the Lungotevere skirting the river.
A LIVELY QUARTER ★. Trastevere remained a predominantly working-class area until the 1960's, when it increasingly came to be seen as a neighborhood of restaurants and nightlife. But in the morning it retrieves some of its traditional character, and the vicoli (small streets) around Santa Maria in Trastevere offer a glimpse of the daily life of the past. The true spirit of the district is revealed in the month of July

THE TRASTEVERE, THE QUARTER OF THE NIGHT ✪
Having attracted travelers and artists since antiquity, the Trastevere is Rome's bohemian quarter par excellence. Today it is frequented most especially by night owls, rivaling the Via Veneto ▲ 302, capital of la dolce vita, and the Piazza Navona ▲ 276 in the number of establishments that stay open until the early hours. It has lost much of its original character after housing speculation in the 1960s drove out the craftsmen, the small local shops and the ordinary working people. However, something of its old spirit returns in July during the Festa de' Noantri ("our own feast"), when restaurant tables invade the sidewalks and processions, concerts, theatrical performances and firework displays fill the small squares and narrow streets.

THE TRASTEVERINI
With their own dialect, the people of Trastevere had always considered themselves the descendants of the ancient Romans. The quarter was frequently a source of uprisings, consequently the popes distrusted the Trasteverini. In 1849 this was the area that continued to defend the short-lived Republic of Rome to the very end.

350

351

At the beginning of each itinerary, the distance, the suggested means of travel and the time it will take to cover the area are indicated beneath the maps:
🚶 On foot
🚤 By boat
⏱ Duration

★ The star symbol signifies sites singled out by the editor for special attention.

● ▲ ◆
The above symbols within the text provide cross-references to a place or a theme discussed elsewhere in the guide.

03

FRONT ENDPAPER Not to be missed
BACK ENDPAPER Rome
02 How to use this guide
06 Introduction to the itineraries
07 The authors

● **Encyclopedia section**

15 NATURE
16 The Tiber
18 Flora and fauna of the ruins
20 Villa Doria Pamphilj
22 The Pineta Sacchetti
24 The trees of Rome

25 THE HISTORY OF ROME
26 Chronology
34 The institutions of Antiquity
36 The sack of Rome
38 The apostolic Church of Rome
40 Archeology in Rome
42 The Roman language

45 ARTS AND TRADITIONS
46 Legends and traditions
48 Festivals
50 The Order of Malta
52 Pontifical ceremonies
54 Restoration work
56 Food: *Carciofi alla Romana*
60 Roman specialties

59 ARCHITECTURE
60 The development of the city
62 Building materials and techniques
64 Roman arches and vaults
66 Buildings for entertainment
68 Water in the ancient town
70 Temples and commemorative monuments
72 Medieval towers and dwellings
74 Churches of the Middle Ages
76 The Roman marble cutters
78 Counter-Reformation architecture
80 Churches: Baroque innovations
82 The art of "trompe-l'œil"
84 Baroque stage effects
86 Renaissance and Baroque palaces
88 Villas and gardens
90 Neoclassicism and Eclectism
92 Fascism and the postwar period
94 The classical orders

95 ROME AS SEEN BY PAINTERS

105 ROME AS SEEN BY WRITERS

▲ Itineraries in Rome

127 THE CAPITOL, THE FORUM AND THE PALATINE
132 The Capitoline museums
136 The Roman Forum
147 The Palatine

153 FROM THE FORUM HOLITORIUM TO THE COLISEUM
162 The imperial forums
170 The Coliseum

175 CIRCUS MAXIMUS AND THE AVENTINE

185 THE COELIAN HILL
193 San Clemente
196 The Latran

201 THE VATICAN
209 St Peter's Basilica
218 The Sistine Chapel
222 The Raphael Rooms
224 The Vatican museums

237 FROM PONTE SANT'ANGELO TO THE GHETTO
240 Via Giulia
247 Around Campo de'Fiori
252 The Ghetto

255 THE CAMPO MARZIO FROM THE GESÙ TO PALAZZO MADAMA
257 The Church of the Gesù
262 The Domes of Rome
264 The Pantheon
270 San Luigi dei Francesi

273 AROUND PIAZZA NAVONA

287 THE QUIRINAL
292 Galleria Nazionale d'Arte Antica
298 Fontana di Trevi

303 IL TRIDENTE
313 Piazza di Spagna
315 The Villa Medici

317 VIA APPIA ANTICA
319 The Baths of Caracalla
324 The Catacombs

331 FROM THE BATHS OF DIOCLETIAN TO SAN PIETRO IN VINCOLI
336 National Roman Museum
342 Basilica Santa Maria Maggiore

349 TRASTEVERE
352 Isola Tiberina
363 The Janiculum

367 FROM VILLA GIULIA TO THE FORO ITALICO
370 Villa Giulia
372 Villa Borghese

379 ROME OUTSIDE THE WALLS
384 Cinecittà

389 TIVOLI AND PALESTRINA
400 The Nile mosaic

403 OSTIA
408 The corporations' mosaics

◆ Practical information

418 Getting there
420 Staying in Rome from A to Z
429 Useful words and phrases
430 Hotels, Restaurants, Cafés and bars selected by Paul Betts of the *Financial Times*
445 Shopping
446 Places to visit
466 Bibliography
470 List of illustrations
480 Glossary
482 Biographical index
491 General index

501 MAP SECTION
502 Street index
  A Monte Mario
  B Villa Borghese
  C Villa Ada, Villa Torlonia
  D Vatican, Trastevere
  E Campo Marzio, Celio
  F Pantheon, Quirinale
  G Around Stazione Termini
  H Testaccio, Ostiense
  I Via Appia Antica
526 Metro plan
528 Bus map of the city center

CAPITOL, FORUM, AND PALATINE ▲ 127
The hub of Roman civilization, between the Capitol, center of political power, and the Palatine, cradle of the city.

FORUM HOLITORIUM TO THE COLISEUM ▲ 153
In the heart of imperial Rome, from the forums to the finest amphitheater in the Roman world.

CIRCUS MAXIMUS AND THE AVENTINE ▲ 175 With its public and monastic gardens, the Aventine is an oasis of quiet and calm, removed from the bustle of the city.

THE COELIAN HILL ▲ 185 The vineyards and orchards on the Coelian Hill are the legacy of the religious orders who settled there in the Middle Ages.

THE VATICAN ▲ 201
The greatest concentration of artistic treasures in the world in the smallest state in Europe, the very center of Christianity.

PONTE SANT'ANGELO TO THE GHETTO ▲ 237
In Campo Marzio, the colorful stalls of Campo dei Fiori, Renaissance palazzi and the narrow streets of the Ghetto.

GESÙ TO PALAZZO MADAMA ▲ 255
Admiring the achievements of Roman builders and genius of architects of the Counter-Reformation.

PIAZZA NAVONA AND AROUND ▲ 273
The finest of piazzas, shaped like a Roman circus, showcase of the genius of the Baroque masters Bernini and Borromini.

THE QUIRINAL ▲ 287
From the corridors of power in the presidential palace to echoes of *la dolce vita* on Via Veneto and the dazzling Fontana di Trevi.

IL TRIDENTE ▲ 303
A place for strolling, a shopper's paradise, and the district of luxury hotels, today's Il Tridente is the product of 19th-century rebuilding.

VIA APPIA ANTICA ▲ 317
This road, 330 miles long, constitutes a necropolis outside the city walls, with columbariums, altars and catacombs.

BATHS OF DIOCLETIAN TO SAN PIETRO IN VINCOLI ▲ 331
A fine example of the great sweep of the centuries that is Rome's fascination.

TRASTEVERE ▲ 349
A center of nightlife, the quarter "across the Tiber" retains its working class spirit in the streets around the Basilica of Santa Maria in Trastevere.

VILLA GIULIA TO FORO ITALICO ▲ 367
From the Villa Borghese, Rome's green lung, and a cluster of museums to Fascism's great sports complex.

ROME OUTSIDE THE WALLS ▲ 379
Memories of Early Christian martyrs, dreams of stardom at Cinecittà and symbols of Fascist Rome at EUR.

TIVOLI, PALESTRINA, AND OSTIA ▲ 389, 398, 403
A visit to Roman towns, with their fine mosaics, and the Villa d'Este, with its 500 fountains.

→ **NUMEROUS SPECIALISTS AND ACADEMICS HAVE CONTRIBUTED TO THIS GUIDE.**

MASTERWORK: CLAUDIA MOATTI

● Encylopedia section

■ **NATURE**
Guido Prola, Livia Tedeschini
■ **HISTORY**
Massimo Bray, Jean-Louis Fournel,
Claudia Moatti, Daniel Nony
■ **LANGUAGE**
Raffaele Simone
■ **ARTS AND TRADITIONS**
Corinne Paul, Simone Pelizzoli,
Mauro Quercioli
■ **ARCHITECTURE**
Oliver Bonfait, Catherine Brice,
Stéphane Guégan, Étienne Hubert
■ **ROME AS SEEN BY PAINTERS**
Antonio del Guercio
■ **ROME AS SEEN BY WRITERS**
Lucinda Gane

▲ Itineraries in Rome

Noëlle de La Blanchardière,
Catherine Brice (modern times),
Filippo Coarelli (Antiquity),
Étienne Hubert (Middle Ages),
Christian Michel (modern times),
Claudia Moatti

◆ Practical information

Grégory Leroy, Corinne Paul,
Angela and Francesca Catello,
Laure Raffaëlli-Fournel. Special thanks
to Paul Betts of the *Financial Times*

EVERYMAN GUIDES
Published by Alfred A Knopf

Completely revised and updated in 2003

Originally published in France by Nouveaux-
Loisirs, a subsidiary of Editions Gallimard,
Paris, 1993. Copyright © 1993 by Editions
Nouveaux-Loisirs

Translated by
Louis Marcelin-Rice and Kate Newton

Practical section translated by
Sébastien Marcelin-Rice

Edited and typeset by
Book Creation Services, London

Printed and bound in Italy by
Editoriale Lloyd

EVERYMAN GUIDES
Gloucester Mansions
140a Shaftesbury Avenue
London WC2H 8HD
guides@everyman.uk.com

ROME
EDITOR
Laure Raffaëlli-Fournel *assisted by* Jean-Louis
Malroux, Corinne Paul, Nathalie Salis, Clarisse
Deniau (architecture)
LAYOUT
Riccardo Tremori,
Michèle Bisgambiglia (nature)
PICTURE RESEARCH
William Fischer *assisted by* Caterina
D'Agostino and Perrine Henri
MAPS : Édigraphie, Éric Gillion,
Eugène Flurey and Catherine Totem (color)
COORDINATION
Eglal Errera
RESEARCH
Laure Raffaëlli-Fournel

ILLUSTRATIONS
Nature: Anne Bodin, Jean Chevallier,
François Desbordes, Claire Felloni, Jean-Michel
Kacédan, Pascal Robin, John Wilkinson
Architecture: Pierre Boutin, Nicolette Castle,
Hugh Dixon, Sandra Doyle, Jean-Marie
Guillou, Jean-Benoit Héron, Olivier Hubert,
Pierre de Hugo, Roger Hutchins, Jean-Michel
Kacédan, Philippe Lhez, Philippe Mignon,
Pierre Poulain, Claude Quiec, Jean-Claude
Sénée, Jean-Louis Serret, Jean-Michel Sinier,
Mike Shœbridge, Tony Townsend
Itineraries: Hubert Goger, Jean-Marie Guillou,
Olivier Hubert, Claude Quiec, Bruno
Lenormand, Jean-Pierre Pontcabare
Computer graphics: Paul Coulbois

PHOTOGRAPHY
Araldo De Luca, Antonello Idini, Marzio
Marzot, Gabriella Peyrot

WE WOULD ALSO LIKE TO THANK
Dominique Fernandes, Francoise
Gaultier, Pierre Gros, Jean Héritier,
Louis Marcelin-Rice, Catherine Metzger,
Claire Sotinel, Florence Valdès-Forain,
and the École Française de Rome

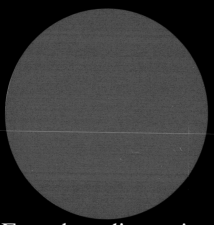

Encyclopedia section

15   Nature

25   The history of Rome

45   Arts and Traditions

59   Architecture

95   Rome as seen by painters

105   Rome as seen by writers

In 1477 the market which for decades had been held in Piazza del Campidoglio and the adjacent streets was moved to Piazza Navona, where it remained and operated every day until 1869. In acquiring the equivalent function of a Piazza del Comune or a Piazza del Duomo, from the 15th century Piazza Navona became the true heart of Rome.

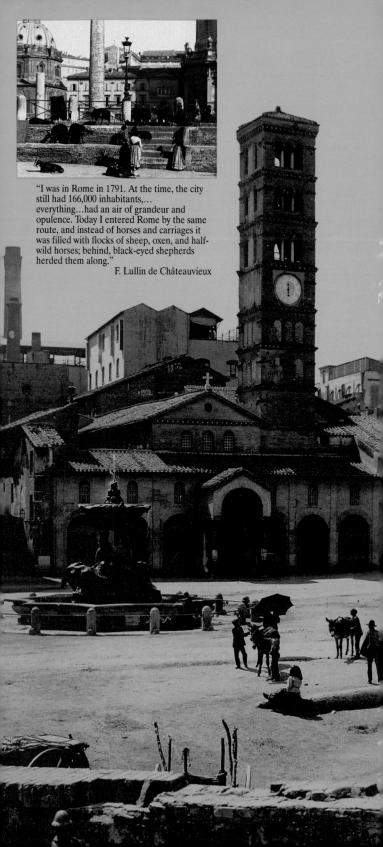

"I was in Rome in 1791. At the time, the city still had 166,000 inhabitants,… everything…had an air of grandeur and opulence. Today I entered Rome by the same route, and instead of horses and carriages it was filled with flocks of sheep, oxen, and half-wild horses; behind, black-eyed shepherds herded them along."

F. Lullin de Châteauvieux

Founded on the left bank of the Tiber, Rome has straddled the river since the Imperial age. From antiquity to the 19th century, when the *muraglioni* (high embankments) were constructed, frequent flooding forced the Romans to build dikes, dredge the riverbed, and build numerous bridges to connect the two banks. These included ancient structures such as the Pons Sublicius (the oldest on record), the Pons Aemilius (the first stone bridge) and the Pons Aelius (the forerunner of the Ponte Sant'Angelo). The newest bridges are the Ponte Duca d'Aosta (opposite the Foro Italico) and the Ponte Principe Amadeo.

Nature

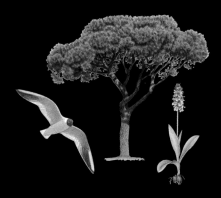

16 The Tiber
18 The flora and fauna
    of the ruins
20 Villa Doria Pamphilj
22 The Pineta Sacchetti
24 The trees of Rome

EEL
So common that the city's last professional
fishermen make their living from eels.

Nicknamed "*il Biondo Tevere*" ("the Blond
Tiber") because of the silt that tinges its waters,
the river, now channeled between embankments, is still a
natural space that shelters a wide range of fish (including carp,
rudd, and eels) and birds (among them cormorants, kingfishers
and various kinds of gulls). On the other hand, there is very
little vegetation apart from the occasional clump of greenery
that the attentive observer wandering along the riverbanks will
notice, where willows or poplars have spontaneously reappeared
on abandoned land.

It was only at the end of the 19th century
that embankments were built in Rome to
channel the Tiber.

MALLARD
A few couples nest regularly on the little
islands in the river.

LITTLE GREBE
These can be seen in winter, especially near
Ponte Sant'Angelo.

At dusk and dawn some eight hundred great cormorants fly over the town, going to or from their roosts.

GREAT CORMORANT
Despite the pollution, in winter it fishes on the river in the very heart of the town.

GREY WAGTAIL
A very useful permanent resident, as it feeds on insects and mosquitoes in the summer.

BROWN RAT
So aggressive even cats fear it, this haunts the sewers, cellars, and streets.

COYPU
Having escaped from a farm in the 1950's, they bred so vigorously on the Tiber they can now be found in the center of Rome.

CARP
This fish was introduced into Europe by the Romans.

PIKE PERCH
Introduced into the Tiber in 1965 and 1966, it has thrived so well that it is now a threat to the native species.

CATFISH
Also an introduced species, it tolerates polluted waters with a low oxygen content.

summer   winter

HERRING GULL
This gull has nested for some years now on the rooftops of palazzi and churches in the city.

BLACK-HEADED GULL
Mainly winter visitors, but a small number now nest on the Tiber.

17

THE FLORA AND FAUNA OF THE RUINS

SICILIAN LIZARD
Also known as "the lizard of the ruins", it sometimes feeds on the remains of tourists' picnics.

The archeological sites all over Rome are protected environments favorable to the development of unusual flora and fauna. Common plant species such as the fig tree and the caper bush (indigenous to the rocks of the Mediterranean) flourish side by side among the ruins. Orchids also frequently grow there. A number of bird species find a choice refuge in ancient Rome.

LITTLE OWL
Particularly common in the forums, where it hunts rodents.

HOOPOE
Sometimes nests on the Palatine, but is being disturbed by the flow of tourists.

BLACK REDSTART
These birds build their nests among the ruins, away from tourists.

Cats are without doubt the most commonly found mammals in the forums.

The Forum is one of the best places to find original flora and fauna, firmly established in the walls and among the ruins.

GREEN LIZARD
This large, relatively uncommon lizard eats insects and sometimes fledglings too.

JACKDAW
Nests in the Coliseum, but is now less common as it is being driven out by crows.

BLUE ROCK THRUSH
A few couples of this superb species nest in the Coliseum and in the tallest ruins of the forums.

CISALPINE SPARROW
This Italian variety of house sparrow can be identified by its brown skullcap.

KESTREL
Nests in bell towers and ruins, where it even hunts bats.

CAPER
This thorny bush with pretty white flowers grows on walls and in crevices between stones.

FIG
Common in the forums. It bears fruit at the end of the summer.

SPLEENWORT
This small fern grows mainly in the cracks between the blocks of stone in the forums.

WALL PELLITORY
Abundant at the foot of walls, this plant swiftly overruns neglected spots.

BUTTERFLY ORCHID
This magnificent orchid is found during April on all dry and chalky ground.

"Ruin-of-Rome" – a tiny and aptly named plant.

19

■ VILLA DORIA PAMPHILJ

EUROPEAN POND TORTOISE
This reptile can occasionally be
observed in the villa's largest lake,
resting on half-submerged branches.

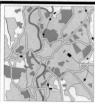

Since antiquity the Romans have been masters of the art of designing superb gardens and country villas, though many of them have been swallowed up by the city. Rome's public parks are an example of these Italian-style gardens where allées, squares, and flowerbeds, bordered by yew, box, or evergreen oak, alternate with groves of such exotic trees as cedars or palms, or with islands of wilder vegetation whose fauna is every bit as interesting as that around various ponds and lakes.

Despite its well-kept Italian-style gardens, the Villa Doria Pamphilj offers shelter to wild flora and fauna that have adapted remarkably well to urban conditions.

RED FOX
At dusk foxes sometimes come to scavenge in the larger parks, but are not very common.

HEDGEHOG
Being shy creatures, hedgehogs only come out at night to hunt for insects and earthworms.

MOORHEN
These birds nest in thick vegetation around the ponds and lakes of Villa Doria Pamphilj.

NUTHATCH
With great agility it creeps down tree trunks, head first.

NARROW-LEAVED CEPHALANTHERA
In May and June this discreet orchid flowers in shady places.

VIOLET BIRDS'-NEST ORCHID
A large orchid that grows in sunny patches of undergrowth on poor soil.

MAGPIE
Never far from man, the magpie population is increasing, especially in Rome's villas.

GREY HERON
Herons visit the small lakes of the Villa Doria Pamphilj in winter to fish.

SPIDER ORCHID
This lovely orchid, which blooms from the month of April, grows on very chalky soil.

PURPLE ORCHID
Twenty-nine species of orchid are found in Rome. This one is fairly common.

EVERGREEN OR HOLM OAK
Unlike other oaks, this tree keeps its leaves all year round.

THE PINETA SACCHETTI

Even today the Pineta Sacchetti still serves as grazing land for sheep, at the very gates of Rome.

Pineta Sacchetti

Vatican City

The Pineta Sacchetti owes its name to the copses of umbrella pines planted on its heights. It stretches along a valley hollowed out by water, the Valle d'Inferno, to the nearby hills a few minutes from the heart of the city. This protected site gives a fairly accurate idea of the original natural environment of Rome. In fact the city developed in a transitional zone, something between a strictly Mediterranean environment, characterized by forests of evergreen trees, and that of the hills farther inland forested with deciduous trees.

Uniforms of the Roman army.

Claudius, the port of Ostia was enlarged in order to improve the capital's food supply. After a devastating fire Nero embarked on town planning on a vast scale, a trend that lasted fifty years and culminated in the building of Trajan's Forum ▲ *165*.

PEACE IN THE 2ND CENTURY.

After Augustus until the time of Septimius Severus new provinces were created, but from London to Arabia most of these were former client-states. This transformation frequently encountered harsh resistance, especially in Judaea. Although the conquests continued under Trajan with his annexation in 107 of Dacia on the right bank of the Danube, Hadrian had to give up Mesopotamia in 117. Antagonism between the Empire's two cultures was lessened thanks to this Greek-loving emperor, and a number of the Greek elite were included in the Imperial administration. By Caracalla's Edict of 212 AD Roman citizenship, previously granted to the notables of the cities and tribes and to the auxiliary soldiers, was finally granted to all free men throughout the Empire.

FIERCE RESISTANCE TO THE BARBARIANS.

In the same period the Empire passed from the offensive to the defensive. Encouraged by interior crises, the army chose emperors such as Maximinus the Thracian, a common soldier brought to power in 235. However, despite a series of epidemics and several rebellions, the Empire remained prosperous and its government stable. The millennium of Rome was celebrated in 248 by Philip the Arab. Then, in 260 Valerian was captured by the Parthians. Despite pressure from the barbarians, the Romans' sense of solidarity, together with Gallienus' genius, enabled them to stem the advance of the Visigoths as far as Greece. But a miscellany of rival generals succeeded him, and eventually in 293 Diocletian attempted to divide up the Imperial power between two Augustuses and two Caesars.

THE CHRISTIAN EMPIRE.

This tetrarchy did not last. In 313, to his own advantage, Constantine started to build a bureaucratic monarchy based on divine right, endowed with a well-organized religion, Christianity, and a new capital, Constantinople. Within a century State paganism vanished, despite its restoration under the Emperor Julian (361–3). The soldier-emperors returned, and on the death of one of them, Theodosius, in 395 the division of the Empire became final. In 406 the Rhine front gave way under pressure from the Suevi and the Vandals. In 410 Rome was sacked by the Visigoths, and in 455 by the Vandals. Puppet emperors succeeded one another in the Western Empire, which was devastated by the barbarians. Germans and Romans formed alliances to repel Attila's Huns, who attempted to invade first Gaul and then Italy. Finally in 476 Odoacer, King of the Heruli, deposed the Emperor of the West, Romulus Augustulus (right), and recognized the fictitious authority of the Emperor of Constantinople. The Western Empire had ceased to exist.

69–71 AD
Revolt of Judaea and the destruction of the temple of Jerusalem.

79 AD
Eruption of Vesuvius destroys Herculaneum and Pompeii.

161–80 AD
Marcus Aurelius repels the Parthians and Marcomanni.

271–5 AD
Construction of the Aurelian Wall.

303–4 AD
The last major persecutions of Christians.

325 AD
The Council of Nicaea.

330 AD
Foundation of Constantinople.

Rome attacked by the Goths.

391 AD
Theodosius bans pagan worship.

THE MAKING OF THE HOLY ROMAN EMPIRE

Gregory I the Great .

476
Odoacer deposes the Emperor of the West in Ravenna.

554
Justinian asserts Byzantine authority in Italy, with Ravenna as its capital.

751
Resumption of Lombard expansion. End of the Ravenna exarchate.

962
Otto the Great, King of Germany, is crowned Emperor.

Charlemagne crowning his son.

FROM THE FALL OF THE EMPIRE TO POPE GREGORY THE GREAT. When the last Emperor of the West was overthrown, Rome was still the most important metropolis in the western world. It emerged barely recognizable from the war (535–55) waged by Justinian, Emperor of Byzantium, who sought to assert Imperial authority over Italy. But from 568 the peninsula was partially lost to the Lombard invasion. In Rome there were rapid changes: the Senate, the last vestige of the ancient order, disappeared. Pope Gregory the Great (590–604) took control, in place of the amorphous Byzantine regime, and laid the foundations of the popes' temporal power.

CAROLINGIAN SUPPORT. The Lombard threat led the Pope to form an alliance with the Franks. The pontiff claimed the territories of Rome and Ravenna. Charlemagne recognized his power, and by having himself crowned in Rome restored the city's prestige as the ideal center of the Christian West.

1075–1122
The War of the Investitures is ended by the Concordat of Worms.

NOBILITY, POPE AND EMPEROR. A long period followed during which the city came under the sway of the great Roman feudal and noble families – the dukes of Spoleto (9th century), the Theophylacts, the Crescentii, then the counts of Tusculum (9th to 10th centuries) – who profited from the weakening of the Carolingians and then from the crisis of pontifical authority and the absence of the Germanic Holy Roman Emperors. In the 11th century a conflict flared up between the Pope and the Emperor. In 1075 Gregory VII referred to a decree banning the Empire's interference in the affairs of the Church, which he intended to reform. In 1084 the Emperor Henry IV responded: he besieged Rome and abducted him. Robert Guiscard, summoned by the Pope, repelled the Emperor and partially destroyed Rome.

THE AGE OF THE COMMUNE

1154–83
Wars between Frederick Barbarossa and the communes. Recognition of the rights of the communes by the Peace of Constance.

1266
Charles d'Anjou establishes an Angevine kingdom in southern Italy.

THE FIRST STEPS. In 1143 a popular revolt against the Pope led to the creation of a Senate independent from the Church and the nobility; thus a commune emerged that was soon to find an ardent champion in Arnaldo da Brescia. The Emperor Frederick Barbarossa had this ringleader executed and restored to the Pope his sovereignty over Rome, which formally recognized the commune.

STRUGGLES BETWEEN LAY AND CHURCH AUTHORITIES. After a flourishing period for the commune in the early 13th century, the post of the only senator in Rome created in 1191 was granted to Charles d'Anjou (1263), before the position

Pope Gregory XI
returning to Avignon.

became a papal appendage. The
failure of the Crusades made
Rome the Christians' first holy
town. But the exile of the popes
to Avignon soon began (1309–77).
The town's institutions benefited by
their banishment. However, as in the
previous century, Rome continued to
be torn by the feuds between two
noble families, the Orsini and the Colonna. Inspired
by the myth of Republican Rome, between 1347 and 1354
Cola di Rienzo ● *XV* endeavored to restore the Republic and
took very severe measures against the nobility. The Pope had
scarcely returned to Rome when the great schism of the West
(1378–1417) undermined his power and caused war to break
out throughout the Church's territory. Rome was left in the
hands of Ladislas of Durazzo.

THE RENAISSANCE

RESTORATION OF PAPAL AUTHORITY. The year 1420
marked the return of the sovereign pontiffs to Rome. During
their absence the city had fallen into decline. It was
unhealthy, short of food and depopulated. The popes
transformed this decaying city into a capital worthy of their
mission and reimposed their authority. The commune of the
people, the nobility, and pontifical power: these were the
poles of Roman political life for three centuries. The popes
opted for an anti-commune policy that provoked violent
reactions during the 15th century and installed a bureaucracy
capable of governing the city directly. The Pope and
College of Cardinals headed a complex administration (the
Curia) consisting of five councils. The great families vied to
join it, while their nepotism led the popes to keep key posts
for their own relations. Alexander VI was even tempted to
carve out a State in central Italy for his son, Cesare Borgia.

A PERIOD OF SPLENDOR. A policy of large-scale building
was initiated at the end of the 15th century. For two centuries
Rome, whose population was increasing, became a vast
building site. The pontifical court was the main center of
humanist culture, and the town welcomed the great
Renaissance artists. The popes of the day (Alexander VI,
Julius II, Leo X, Clement VII) became great princes who
took part in the alliances of Italy's wars, encouraging France

or its adversaries in turn. The Sack of Rome ● *36* (1527)
seemed likely to put an end to this splendor. But the
pontificate of Paul III and preparations for the Council of
Trent restored Rome's cultural and political importance.

1339
*Beginning of the
Hundred Years War.*

Cola di Rienzo.

1348
*The Black Death in
Europe.*

1453
*The Turks capture
Constantinople.*

1454
*Peace of Lodi between
the great Italian States.*

1494
*Charles VIII sets out to
conquer the Kingdom
of Naples: start of the
Wars of Italy.*

Pope Julius II.

1517
*Beginning of the
Lutheran Reformation.*

1530
*Charles V is
consecrated Emperor
in Bologna.*

The Sack of Rome
(left).

1545–63
*The Council of Trent.
Counter-Reformation.*

31

THE COUNTER-REFORMATION

1559
Treaty of Cateau Cambrésis: France relinquishes Italy.

THE ALL-POWERFUL PAPACY AND THE FRAGILITY OF THE STATE. Nevertheless, the disruption created by Protestantism in the Christian world and the transfer of the great trading centers from the Mediterranean to the Atlantic and Northern Europe forced Rome to somewhat reduce its universal ambitions. The Pontifical State owed its survival less to real strength than to the logic of the Counter-Reformation, which found a powerful ally in the Spanish monarchy. But the Pope reigned as a king, and the Curia saw its role in local affairs increase. The former cooperation between the aristocracy and the high-ranking clergy lasted until the end of the 17th century – leaving little room for the bourgeoisie, who therefore asserted their position in other capitals.

POVERTY AND GRANDEUR. The popes – especially Sixtus V (left), Paul V and Urban VIII, who between them commissioned many of Rome's Baroque treasures – pursued an active policy of promoting the arts. Patronage encouraged culture while censure stifled it. Opulence and misery rubbed shoulders in this densely populated town: aristocrats, prelates and powerful foreigners measured their prestige according to the number of poor who knocked at their doors and the quantity of servants and peasants they employed.

TO THE NAPOLEONIC AGE

1618–48
The Thirty Years War.

1702–12
The War of the Spanish Succession.

1796–7
Napoleon's Italian campaign.

1799
The Austrians occupy much of the peninsula.

1800–1
French victory at Marengo. The Peace of Lunéville puts the peninsula back under French hegemony.

IMMOBILISM AND CONFORMITY. Clement XI seemed for a time to wish to involve the Pontifical State in the War of the Spanish Succession. But the military and political impotence of the Holy See obliged it to remain neutral. Cut off from mainstream European politics, Rome was forced to content itself with its religious, artistic and archeological prestige.

THE NAPOLEONIC HURRICANE. The French Revolution and its repercussions were to revive political life. In 1798 the French occupied the town. A Roman republic was born, and the Pope was exiled. On his return to Rome in 1800, he accepted all the arrangements. In 1808 French troops again occupied Rome and dismantled the former administration. The following year, his temporal power abolished, the Pope was again forced into exile. Finally on May 24, 1814, he regained the Papal States, and in 1815 the Congress of Vienna restored their former frontiers.

FROM THE RESTORATION TO ITALIAN UNITY

1806
Napoleon proclaimed Emperor of Rome. Proclamation of the Kingdom of Italy.

1814
The fall of the Empire.

Pius IX (right).

THE FIRST WAR OF INDEPENDENCE.
Political liberalism, patriotic aspirations and social claims made headway in the first half of the 19th century. In the revolutionary outburst of 1848 temporary governments flourished in several Italian cities, including Rome. For two years it seemed that Pius IX wished to be the spokesman for these new aspirations. However, he recalled his troops

Giuseppe Garibaldi.

involved in the First War of Independence and left his State. On February 9, 1849, Mazzini's supporters proclaimed the abolition of temporal power and the Roman Republic. In reply, France intervened in the Pope's favor and occupied Rome.

ROME BECOMES THE CAPITAL. In 1859, at the end of the Second War of Independence, the new Kingdom of Italy extended to within a few miles of Rome. France occupied the city, blocking the Roman question, and Garibaldi twice tried in vain to take it. Finally, when the French troops were evacuated, the Piedmontese entered the city on September 20, 1870. Annexed by plebiscite on October 2, Rome was proclaimed the capital of the kingdom.

1848
Revolutions in Europe. First War of Italian Independence. Defeat by the Austrians.

1860
The King of Piedmont is declared King of Italy.

The first Italian flag.

1861
Proclamation of the Kingdom of Italy.

FROM UNITY TO THE PRESENT DAY

THE RISE OF FASCISM IN ROME. Having inherited an extremely weak economy in 1870, the new capital experienced various difficulties until World War One, despite the laws in its favor introduced by the Giolitti government. The Fascist government, which assumed power two years after the March on Rome, was to bring about both a rhetorical rehabilitation of the Eternal City and a reconciliation with the Church by signing the Lateran Treaty, thus putting an end to dissension between the Church and the State.

1915
Italy enters the war on the side of the Allies.

The March on Rome (center).

1924
The Assassination of Matteotti.

1924–43
The Fascist regime.

1933
Hitler comes to power in Germany.

1946
The first Italian Republic.

FROM WORLD WAR TWO TO TODAY. The Fascist government abandoned the city as soon as the armistice was declared on September 8, 1943. Caught between its status as an open city and the Nazi occupation, Rome's inhabitants began intense underground activity, and the city served as one of the two headquarters of the National Liberation Committee until June 1944. The signing of the Treaty of Rome (1957), the Holy Years (1950 and 1975) and the Olympic Games (1960) brought Rome into the limelight. This city where the service sector is so dominant has been a victim of its own sudden growth: it lacks basic amenities and exists in a state of urban chaos, which the municipality has been unable to remedy despite efforts made since 1975.

Pope John XXIII.

In 509 BC a revolution rid Rome of its kings and established a government that entrusted the State to the Senate and the Roman people, as well as to a body of magistrates. The oligarchic Republic continued until the end of the 1st century AD, despite the expansion of the City-State and the birth of a gigantic empire. In 27 BC power passed into the hands of a single man, the *princeps* or Emperor. The Roman Empire remained undivided until the 4th century AD. Subsequently, due to the threat of barbarian invasions, a division of authority was imposed – which led to the collapse of the Western Empire in 476, while in the East the Byzantine State was asserting itself.

"PROVOCO"
"I appeal to the people" was the ritual formula that a citizen (on the left) condemned to death by a magistrate (center) had to pronounce in Republican times to place himself under the protection of the people.

The augurs, recognizable by their sacred crook (the *lituus*), interpreted the omens (*auspicae*) before any public act, such as elections or war.

THE COMITIUM
An approximate reconstruction. The layout of the Comitium admirably reflected the political institutions of the Republic. The Curia housed the sessions of the Senate, which possessed great authority. Assemblies of the people (*populus*) were held on the circular tiers of steps; although theoretically sovereign, they were only permitted to gather to vote when summoned by the superior magistrates. Finally, the magistrates (consuls, praetors, tribunes of the people, etc.) harangued the crowd from the *rostra* ▲ *140*, which faced the Curia.

THE CENSUS OF CITIZENS
Under the Republic this took place every five years. First the father of the family (standing on the left) declared his assets. Then he was assigned his status in the social and military hierarchies (second scene). A religious ceremony accompanied by a sacrifice concluded the process.

> "In this constitution…everything was organized in such an equitable manner that it was impossible to say whether the regime was aristocratic, democratic or monarchic."
>
> Polybius

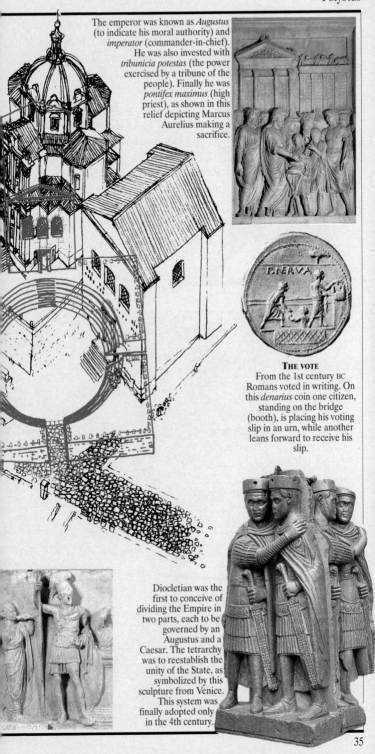

The emperor was known as *Augustus* (to indicate his moral authority) and *imperator* (commander-in-chief). He was also invested with *tribunicia potestas* (the power exercised by a tribune of the people). Finally he was *pontifex maximus* (high priest), as shown in this relief depicting Marcus Aurelius making a sacrifice.

THE VOTE
From the 1st century BC Romans voted in writing. On this *denarius* coin one citizen, standing on the bridge (booth), is placing his voting slip in an urn, while another leans forward to receive his slip.

Diocletian was the first to conceive of dividing the Empire in two parts, each to be governed by an Augustus and a Caesar. The tetrarchy was to reestablish the unity of the State, as symbolized by this sculpture from Venice. This system was finally adopted only in the 4th century.

35

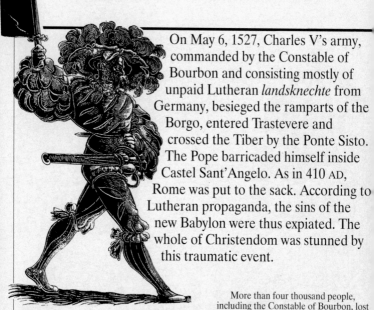

On May 6, 1527, Charles V's army, commanded by the Constable of Bourbon and consisting mostly of unpaid Lutheran *landsknechte* from Germany, besieged the ramparts of the Borgo, entered Trastevere and crossed the Tiber by the Ponte Sisto. The Pope barricaded himself inside Castel Sant'Angelo. As in 410 AD, Rome was put to the sack. According to Lutheran propaganda, the sins of the new Babylon were thus expiated. The whole of Christendom was stunned by this traumatic event.

More than four thousand people, including the Constable of Bourbon, lost their lives in combat and during the siege.

THE LOOTING
For several weeks the city was systematically plundered by the troops.

THE PEACE TREATY
In Madrid, Emperor Charles V feigned regret over the conduct of his troops by not holding victory celebrations, but he knew full well how to reap the profits and only agreed to meet Clement VII to sign a peace treaty on June 20, 1529, in Barcelona.

THE POPE IN CASTEL SANT'ANGELO

n June 6, 1527, the Pope capitulated and agreed to pay a very high ransom, but the Spaniards
kept him prisoner in Castel Sant'Angelo until December 8. In spite of the plague that was
mating both the inhabitants and the army, the destruction of the city continued for six months.

THE GRAFFITI
Frescoes and the walls
of palazzi still bear
traces of the soldiers'
graffiti ▲ 360.

Tu es Petrus et super hanc petram aedificabo ecclesiam meam ... Tibi dabo claves caelorum ("You are Peter and on this rock I will build my Church ... I will give you the keys of the kingdom of heaven," *Matthew* 16:18–19). As Peter's successor, the Pope is the basis of the community of believers, the head of the Roman Church (*Ecclesia romana*). Originally he was aided by deacons (who administered the charitable works of the Church), the parish priests of Rome and the bishops of the suburbicarian dioceses (Ostia, Albano, Palestrina, Frascati, Sabina and Porto). These prelates, who were the Pope's close advisers, constituted the original College of Cardinals, which since the 12th century has had the task of electing the Pope. As successors to the apostles, the bishops (*episcopoi*) used to be elected by the religious community; today they are appointed by the Pope.

CARDINAL
Appointed by the Pope to assist in governing the Church.

BISHOP
"Prophet, pontiff and pastor", responsible for the Christians in a diocese.

PRIEST
Ordained by the bishop, who invests him with his powers. He assists the bishop in his tasks, particularly in administering the sacraments.

CAGLIOSTRO AND LORENZA

It is said that on certain misty nights, a strange figure can be seen skirting the walls of the vicoli in Trastevere ▲ 349, crossing Ponte Garibaldi and making its way to Piazza di Spagna. With a peel of sardonic laughter, the name "Lorenza!" then booms out. Could this not be the ghost of Lorenza Feliciani, who denounced her husband, Count Cagliostro, whose real name was Giuseppe Balsamo? After his arrest in Piazza di Spagna he was imprisoned in the San Leo fortress. Far from gaining her freedom, his wife was shut away in a Trastevere convent and conveniently forgotten.

THE BOCCA DELLA VERITÀ

Beneath the portico of Santa Maria in Cosmedin ▲ 155 there is the enormous face of a Triton, which came from a fountain. Its large mouth was thought in the Middle Ages to be the mouth of an oracle, but it was mainly used for submitting liars to the judgment of God. Forced to put their hand into the orifice, the innocent escaped unharmed while the guilty lost their hand. It is said that the judges may have "helped" God to pass judgment when they were convinced that the accused was guilty.

MADAMA LUCREZIA

This is the only female figure in the congregation of *spiriti arguti* ("witty spirits"), as the family of talking statues are called in Rome.

This gigantic female bust could be either the goddess Isis or Lucrezia, the very beautiful mistress of King Alfonso of Aragon.

47

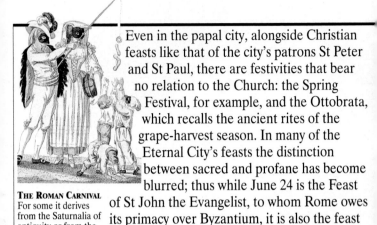

Even in the papal city, alongside Christian feasts like that of the city's patrons St Peter and St Paul, there are festivities that bear no relation to the Church: the Spring Festival, for example, and the Ottobrata, which recalls the ancient rites of the grape-harvest season. In many of the Eternal City's feasts the distinction between sacred and profane has become blurred; thus while June 24 is the Feast of St John the Evangelist, to whom Rome owes its primacy over Byzantium, it is also the feast of the summer solstice.

THE ROMAN CARNIVAL For some it derives from the Saturnalia of antiquity or from the feasts dedicated to Sol Invictus of the late Empire. For others it is simply linked to the Christian calendar. It disappeared at the end of the 19th century when freedom of expression was stifled because of social unrest.

CARNIVAL REVELS AND DISGUISES
Revelers wore nose masks during the Roman Carnival, which ended with the Festa dei Moccoletti, when everyone tried to snuff out everyone else's candles. The smaller-scale Ronciglione Carnival has *nasi rossi* (red noses) instead.

THE FEAST OF SAN GIUSEPPE
This has become the feast of the Trionfale quarter, just behind St Peter's Basilica. Today the traditional stalls that sell deep-fried *bignè* (fritters) on March 19 compete with the traffic, parked cars and other stalls, which sell things all year round.

THE FEAST OF SAN GIOVANNI
Certain scholars link this feast to the grain-harvest festivals of antiquity, during which sacrifices were offered to Ceres. "On the eve one goes to St John the Lateran to pray and to eat snails … Outside the walls, near the Salita degli Spiriti, there was a witches' tavern where we would dine." (Gigi Zanazzo)

THE SPRING FESTIVAL
This is not so much a feast as a general decoration of the city each year in the month of April. The Spanish Steps are turned into a cascade of azaleas.

THE OTTOBRATA
the 19th century the grape harvests were celebrated with feasts during which songs in Romanesco 42 were sung and the *saltarello* was danced.

THE ORDER OF MALTA

The eight points of the Maltese cross represent the eight Beatitudes. Also, eight powerful European states presided over the Order's creation, namely Provence, Auvergne, France, Italy, Aragon, England, Germany and Castile.

Rome is the only city in the world that can claim to be a capital three times over. Besides being the capital of Italy, it contains the Vatican State and the Sovereign Order of the Knights of Malta. Created to welcome and care for pilgrims arriving in the Holy Land, the Order of Hospitalers of St John of Jerusalem received papal recognition in 1113 and was given the task of defending the Holy Sepulcher by Calixtus II in 1120. Its original vocation thus became overlaid by a military function, like that of other orders of knighthood.

FROM JERUSALEM TO RHODES
First established in Jerusalem, the Order was transferred to St John of Acre in 1187. After being defeated by the Sultan of Egypt, it left the Holy Land and settled in Cyprus in 1290, then moved to Rhodes, which it captured in 1310.

FROM RHODES TO MALTA
Chased from Rhodes by Sultan Suleiman's Turks, in 1523 the Order petitioned the Pope for a new base and was granted Malta. This was confirmed in 1530 by a treaty between the Pope and Charles V. The Order exercised sovereignty over the island for several centuries.

FROM MALTA TO ROME
In 1798 Napoleon seized the island without opposition on his way to Egypt. Lacking a home, the Order moved to Russia and then various places in Italy before settling in Rome in 1834.

"IT TAKES A PIRATE AND A HALF TO BEAT A PIRATE!"
This was the rallying cry of the Order of the Knights of Malta, who reacted blow by blow to the Moorish and Turkish offensives. In fact, their methods and objectives were similar to those of the Barbary Coast pirates.

Before frescoes can be restored, chemical testing is required. Color samples are needed in order to determine which pigments were originally used, and to discover what parasitical materials have been deposited on the surface of the painting.

THE SISTINE CHAPEL

Layers of greasy dust, soot from candles used in ceremonies and especially a film of animal glue had altered and seriously darkened the colors. Furthermore, certain figures had been retouched when this varnish was applied to protect them. Finally, the infiltration of rainwater from the roof had left whitish saline deposits on the ceiling. The restoration, carried out by Vatican experts, was undertaken when it was discovered that microclimatic variations were contracting the varnish in such a way that it was lifting the painted surface in certain places. The operations were minimal; in fact the main work consisted in cleaning the frescoes, for which the solvent AB 57 was used. The frescoes have now been restored to their original colors.

FONTANA DI TREVI

The fountain was suffering from static problems due to the materials from which it was made, and also from general degradation associated with a highly polluted environment (such as ingrained dirt and disintegration due to polluting agents).

In particular, it was covered with calcium deposits and algae formations. After general strengthening and cleaning work (sandblasting and ultrasound), plus localized biocidal cleansing, it was equipped with a water processing unit.

Roman cuisine combines the country cooking of Lazio and the Abruzzi region with popular culinary traditions featuring pasta, fresh and dried vegetables, salt cod, offal and pork. Although some of the recipes of antiquity have been handed down (mainly dishes blending sweet and savory flavors), the character of Roman cooking is largely due to the use of condiments (garlic, herbs and spices), sometimes combined with *pecorino* (a sharp sheep cheese), which give a delightful texture, taste and smell to even the simplest dishes.

2. Remove the toughest leaves and cut off the stems.

3. Using a small sharp knife, pare the artichokes into a conical shape.

7. Season them again with a little salt, and let them simmer uncovered over a low flame. When they are half done, turn the artichokes onto their sides.

6. Place the artichokes prepared in this way on their bases in a pan or dish. Cover with the glasses of water (according to the number of artichokes) and half a glass of olive oil.

MEDIEVAL ROME

During the late Middle Ages, with the decrease in population, a major part of the area within the Aurelian Wall fell into disuse. The Vatican, fortified in 854, became the political and religious center. From the 10th century to the end of the 13th century, the inhabited area was concentrated around the Tiber as well as the Forum. In the 14th century catastrophes and epidemics decimated the population, but it soon increased again due to a surge of immigration.

THE TOWN PLANNING OF SIXTUS V

During the five years of his pontificate, with Domenico Fontana as his chief architect, Sixtus V (1585–90) implemented a huge urban plan which was to make Rome Europe's first modern city.

BUILDING UNDER SIXTUS V

The Pope had new palaces and religious buildings erected, constructed important roads such as the Via Felice, and created vast squares decorated with columns, fountains and obelisks.

ROME THE CAPITAL

1870: When Rome became the capital, there were only 200,000 inhabitants.
1910: Its new role accelerated building activity. The city spread mainly eastward, and the popular neighborhood of Testaccio sprang up in the south.
1930: Rome's expansion gathered momentum. Suburbs developed far from the center, isolated in the countryside.
1960: The great parks were now the only areas free from buildings.

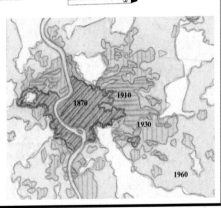

61

Roman architecture relied for a long time on the assembly of large quadrangular blocks, but masonry characterized by the difference between its facing materials and its internal composition appeared at an early date. The fill, or *opus caementicium*, made of rubble mixed with lime mortar, was highly resistant but rather ungainly. At first it was faced with *opus incertum*; then with *opus reticulatum*, which was soon replaced by *opus testaceum*, a brick facing rapidly adopted for all Roman walls.

A. Step quarrying
B. Quarry face
C. Residual pillar
D. Stone face
E. Natural cleft
F. Transporting a block on rollers

TRAVERTINE
A whitish calcareous stone from the Tivoli area.

TUFA
A compound of volcanic rocks of varying colors.

QUARRYING FOR STONE
Once the soil covering the rock had been stripped away, the quarrymen scored the rough outline of the blocks on the stone so that, while it was being extracted, it could be hewn into the shape and size required by the architect.

A ROMAN LEWIS

HOIST
A winch operated by a lever was used to lift and position stones.

TECHNIQUES FOR TRANSPORTING AND POSITIONING THE BLOCKS
1. Tenons (projections) were left on the face of the stone so ropes could be attached.
2. Small cavities were carved symmetrically in the blocks so they could be lifted by GRIPS.
3. A dovetail cavity was sunk into the top of the block so a LEWIS could be inserted.

CIRCUSES

These were less costly structures than amphitheaters, and their technical requirements were more modest. The Circus Maximus and Circus Flaminius fulfilled an important role in the Rome of the 4th and 3rd centuries BC due to their link with the triumphal rituals.

CROSS-SECTION AND PLAN OF THE CIRCUS OF MAXENTIUS ▲ 328
Circuses were built with a long, low central wall, the *spina* ▲ 178, around which the chariots raced. Each end was marked by a turning point known as a *meta*.

THEATERS

Roman theaters were modeled on theaters of the Hellenistic period in Sicily and southern Italy. But whereas the Greek theaters were left open, facing the natural landscape, with their *cavea* resting on the slope of a hill, Roman ones were enclosed buildings erected on architectural substructures with monumental stage fronts.

STAGE FRONT AND CROSS-SECTION OF POMPEY'S THEATER ▲ 248

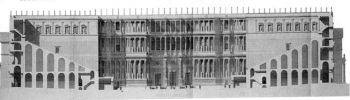

3 OUTER WALLS
In amphitheaters and theaters the external façade of the *cavea* consisted of superimposed arcades framed by engaged columns and separated by friezes.

4 The three lower levels of the Coliseum's façade are made up of (from the bottom) Tuscan Doric, Ionic and Corinthian columns. The fourth level is blind and is decorated with pilasters.

PLAN OF MARCELLUS' THEATER ▲ 157
The *cavea* of Roman theaters never went beyond a semicircle.

PLAN OF THE COLISEUM
These drawings show the internal and external structure.

In Imperial times, Marcellus' theater served as a model for theaters in the Western Provinces.

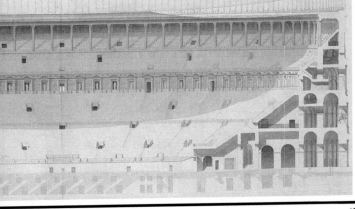

● WATER IN THE ANCIENT TOWN

The control and regular distribution of water to large cities was one of Rome's most remarkable urban innovations. Nothing brought a more radical modification to lifestyles than the abundance of running water in towns, with all the public and private infrastructures this implied. Roman engineers were not the inventors of aqueducts, but the challenges Rome had to face in order to harness sometimes quite remote water sources gave rise to the construction of some remarkable buildings.

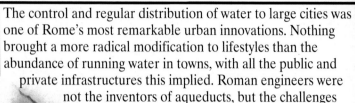

"CASTELLUM DIVISORIUM" (WATER TOWER)
This enabled water to be distributed within the town. A circular basin was constructed to receive the water, through a grating, from the aqueduct. Lead piping carried the water from the basin to different parts of the town.

PIPES
Water pipes were generally made out of lead sheets rolled around a caliber and welded with a lead seal secured by a strip of clay. The Roman architects Vitruvius and Frontinus established precise standards for their calibration.

BATHS
In the *tepidaria* and *caldaria* the floor and the bottom of the swimming pools were supported by small terracotta pillars around which air heated by an oven could circulate. This space was called the *hypocaustum*. Beneath the marble facing of the walls a very thick coating of cement covered rectangular ceramic piping (*tubuli*), which served as vents for hot air or steam.

68

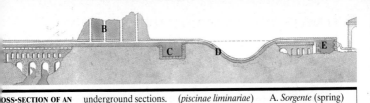

CROSS-SECTION OF AN AQEDUCT
...m the spring *...rgente*) to the *...ellum divisorium*, ...sed sections with ...hes alternated with underground sections. The latter could be maintained and examined through inspection vents (*lumina*) at regular intervals. Settling sumps (*piscinae liminariae*) allowed the water of the *specus*, as the channel of the aqueduct was called, to be purified before it reached the town. Steep dips in the terrain were traversed by means of siphons, but generally the aim was, wherever possible, to avoid supplying water under pressure.

A. *Sorgente* (spring)
B. *Lumina* (inspection vents)
C. *Piscina liminaria* (settling sump)
D. *Sifone rovescio* (siphon)
E. *Castellum divisorium* (water tower)

PUBLIC FOUNTAINS
These were rarely more than 260 feet apart, so that no one ever lived more than 130 feet away from one. The lead supply pipe came up through a stone fixed in the sidewalk and flowed into a basin made of stone slabs set in the street.

"DOMUS"
This Pompeian *domus* is a good example of a sophisticated house with an *atrium* and a peristyle laid out as a garden.

"INSULA"
This *insula* ▲ 410 in Ostia is one of the most remarkable examples of a large multistoried apartment building with a staircase that opens on to a central courtyard with arcades. It has the unusual feature of a thermal bath connected to it for the use of residents.

It was situated opposite a public fountain and possessed an *impluvium* (1), or cistern, for the collection of rainwater. Some houses were even equipped with running water and had a decorative fountain in the peristyle (2).

THE DISPOSAL OF WASTE WATER
Not all Roman towns had a network of underground sewers. In Rome the main sewer, the *cloaca maxima* ▲ 156, which is very ancient, remained an open sewer for a long time. It permitted all the water in the city to be drained into the Tiber.

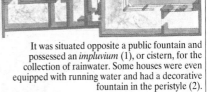

● TEMPLES AND COMMEMORATIVE MONUMENTS

THE TROPHIES OF MARIUS
These figures displayed reproductions of arms and armor stripped from Rome's enemies as a symbol of victory.

In Rome, as in all the great cities of the Empire, the religious buildings gave the urban landscape a sense of order and hierarchical significance. They were the richest and most diverse buildings in the whole array of ancient monuments. Triumphal arches, which were another characteristic of Roman towns, stood at each of the key points in the metropolis. Great mausoleums also adorned the city, commemorating the emperors as if they were Hellenistic sovereigns.

ETRUSCAN TEMPLES
The most ancient temples belonged to the Italo-Etruscan tradition, of which the venerable Temple of Jupiter Capitolinus ▲ *128* was the best example. Three halls of worship (*cellae*) opened onto a deep portico with widely spaced columns.

QUADRANGULAR TEMPLES OF HELLENIC ORIGIN
These made use of all the Greek architectural resources in an essentially decorative form, as can be seen in the Temple of Portunus ▲ *155*.

ROUND TEMPLES
The Temple of Vesta ▲ *155* in the Forum Boarium is the oldest instance in Rome of an entirely Greek design (the *tholos periptera*).

TRIUMPHAL ARCHES
The most striking examples of these symbols of Rome's military supremacy have three bays, like the Arch of Constantine ▲ *169*. This displays all the traditional signs of solemnity: the bays are framed by Corinthian columns on pedestals, a high attic crowns the whole structure, and every available space is decorated with reliefs.

A. Plan of the Temple of Jupiter Capitolinus.

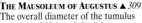 **B.** Plan of the Temple of Portunus.

 C. Plan of the Temple of Venus and Rome.

 D. Plan of the Temple of Vesta.

THE MAUSOLEUM OF AUGUSTUS ▲ 309
The overall diameter of the tumulus was about 285 feet. It had three levels: a vast cylindrical podium planted as a "sacred forest", the cylindrical drum of the mausoleum itself surrounded by a colonnade, and finally a truncated pyramid erected on the top, supporting a colossal statue of the Emperor. The door leading into the mausoleum was framed by two obelisks.

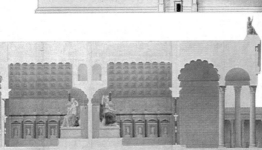

THE "CELLAE"
Porphyry, polychrome marbles and gilded coffers adorned the *cellae*.

THE TEMPLE OF VENUS AND ROME ▲ 146
This double sanctuary was made up of two temples placed back to back along a longitudinal axis. It was the largest religious building in the Graeco-Roman world.

THE PLAN OF THE PANTHEON
The vast rotunda is preceded by a great quadrangular portico (*pronaos*) with sixteen majestic columns.

THE INTERIOR OF THE PANTHEON ▲ 264
The monumental rigor of this building is due to the harmonious juxtaposition of two simple geometrical figures: the cylinder and the hemisphere.

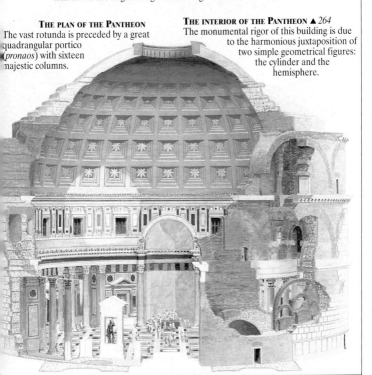

MEDIEVAL TOWERS AND DWELLINGS

During the 11th and 12th centuries the Roman nobility developed an architectural idiom that combined fortifications, towers and ramparts with dwellings. Palaces, surrounded by the houses of relatives and servants, and towers (the military scope of which soon became merely emblematic), were the homes of the grandees until the end of the Middle Ages.

CASA DEI CRESCENZI
This house was built in the 11th century by Nicolò di Crescenzio with a view to "reviving the ancient setting of Rome", as an inscription set above the door proclaims. It is a good example of the reuse of classical architectural and decorative materials and elements within the medieval, domestic, architectural idiom.

TORRE ANGUILLARA ▲ *356*
This 13th-century tower in Trastevere was rebuilt around 1455. Its crenelations are the product of a 19th-century restoration.

THE TOMB OF CECILIA METELLA
▲ *330* Certain tombs on the Via Appia were used as foundations for medieval fortifications.

THE FORTIFICATION OF THE MAUSOLEUM
The Tomb of Cecilia Metella is a vast two-floored structure. In 1302 it was turned into a gigantic dungeon by Pietro Caetani. The Ghibelline crenelations were added at that time. However, its spacious balcony and broad windows make this fortress less severe.

TORRE DELLE MILIZIE ▲ 168
This very tall tower, the symbol of "Roma turrita", was erected at the beginning of the 13th century on the ruins of Trajan's market. The 1348 earthquake destroyed its upper floors.

TORRE DEI CAPOCCI
This was built in the 13th century as a part of one of the largest fortified complexes, using building materials and bricks from

A MEDIEVAL TOWN HOUSE
The house standing at No. 14 Via dell'Atleta (a delightful street in Trastevere ▲ 353) is one of the best examples of Roman medieval architecture. Its brick and tufa-rubble façade is adorned with a loggia with a twin arcade supported by marble columns, while above, a frieze of smaller ogival arches rests on travertine corbels.

PLAN OF THE FORTIFIED COMPLEX
The Tomb of Cecilia Metella was surrounded by a rectangular wall originally buttressed by sixteen protruding quadrangular guard towers. It extended over both sides of the Via Appia, which it controlled. The layout of the buildings within these battlements indicates the degree to which the highway had been "privatized", with the castle on one side of the road and its chapel, San Nicola da Bari, on the other.

A STRATEGIC POSITION
Many ancient monuments that were turned into citadels in the Middle Ages had strategic advantages. The Tomb of Cecilia Metella afforded control over an important route into the city.

73

● CHURCHES OF THE MIDDLE AGES

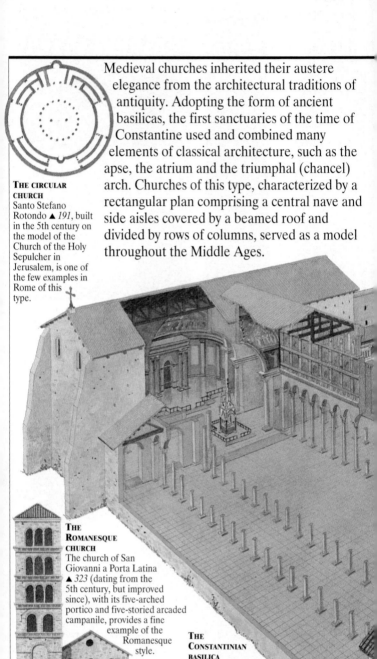

Medieval churches inherited their austere elegance from the architectural traditions of antiquity. Adopting the form of ancient basilicas, the first sanctuaries of the time of Constantine used and combined many elements of classical architecture, such as the apse, the atrium and the triumphal (chancel) arch. Churches of this type, characterized by a rectangular plan comprising a central nave and side aisles covered by a beamed roof and divided by rows of columns, served as a model throughout the Middle Ages.

THE CIRCULAR CHURCH
Santo Stefano Rotondo ▲ 191, built in the 5th century on the model of the Church of the Holy Sepulcher in Jerusalem, is one of the few examples in Rome of this type.

THE ROMANESQUE CHURCH
The church of San Giovanni a Porta Latina ▲ 323 (dating from the 5th century, but improved since), with its five-arched portico and five-storied arcaded campanile, provides a fine example of the Romanesque style.

THE CONSTANTINIAN BASILICA (4TH CENTURY)
Despite its total reconstruction, the best model of a standard Roman basilical church is San Paolo fuori le Mura ▲ 382. Its basic structure consists of a vast central nave with four side aisles. At the top end a triumphal arch leads into the transept crossing and the choir. In the crossing stands the ciborium built by Arnolfo di Cambio in 1285.

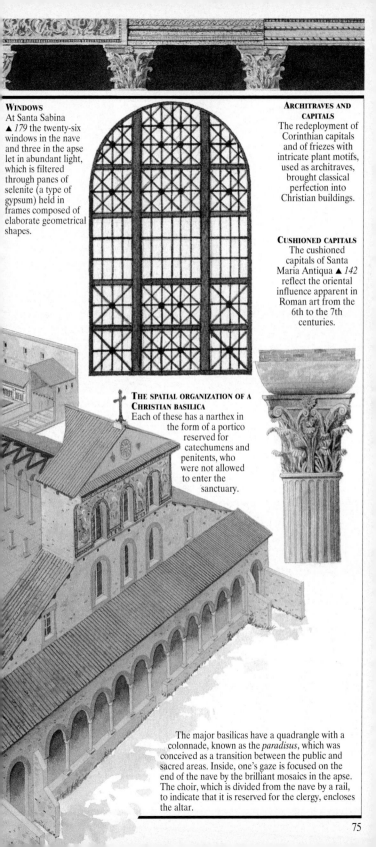

WINDOWS

At Santa Sabina ▲ *179* the twenty-six windows in the nave and three in the apse let in abundant light, which is filtered through panes of selenite (a type of gypsum) held in frames composed of elaborate geometrical shapes.

ARCHITRAVES AND CAPITALS

The redeployment of Corinthian capitals and of friezes with intricate plant motifs, used as architraves, brought classical perfection into Christian buildings.

CUSHIONED CAPITALS

The cushioned capitals of Santa Maria Antiqua ▲ *142* reflect the oriental influence apparent in Roman art from the 6th to the 7th centuries.

THE SPATIAL ORGANIZATION OF A CHRISTIAN BASILICA

Each of these has a narthex in the form of a portico reserved for catechumens and penitents, who were not allowed to enter the sanctuary.

The major basilicas have a quadrangle with a colonnade, known as the *paradisus*, which was conceived as a transition between the public and sacred areas. Inside, one's gaze is focused on the end of the nave by the brilliant mosaics in the apse. The choir, which is divided from the nave by a rail, to indicate that it is reserved for the clergy, encloses the altar.

PAVEMENTS. Rich geometrical patterns surround disks of porphyry sliced from the shafts of ancient columns.

These proud heirs of the arts of antiquity and early Christianity, who described themselves as "very learned Roman masters", combined the science of the architect, the art of the sculptor and the refinement of the mosaic artist. Their campaniles, pavements, colonnades, cloisters and furniture adorn Rome's churches. The Vassalletto and Cosmati workshops were the two most famous of the many active from the 12th to the 13th century in the expressive, elegant and refined decorative art form known as the "Cosmatesque".

THE EPISCOPAL THRONE OF SAN LORENZO FUORI LE MURA ▲ *381*

This throne, designed in the 13th century for the Pope as Bishop of Rome, is a symbol of the papacy's political theology. Instead of very explicit symbolic motifs, it aims at rich decorative and chromatic effects. The great central disk resembling a nimbus evokes sanctity, while the three-lobed design above it exalts the theocratic ideas dear to Pope Innocent IV.

DETAIL OF INLAID FRIEZE IN THE CLOISTER OF SAN PAOLO FUORI LE MURA

Polychrome decorations, geometrical designs and mosaics emphasize the architectural features, which glitter with marble, porphyry and serpentine taken from the ruins of antiquity.

COLUMNS FROM THE CLOISTER OF SAN PAOLO FUORI LE MURA

The Roman marble cutters explored every possibility in the decoration of columns, ranging from the rectilinear to the twisted and entwined, enhancing their rhythm with inlaid patterns.

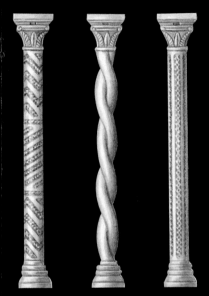

THE CLOISTER OF SAN PAOLO FUORI LE MURA ▲ *382*

This cloister, probably designed by one of the Vassalletti, is among the great architectural and decorative achievements of the 13th century in Rome. Each of its four galleries consists of four or five arcades separated by pilasters topped by a pseudo-Corinthian capital.

CARVED MARBLE PASCHAL CANDELABRA

Coat of arms of the order of Jesuit fathers.

The rapid development of religious architecture was given a further impetus by the Council of Trent (1545–63), under the militant leadership of newly founded Orders such as the Society of Jesus (the Jesuits). The perfection of the centrally planned church was renounced in reconciling it with the Latin-cross layout, which was better suited to the Church's new liturgical priority: the promotion of preaching. The design of the Gesù, the building of which began in 1568, was based on the total integration of the nave, transept and choir. In the 17th century, church architecture also reaped the benefits of Bernini, Cortona and Borromini's liberating experiments with curves and dynamic effects.

THE GESÙ
▲ 257
For the Jesuits' first large church, Vignola adapted a layout made famous by Alberti's Church of Sant'Andrea, in Mantua. He set off the vast nave with a huge cupola, abundantly lit by the bays in the drum. The wide nave blends into a non-protruding transept, creating a grandiose space of spectacular unity that contributes greatly to the effect of services and sermons by emphasizing the majesty of the choir. The church's minimal decorations – marble altars and frescoes on the cupola and pendentives – were copiously enriched at the end of the 17th century.

 A B  C

Renaissance | Counter-Reformation | Baroque

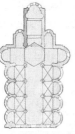 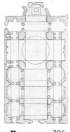 

B. Sant'Ignazio
▲ *261* The layout and façade of the Gesù were virtually copied when this church was constructed in 1626. Only its lavish decorations distinguished it from its model, built in the austere spirit of the Counter-Reformation, before the innovations of the 17th century.

C. Sant'Andrea al Quirinale ▲ *296*
In this small elliptical church Bernini developed elegant dynamic effects by means of contrasting curves and the tension created by his use of limited space.

A. Santa Maria del Popolo ▲ *306*
This church's ground plan in the shape of a Latin cross and its façade divided into three sections reflect the internal layout of a nave with two aisles, reminiscent of the pure Renaissance style of Santa Maria Novella in Florence, the façade of which was designed by Alberti in 1458.

The façade of the Gesù
In the rational tradition of the early Renaissance, Giacomo Della Porta's façade, with its two levels linked by consoles, reflects the interior layout of the church. Three doors open into the single nave. The lateral sections contain chapels. This particular feature is echoed on the first level by the grouping of the pilasters and the projection of the columns supporting the main door's double pediment. The longitudinal axis is thus emphasized.

Profile of a Counter-Reformation façade
Unlike later, Baroque churches, the Gesù has a flush façade with only slight projections.

THE PANTHEON ▲ 264
This cupola (2nd century BC) became the model for the "concrete vault". The extrados (outer surface) serves as a complete covering.

While Bernini and Borromini shared the same classical and Renaissance background and pursued a similar goal in seeking to give life to the principles of composition, they differed in their manner of interpreting these traditions – the one theatrical and the other architectural.

The cupola, or dome, was the essential element in the new challenges of religious architecture and underwent unprecedented variations in this period.

THE CUPOLA OF SANT'IVO
The drum supports a stepped cupola surmounted by a lantern at the apex of powerful ribs. A spiral enhances the upward movement.

SANT'IVO ALLA SAPIENZA ▲ 272
In Borromini's masterpiece, begun in 1642, the dynamic tension generated by the contrasting concave and convex surfaces is brought to a climax. Externally the hexagonal drum appears even more powerful because it inverts the design of the façade, whose curve is extended by the two arcades of the courtyard. Inside, six apses facing each other in pairs, in accordance with the building's interplay of contrasts, reveal the star-shaped ground plan.

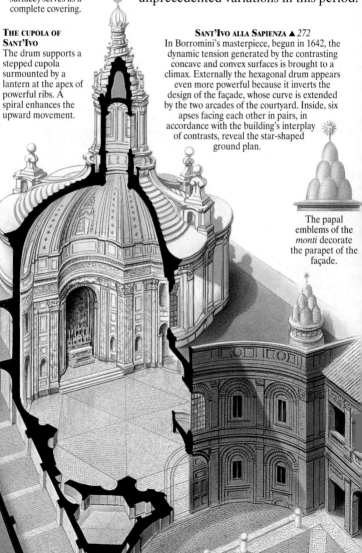

The papal emblems of the *monti* decorate the parapet of the façade.

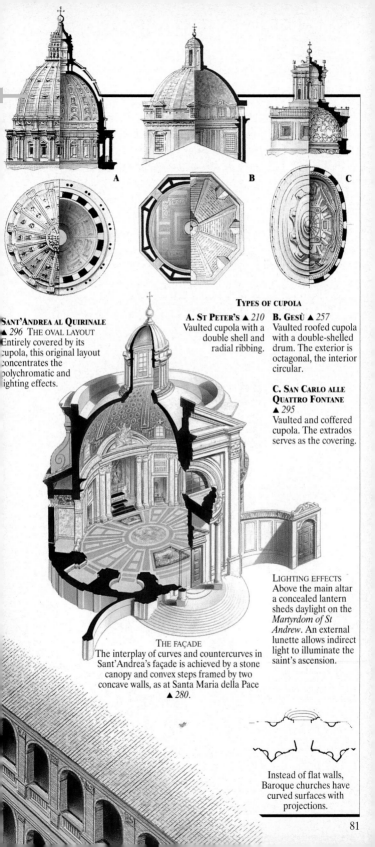

TYPES OF CUPOLA

A. St Peter's ▲ *210*
Vaulted cupola with a double shell and radial ribbing.

B. Gesù ▲ *257*
Vaulted roofed cupola with a double-shelled drum. The exterior is octagonal, the interior circular.

C. San Carlo alle Quattro Fontane ▲ *295*
Vaulted and coffered cupola. The extrados serves as the covering.

Sant'Andrea al Quirinale
▲ *296* The oval layout
Entirely covered by its cupola, this original layout concentrates the polychromatic and lighting effects.

Lighting effects
Above the main altar a concealed lantern sheds daylight on the *Martyrdom of St Andrew*. An external lunette allows indirect light to illuminate the saint's ascension.

The façade
The interplay of curves and countercurves in Sant'Andrea's façade is achieved by a stone canopy and convex steps framed by two concave walls, as at Santa Maria della Pace ▲ *280*.

Instead of flat walls, Baroque churches have curved surfaces with projections.

81

THE ART OF "TROMPE L'ŒIL"

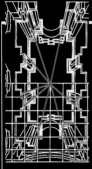

Preparatory cartoon showing the *trompe l'oeil* effect on a squared surface, with a central vanishing point.

In the 17th century many Roman ceilings were covered with princely apotheoses, celestial glories and *quadrature* (painted architectural elements). Cupolas reveal Baroque cloud formations that sweep architecture, paintings and sculptures up into their luminous vortex. One of the most spectacular masterpieces of this art of illusion, the absolute mastery of the rules of perspective, is the Church of Sant'Ignazio ▲ *261*, where Andrea Pozzo painted a *trompe l'oeil* cupola and, in the nave, a magnificent fresco in which earthly architecture seems to reach heavenly heights.

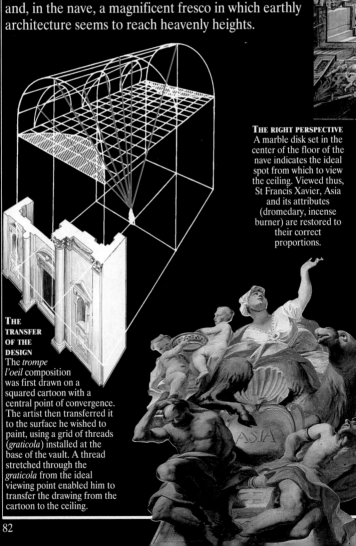

THE RIGHT PERSPECTIVE
A marble disk set in the center of the floor of the nave indicates the ideal spot from which to view the ceiling. Viewed thus, St Francis Xavier, Asia and its attributes (dromedary, incense burner) are restored to their correct proportions.

THE TRANSFER OF THE DESIGN
The *trompe l'oeil* composition was first drawn on a squared cartoon with a central point of convergence. The artist then transferred it to the surface he wished to paint, using a grid of threads (*graticola*) installed at the base of the vault. A thread stretched through the *graticola* from the ideal viewing point enabled him to transfer the drawing from the cartoon to the ceiling.

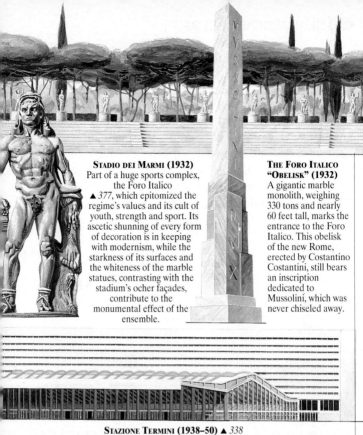

STADIO DEI MARMI (1932)
Part of a huge sports complex, the Foro Italico ▲ *377*, which epitomized the regime's values and its cult of youth, strength and sport. Its ascetic shunning of every form of decoration is in keeping with modernism, while the starkness of its surfaces and the whiteness of the marble statues, contrasting with the stadium's ocher façades, contribute to the monumental effect of the ensemble.

THE FORO ITALICO "OBELISK" (1932)
A gigantic marble monolith, weighing 330 tons and nearly 60 feet tall, marks the entrance to the Foro Italico. This obelisk of the new Rome, erected by Costantino Costantini, still bears an inscription dedicated to Mussolini, which was never chiseled away.

STAZIONE TERMINI (1938–50) ▲ *338*
The rebuilding of Rome's main station spanned the Fascist period and the postwar years. It provides a good illustration of the transition of architectural styles during this period of political change. The two rigid lateral buildings with false arches faced in Travertine were the first to be built, and evoke the paintings of Giorgio De Chirico▲ *387* in no uncertain way. The grandiose main hall (opened in 1950), on the other hand, is striking because of the dynamic use of materials in its powerfully ribbed undulating roof.

PALAZZETTO DELLO SPORT (1956–8)

Cross-section of the Palazzetto and the framework of the dome.

The Palazzetto was designed by Annibale Vitellozzi and Pier Luigi Nervi, the master of Italian rationalism.

This circular building was designed in such a way as to make it adaptable for different types of sport and to accommodate the maximum number of spectators. The dome, which took only thirty days to assemble, consists of a sheet of prefabricated concrete lozenges. Tall Y-shaped weight-bearing trestles, characteristic of Nervi, are treated as a feature and constitute the only decorative motif of the Palazzetto, which is otherwise devoid of adornments.

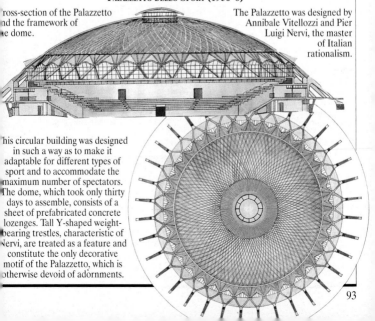

93

● THE CLASSICAL ORDERS

2

3

4

5

Using an architecture of columns, the Greeks developed the Doric, Ionic and Corinthian styles, which provided aesthetic solutions to every kind of building. In Rome during the 1st century BC Vitruvius formulated a theory concerning the classical orders at a time when the development of the arch and the vault had reduced columns to a more decorative function. These styles and their variants were destined to become the basic orders of western architecture.

SUPERIMPOSED ORDERS
In all periods the orders were always superimposed in the same sequence. From the bottom: Doric or Tuscan (1 and 2), Ionic (3), Corinthian (4) and Composite (5).

Doric capital with ovolo molding.

II. ENTABLATURE
1. Architrave: smooth in the Doric style, but divided into three bands or *fasciae* in the Ionic and Corinthian.
2. Taenia (fillet).
3. Frieze: (left to right)
– Ionic, sometimes omitted from the entablature, sometimes plain.
– Doric, always consisted of alternating metopes (**a**) and triglyphs (**b**), each crowned by a mutule and anchored under the taenia by a *regula* with *guttae*.
– Corinthian, could be adorned with figurative motifs (**c**), animals or plants.
4. Cornice.

I. PEDIMENT AND ROOF
1. Tympanum. 2. Raking cornices.
3. Bases for gable and angle *acroteria*: these often took the form of sculptures.

I. PEDIMENT

II. ENTABLATURE

III. COLUMNS
Columns have three parts: the base (**a**), the shaft (**b**), which can be smooth or fluted, and the capital (**c**). Their proportions and decorations vary according to the order they belong to:
1. Doric (normally has no base).
2. Tuscan Doric (with a base).
3. Ionic.
4. Corinthian.
5 and 6. Composite.

III. COLUMNS

IV. SUBSTRUCTURE
1. Bases flanking steps. 2. Podium: unlike the Greeks, the Romans generally erected temples on massive stone platforms.

Rome
as seen by painters

Both a painter
and an architect,
GIOVANNI PAOLO
PANNINI
(c. 1691–1765), was
one of the most
representative artists
of the 18th century.
Like many of his
contemporaries, he
used painting as a
means to show reality:
cities, palaces, the
private apartments of
the nobility and the
dwellings of the
common people. In hi
*Galleries of Views of
Ancient Rome* (1) and

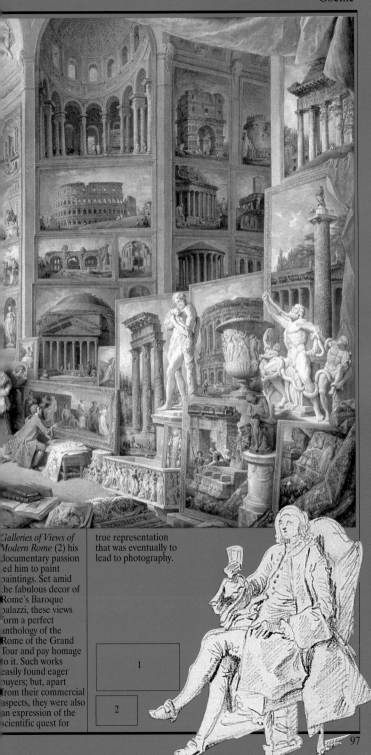

"At each step, a palace, a ruin, a garden, a desert, a little house, a stable, a triumphal arch, a colonnade, and all these so close together that one could draw them on a small sheet of paper."

Goethe

Galleries of Views of Modern Rome (2) his documentary passion led him to paint paintings. Set amid the fabulous decor of Rome's Baroque palazzi, these views form a perfect anthology of the Rome of the Grand Tour and pay homage to it. Such works easily found eager buyers; but, apart from their commercial aspects, they were also an expression of the scientific quest for true representation that was eventually to lead to photography.

1

2

ROME AS SEEN BY PAINTERS

Even when he decided to portray a real place, as in this *View of the French Academy in Rome* (1), GUSTAVE MOREAU (1826–98) never forgot his overriding artistic aim: to suggest more than the visible. Built up in monochrome masses, the various parts of this picture (trees, flowerbed, buildings) amount to a "vision" rather than a "view". A very well known place, painted many times, thus acquires a certain mystery, which the time of day chosen by Moreau – a gentle twilight – accentuates and makes more magical.

Although as a writer Goethe (1749–1832) offers a totally romantic idea of Rome and Italy, during his visit to Rome in 1784 he admired David's *The Oath of the Horatii*, a pictorial manifesto of neoclassicism. In contrast, David's *The Pyramid of Caius Cestius in Rome* (2) – a nocturnal view of a strangely eerie and exotic place – clearly belongs to the poetry of the ruins which Mantegna had already explored in the 15th century and which the Romantics made their own.

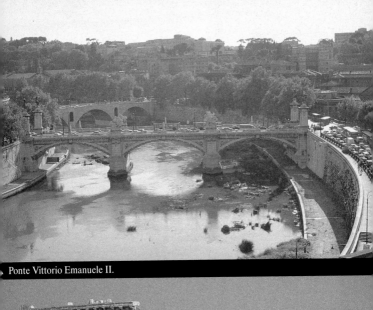

Ponte Vittorio Emanuele II.

▲ The Coliseum. The Fountain of Neptune in Piazza Navona. ▼

▲ An ice-cream shop in Trastevere.

▲ Metro sign.

Monks and nuns at the Vatican. ▼

BUST OF COMMODUS
The artist applied great technical virtuosity in portraying the emperor who, at the end of his reign, saw himself as Hercules. This bust bearing the emblems of the "Conqueror of the World" (the lion skin and club) seems to float weightlessly above two cornucopias, borne by Victories, surmounting a celestial globe.

"BUST OF JUNIUS BRUTUS"
Ivory-and-glass inlays give a lifelike look to the eyes of this 3rd-century head (erroneously identified as that of L. Junius Brutus, Rome's first consul), supported on a modern bust. The calm, strict facial expression nevertheless corresponds to the ideal image of a man of the Roman Republic.

THE WOLF OF THE CAPITOL
This bronze from the early 5th century BC portrays the animal totem of Rome and illustrates one of the city's best-known legends. Its naturalism combines with a keen abstract sensitivity: the dilated nostrils, the wide-open eyes and the three furrows on the forehead convey a strong sense of realism, whereas the rest of the body is highly stylized. The twins, Romulus and Remus, were Renaissance additions.

"THE TRIUMPH OF BACCHUS"
Among the works painted by Pietro da Cortona around 1620 for his patron, the Marchese Sacchetti, this is probably the one most clearly influenced by Titian's *Bacchanals* – a series of paintings that da Cortona had admired when they were acquired by Cardinal Ludovisi.

"THE DYING GAUL"
Hellenistic art was prone to the representation of certain ethnic types, such as the Galatian warriors with rough features and thick bushy hair that the sculptors of Pergamon, in Asia Minor, excelled in depicting. This wounded Gaul, with his poignant expression, corresponds exactly to the dominant style of the 3rd century BC. The statue was discovered in the gardens of Villa Ludovisi.

15

TEMPLE OF THE DIVINE JULIUS AND THE ARCH OF AUGUSTUS. After Caesar's assassination in Pompey's Curia ▲ *248*, his body was brought to the Forum and cremated. A column with the inscription *Parenti patriae* ("To the father of the nation") and a temple, dedicated by Augustus in 29 BC, were erected on this spot. This was the first posthumous deification in Rome, but all that has survived of the temple are parts of the podium and of the tribune built in front of it to display the figureheads of Anthony and Cleopatra's fleet, defeated by Octavian at Actium in 31 BC. Beside the temple lie the scant remains of the ARCH OF AUGUSTUS. This had three openings and is almost certainly the monument built by the Senate in 29 BC to commemorate the victory at Actium.

THE REGIA. The construction of the "Royal house" is attributed to Numa Pompilius ● *26*, the second king of Rome, who is said to have used it as his residence. It included the House of the Vestals and the building reserved for the *rex sacrorum*, a title which in early Republican times conferred the priestly attributes of the ancient kings. Later it became the residence of the *pontifex maximus*, Rome's

show Christ and the saints. Only a few fragments of the right aisle's murals can still be seen. They include a niche with a *Virgin and Child*, and the apse with a *Crucifixion* above and *Christ Giving His Blessing* below; on his right is Pope Paul I (757–67).
San Teodoro.

143

TEMPLE OF ANTONINUS AND FAUSTINA
The temple's transformation into a church saved it from destruction. Its fine façade, with steps and cipollino columns, has been preserved. The *cella's* magnificent frieze, featuring griffins and ornate candelabra (see top of facing page), recalls the temple's funerary vocation.

highest priestly functionary. After a fire and two reconstructions in the early years of the Republic, it acquired the appearance it was to keep throughout Imperial times.

THE TEMPLE OF VESTA AND THE HOUSE OF THE VESTALS ★. The temple of the goddess Vesta stands in front of the Regia. This sanctuary and the House of the Vestals were designed as a single unit, the Atrium Vestae. A substitute for the royal hearth (perceived as symbolizing all others and representing the permanence of the State), the Temple of Vesta housed the city's sacred fire. Tending this fire was originally the task of the king's daughters, but under the Republic the duty was conferred upon six specialized priestesses known as Vestals. They had to be from patrician families and were selected for this function at the age of six. They were obliged to keep their virginity throughout the time of their priesthood, which lasted for thirty years. The penalty for breaking this vow was to be buried alive in the Campus Sceleratus on the Quirinal Hill (their accomplice merely suffered flagellation in the Comitium ▲ *138*). The temple also housed the "pledges" of the permanence of Rome's universal empire said to have been brought from Troy by Aeneas. The most important of these was the Palladium, an archaic effigy of Minerva reputed to preserve the city that possessed it. The present ruins of the temple, entirely made of brick, date from the end of the 2nd century, as do those of the House of the Vestals. This was a vast building several floors high, with rooms overlooking a rectangular courtyard, itself adorned with three basins and surrounded by statues of the greatest Vestals.

THE OTHER SIDE OF THE VIA SACRA

The Via Sacra was the Forum's most ancient thoroughfare, and its most prestigious. The triumphal parades of victorious generals used it to reach the Temple of Jupiter on the Capitol.

TEMPLE OF ROMULUS. This small domed temple was dedicated to Maxentius' son Romulus ▲ *329*, who died and was deified in 309 AD. Later it was used as the vestibule to the Church of Santi Cosma e Damiano ▲ *168*. The temple was originally erected at street level, but archeological digs in the 19th century exposed its foundations.

From the Forum Holitorium to the Coliseum

154 The Forum Holitorium and Forum Boarium

157 The Circus Flaminius area

160 Piazza Venezia

162 The Imperial Forums

167 From Trajan's Markets to the Coliseum

170 The Coliseum

174 The Domus Aurea

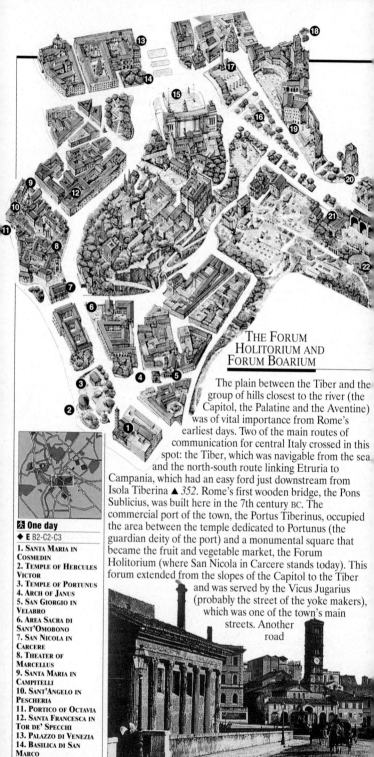

THE FORUM HOLITORIUM AND FORUM BOARIUM

The plain between the Tiber and the group of hills closest to the river (the Capitol, the Palatine and the Aventine) was of vital importance from Rome's earliest days. Two of the main routes of communication for central Italy crossed in this spot: the Tiber, which was navigable from the sea, and the north-south route linking Etruria to Campania, which had an easy ford just downstream from Isola Tiberina ▲ *352*. Rome's first wooden bridge, the Pons Sublicius, was built here in the 7th century BC. The commercial port of the town, the Portus Tiberinus, occupied the area between the temple dedicated to Portunus (the guardian deity of the port) and a monumental square that became the fruit and vegetable market, the Forum Holitorium (where San Nicola in Carcere stands today). This forum extended from the slopes of the Capitol to the Tiber and was served by the Vicus Jugarius (probably the street of the yoke makers), which was one of the town's main streets. Another road

⏳ One day

◆ E B2-C2-C3

1. SANTA MARIA IN COSMEDIN
2. TEMPLE OF HERCULES VICTOR
3. TEMPLE OF PORTUNUS
4. ARCH OF JANUS
5. SAN GIORGIO IN VELABRO
6. AREA SACRA DI SANT'OMOBONO
7. SAN NICOLA IN CARCERE
8. THEATER OF MARCELLUS
9. SANTA MARIA IN CAMPITELLI
10. SANT'ANGELO IN PESCHERIA
11. PORTICO OF OCTAVIA
12. SANTA FRANCESCA IN TOR DE' SPECCHI
13. PALAZZO DI VENEZIA
14. BASILICA DI SAN MARCO
15. VICTOR EMMANUEL II MONUMENT

bronze at the foot of the stairway portray *Thought* and *Action*. Two great fountains frame it: *The Tyrrhenian Sea* and *The Adriatic*. Above the fountains, from left to right, are marble sculptures: *Strength, Concord, Sacrifice* and *Law*. On the first level the *Altare della Patria*, the work of the sculptor Angelo Zanelli, shows the *Triumphal Processions of Work* and *Love for the Fatherland*, which converge toward the statue of the goddess Rome. Finally, crowning it all, is the colossal equestrian statue of Victor Emmanuel, in bronze that was originally gilded, sculpted by Enrico Chiaradia. The portico is dominated by statues representing the regions of Italy. Adding the finishing touches to this powerful tribute to the united nation, two gigantic bronze *quadrigae*, driven by winged Victories symbolizing *Freedom* and *Italian Unity*, rise above the *propylaea* (porticos). Inside the monument are the MUSEO CENTRALE DEL RISORGIMENTO, devoted to the history of the country's unification, and the MUSEO DELLE BANDIERE (Flag Museum) devoted to Italian military history.

Part of a Garibaldi uniform in the Museo Centrale del Risorgimento.

PALAZZO DELLE ASSICURAZIONI GENERALI DI VENEZIA.
Designed by Guido Cirilli to counterbalance Palazzo Venezia, this neo-Renaissance palace was built between 1902 and 1906 on the site of Palazzo Torlonia, which was demolished when the square was revamped. Its façade is decorated with a 16th-century winged lion, the symbol of the Serenissima (Venice).

PALAZZO VENEZIA. Pietro Barbo decided to build this palace when he became titular cardinal of San Marco in 1451; and in 1464, when he became Pope Paul II, he resolved that his residence should reflect the importance of his office. After his death, work on it continued until the 16th century. Pius IV granted part of the palazzo to the Venetian ambassadors, who resided there from 1564 to 1797, and it was then that the building acquired its present name. In 1806, by order of Napoleon I, it became the headquarters of the French administration. The building inherited its powerful corner tower and crenelations from the medieval fortresses, but the mullioned windows in marble on the *piano nobile*, the great doorway on Piazza Venezia, the elegant courtyard and the decoration of the rooms all display the finesse of the Renaissance. A MUSEUM now occupies the apartments of Paul II and part of the PALAZZETTO VENEZIA (built by the same Pope at the foot of the tower, but moved to the rear of the palace in 1911 to improve the landscaping of the new square). Its collection

PALAZZO VENEZIA
Mussolini's offices were in the palace from 1929 to 1943. He used to stand on the balcony overlooking the piazza in order to harangue the crowd below.

The courtyard of Palazzo Venezia.

161

▲ FROM THE FORUM HOLITORIUM TO THE COLISEUM

1. Trajan's Column
2. Trajan's Markets
3. Caesar's Forum
4. Augustus' Forum
5. Nerva's Forum
6. Temple of Peace

THE "RECONCILIATION" Priests filing past Mussolini at the head of a parade of Fascist youth organizations in the Imperial Forums.

includes tapestries, ceramics, weapons, works in silver and gold, sculptures and numerous paintings. The most remarkable rooms in the palace are the Sala Regia, where the ambassadors met before being received in audience by the Pope; the Sala del Concistorio, where the cardinals used to meet; and the Sala del Mappamondo, in which Mussolini installed his study. On Piazza San Marco is a figure of a woman, known as Madama Lucrezia, perhaps originally from the neighboring Temple of Isis, that became one of the famous talking statues of Rome● 47.

BASILICA DI SAN MARCO. This church was founded in 336 by Pope Mark, who dedicated it to the evangelist. In the 9th century it was rebuilt by Gregory IV, and in the 12th century a campanile was added. It underwent further modifications when Pope Paul II included it in the new Palazzo di Venezia. The outer portico with elegant arcades and the Loggia of the Benediction, which date from this period, form one of the city's most successful Renaissance façades. The interior, designed as a traditional basilica with three naves, has survived, as has part of the Cosmatesque paving ● 76. But the beautiful coffered ceiling decorated with the coat of arms of Paul II was added in the 15th century, and the stucco decoration and paintings in the central nave date from the 18th century. These illustrate the story of St Abdon and St Sennen, two Persian martyrs venerated in the Middle Ages whose relics are preserved in the crypt, together with those of the basilica's founder. The large mosaic with a gold background in the apse dates from the 19th century and was inspired by the one in the Church of Santi Cosma e Damiano ▲ 168.

THE IMPERIAL FORUMS

At the end of the Republic it was realized that the Forum was not large enough to meet the needs of the capital of an immense empire. Julius Caesar

Julius Caesar.

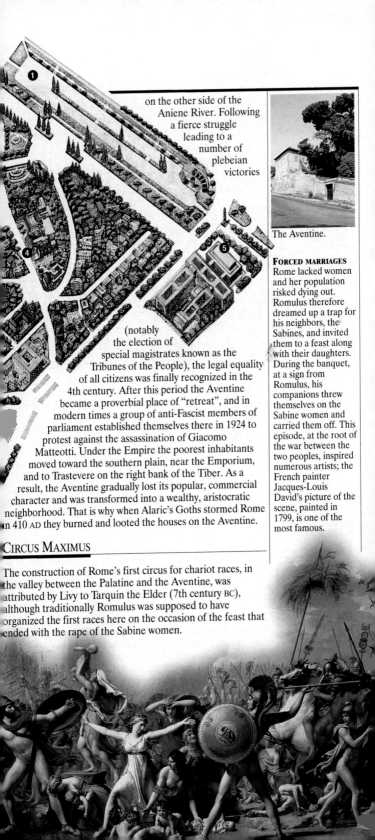

on the other side of the Aniene River. Following a fierce struggle leading to a number of plebeian victories

The Aventine.

FORCED MARRIAGES
Rome lacked women and her population risked dying out. Romulus therefore dreamed up a trap for his neighbors, the Sabines, and invited them to a feast along with their daughters. During the banquet, at a sign from Romulus, his companions threw themselves on the Sabine women and carried them off. This episode, at the root of the war between the two peoples, inspired numerous artists; the French painter Jacques-Louis David's picture of the scene, painted in 1799, is one of the most famous.

(notably the election of special magistrates known as the Tribunes of the People), the legal equality of all citizens was finally recognized in the 4th century. After this period the Aventine became a proverbial place of "retreat", and in modern times a group of anti-Fascist members of parliament established themselves there in 1924 to protest against the assassination of Giacomo Matteotti. Under the Empire the poorest inhabitants moved toward the southern plain, near the Emporium, and to Trastevere on the right bank of the Tiber. As a result, the Aventine gradually lost its popular, commercial character and was transformed into a wealthy, aristocratic neighborhood. That is why when Alaric's Goths stormed Rome in 410 AD they burned and looted the houses on the Aventine.

CIRCUS MAXIMUS

The construction of Rome's first circus for chariot races, in the valley between the Palatine and the Aventine, was attributed by Livy to Tarquin the Elder (7th century BC), although traditionally Romulus was supposed to have organized the first races here on the occasion of the feast that ended with the rape of the Sabine women.

▲ Circus Maximus and the Aventine

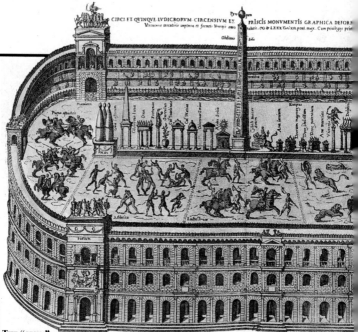

CIRCI ET QVINQVE LVDICRORVM CIRCENSIVM EX... PRISCIS MONVMENTIS GRAPHICA DEFORM...

THE "SPINA"
On the *spina*, as well as two obelisks and the seven eggs and seven dolphins that served to mark the laps, there were various small buildings and shrines.

Subsequently stone steps with wooden seats were added. In 4 BC Julius Caesar had the circus enlarged substantially, but the most important event was the erection on the *spina* – the long low central wall that linked the two turning posts – of the obelisk of Ramses II, brought from Heliolopolis by Augustus (in 1589 it was moved to Piazza del Popolo ▲ *306*). Much later Constantius II added a second obelisk, that of Tutmoses III, from Thebes (also removed by Sixtus V in 1587, to be re-erected in Piazza San Giovanni in Laterano ▲ *196*). The circus was nearly 2,000 feet long and was said to have a capacity of more than 300,000 spectators. Substantial remains are to be seen at the curved end on the Palatine side; they correspond to the middle of the *cavea* (steps) and date from the time of Hadrian (117–38 AD).

THE GAMES. Caesar organized a mock battle with a thousand infantry, six hundred horsemen and forty elephants. The *spina*, which the *quadrigae* (two-wheeled chariots drawn by four horses) had to circle counterclockwise seven times, was just over 1,100 feet long. The most important races took place during the Ludi Romani (Roman Games), from September 14 to 18. The four *factiones* (teams) of charioteers, Albata, Russata, Prasina and Veneta, with their white, red, green and blue colors, eventually developed the characteristics of full-blown political parties. The last races in the Circus Maximus were held in 549, during the reign of Totila.

AT THE FOOT OF THE AVENTINE. In line with the Circus Maximus, silhouetted against the sky are the buildings of the F.A.O. (Food and Agriculture Organization of the United Nations), inaugurated in 1951, and the obelisk of Axum (4th century AD) transported from the Ethiopian city to Rome in 1937. THE STATUE OF GIUSEPPE MAZZINI (1805–72) that adorns the Piazzale Ugo La Malfa has had an eventful history. The Freemason sculptor Ettore Ferrari was commissioned to make it in 1890, but because of Mazzini's militant republicanism and controversial political image it was not inaugurated until 1949. (Return to the Tiber, turn left,

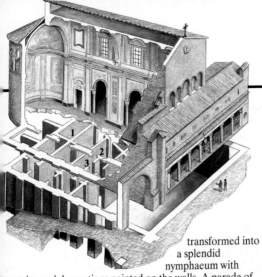

transformed into a splendid nymphaeum with fountains and decorations painted on the walls. A parade of cupids riding sea serpents can still be seen on the right. But the most remarkable element is a large fresco on one of the walls depicting Proserpina returning from Hades. From the court of the nymphaeum you reach the ground-floor rooms, which lead to the Clivus Scauri (1). On a well-preserved vault can be seen a fresco in twelve sections showing male figures carrying scrolls, and pairs of sheep. A praying figure painted in one of the lunettes gives evidence of the Christian character of the house at that time. At the top of a small staircase is the "confessio", a sort of alcove entirely decorated with frescoes from the second half of the 4th century, depicting scenes of martyrdom (arrests, decapitation, and general violence); these describe the passions of John and Paul and also those of Crispus, Crispinianus and Benedicta, who were all executed under Julian the Apostate and whose bodies were buried in this house.

THE TEMPLE OF CLAUDIUS. At the western top of the Coelian Hill, overlooking the Palatine, stand the remains of a temple dedicated to the Emperor Claudius, who was deified by his wife Agrippina soon after his death in 54 AD. The temple was built on top of the ruins of a rectangular building. The western wall, which can be seen between the campanile and the monastery of Santi Giovanni e Paolo, belongs to the oldest part of the monument. To the east, the supporting walls that run along the Via Claudia down toward the Coliseum were built by Nero as a frame for the monumental gardens of the Domus Aurea ▲ 174.

▲ 174.

THE HOUSE OF THE SAINTS JOHN AND PAUL
This is painted with remarkable decorations on a white background showing youths supporting green bowers in which there are peacocks and other large birds. The vault is adorned with cupids and birds rampaging in the foliage. Later decorations, which probably date from the 4th century AD, are to be seen in rooms (2) and (3).

CLAUDIUS
The Emperor Claudius (41–54 AD) was often ridiculed, but he was in fact a scholar and a great administrator. As a soldier he pursued Augustus' policies and succeeded in conquering Britain. But this man who stammered and walked with a limp had the misfortune of marrying first Messalina, notorious for her debauchery, and then Agrippina, who had him assassinated to ensure her son Nero's succession to the throne.

SANTA MARIA IN DOMNICA

The aqueduct built by Nero (54–68 AD) started at Porta Maggiore and brought water to the Palatine Hill.

THE ARCH OF DOLABELLA AND THE AREA AROUND SANTA MARIA IN DOMNICA. From Piazza Santi Giovanni e Paolo, the Via San Paolo della Croce rises between high walls, along the side of the Villa Celimontana, toward a travertine arch supporting Nero's aqueduct. The attic bears an inscription (10 AD) giving the names of the consuls Publius Cornelius Dolabella and Caius Junius Silanus. This arch was no doubt originally the Porta Caelimontana, one of the gates in the

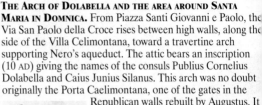

Republican walls rebuilt by Augustus. It opens onto a very typical Roman scene. To the left is the isolated brick silhouette of a pilaster from Claudius' aqueduct; behind the trees in the background stand the round Church of Santo Stefano; and in the center is the NAVICELLA, a marble ship on a base plate bearing the insignia of Pope Leo X (1513). It has since been transformed into a fountain. A portico built in the same period by Sansovino gives access to Santa Maria in Domnica.

"The park [of the Villa Celimontana], almost unique in its variety and fantasy among Roman parks, follows the folds of the Coelian Hill, on the ridge of which it stands."
Gabriel Fauré

SANTA MARIA IN DOMNICA. No mention of this church can be found earlier than the time of Pope Leo III (795–816), but its foundation, on the remains of the barracks of the 5th cohort of *vigiles* ▲ 356, probably goes back to the 7th century. The present building dates from the pontificate of Pascal I (817–24), as do the beautiful mosaics in the apse: the chancel arch portrays the Savior seated on the vault of heaven between two angels, while below this the apostles are shown being led by Peter and Paul, Moses and Elijah. At the back of the apse there is a hieratic Byzantine image of the *Virgin and Child* seated in the midst of a crowd of angels, while the Pope (distinguished by the square nimbus of the living) humbly touches her foot. To the left of the church, a monumental door opens onto the Villa Celimontana.

"VIRGIN AND CHILD" With its vivid colors and iconographic freedom, which combines the Hellenistic and Byzantine styles, this mosaic is one of the finest Carolingian works in Rome.

VILLA CELIMONTANA. On sunny days this villa's magnificent trees are an invitation to walk in their shade among the flowers and fountains. The park, which is now open to the public, has been in existence since the 15th century. It was later the garden of the Villa Mattei ▲ 369, which had been conceived as a pleasure palace and adorned with ancient sculptures collected by its owners. The *casino* was built between 1581 and 1586 by Jacopo del Duca, and an obelisk was erected in the garden. This had previously stood on the Capitol and was given in 1584 to Prince Mattei by the Senate of Rome in gratitude for his good works. Between the 16th and the 19th centuries the villa was open to the public one day a year: during the pilgrimage to the Seven Churches ▲ 381, rehabilitated by St Philip

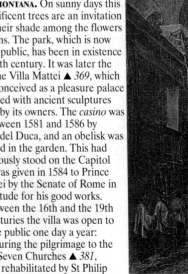

The cloister of the basilica is the work of the Vassalletto family.

The statues crowning the basilica's façade portray Christ, St John the Evangelist, St John the Baptist and the Fathers of the Church.

...osaics in the chapels dedicated to St ...ohn the Evangelist (5th century) and St ...enanzio (7th century) afford proof of ...e building's age. The font (in the ...enter) is a huge green basalt urn ...riginally used for the total ...mmersion of those being baptized; it is ...urrounded by eight porphyry columns ...nd has a bronze cover made between ...677 and 1678.

HE SCALA SANTA AND SANCTA ...ANCTORUM. The steps of the Scala Santa ...re said to be the ones on which Christ stood ... Pontius Pilate's palace during his trial, and ... Helena is supposed to have brought them to ...ome. Pilgrims climb these twenty-eight steps ...n their knees as an act of veneration. Sixtus V ...ad them erected as a stairway to the private ...hapel of the popes, San Lorenzo in Palatio. This ...hapel, which was part of the medieval palace, ...wes its other name, the Sancta Sanctorum ..."Holy of Holies"), to the precious relics it ...ontains. The most famous of these is an *...cheiropoieton*, an image of Christ "not made by ...uman hands", which Innocent III (1198–1216) ...ad covered with silver leaf. (Proceed along ...iale Carlo Felice.)

THE CASTRENSE AMPHITHEATER

The amphitheater owes its survival to its incorporatation into the Aurelian Wall, although only one of

its three levels is well preserved. The name comes from the late Latin *castrum*, meaning "Imperial palace".

CIRCUS VARIANUS

This circus derives its name from the family of the Emperor Heliogabalus, the Varii. It was recently discovered at the northern end of the ssorium, running allel to Claudius' duct and the ian Wall. On the as placed the hat must ned the adrian's tinous, on the rmer

arther ably ast

SANTA CROCE IN GERUSALEMME

The most important ancient remains in this area – the Castrense Amphitheater, the Baths of Helena, the Circus Varianus and the hall converted to create Santa Croce in Gerusalemme – were all part of a single Imperial villa, the Sessorium, begun by Septimius Severus and completed by Heliogabalus in the 3rd century AD. The Baths of Helena were covered over by the construction work for the Via Felice instigated by Sixtus V ● *61*.

BASILICA OF SANTA CROCE IN GERUSALEMME.

Tradition has it that Santa Croce, one of the major basilicas, was built by Constantine in 320 AD to house the relics brought back from Jerusalem by his mother, St Helena. After frequent restorations in the Middle Ages, it was almost completely rebuilt in 1743 by Domenico Gregorini. Behind its convex façade there is an unusual oval atrium with an elliptical ambulatory (pictured on the left). The ancient columns separating the nave from the two aisles alternate with Baroque pillars. The whole of the interior is adorned with stucco decorations. The frescoes on the main vault of the church and the walls of the choir were painted by Corrado Giaquinto in 1745. The choir vault still has its late-15th-century decorations. The mid 18th-century *baldacchino* rests on the columns of the original medieval ciborium. The underground chapel of St Helena, below the nave, is adorned with a splendid 15th-century mosaic designed by Melozzo da Forlì.

THE CHAPEL OF THE RELICS.

Of all the churches in Rome, Santa Croce has one of the richest collections of relics. A special chapel was therefore built for them in 1930. A staircase to the left of the choir leads to this chapel, where one can see three pieces of the True Cross, one of its nails, a

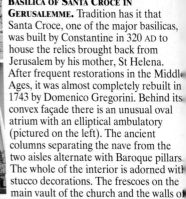

fragment of the INRI ("Jesus of Nazareth, King of the Jews") inscription, two thorns from Christ's crown of thorns, a piece of the sponge that was held up to him, one of the silver pieces paid to Judas, St Thomas's finger which touched the wounds of Christ, and the crossbar from the Good Thief's cross. The paving stones are said to have been laid on a substantial amount of earth from Golgotha.

The Vatican

209 St Peter's Basilica

210 The greatest church in Christendom

214 Inside the Vatican

218 The Sistine Chapel

222 The Raphael Rooms

224 The Vatican Museums

232 The Borgo and Via della Conciliazione

233 Castel Sant'Angelo

236 Prati

▲ The Vatican

⚐ One day

◆ **D** A2-A3-A4

1. Piazza San Pietro
2. St Peter's Basilica
3. Sistine Chapel
4. Cortile del Belvedere
5. Cortile della Pigna
6. Entrance to the Vatican Museums
7. Pinacoteca (Vatican Picture Gallery)
8. Casina di Pio IV
9. Vatican Library
10. Palazzo del Governatorato
11. Vatican Radio
12. Vatican Station
13. Papal Audience Hall
14. Passetto
15. Via della Conciliazione
16. Castel Sant'Angelo ✪
17. Palazzo di Giustizia

A STATE WITHIN A CITY ✪

Vatican City may be Europe's smallest state, covering less than one fifth of a square mile, and having 282 permanent residents, plus 110 Swiss Guards, but it is also the most visited: 6 million pilgrims and tourists pass through its gates every year. Neither ticket nor pass is necessary to enter St Peter's Basilica and the museums (you may have to return several times, as opening times are unreliable). Those wishing to visit Vatican City should contact the Ufficio Informazioni Pellegrini e Turisti (in St Peter's Square) to book a guide (one visit per day, except Wednesdays and public holidays).

The Vatican City is the smallest State in Europe (less than one fifth of a square mile). Its bound were fixed on February 11, 1929, by the Latera Treaty, which recognized the Pope's sovereign over his territory. The treaty also gave extraterritorial status to a number of buildings including the three other great patriarchal bas of Rome (San Giovanni in Laterano, San Paolo fuori le Mura and Santa Maria Maggiore), as w as the papal villa of Castel Gandolfo and the Palazzo della Cancelleria.

ST PETER'S KEYS
The coat of arms of the popes includes the tiara (the triple papal crown: father of kings and princes, king and rector of the world, and vicar of Christ) and the keys of the Kingdom of Heaven, entrusted by Jesus to St Peter.

THE SWISS GUARDS
The institution of the Swiss Guards (officially the *Cohors pedestris Helvetorium a sacra custodia Pontificis*) goes back to Julius II. In 1505 the pontiff obtained a personal guard composed of two hundred Swiss soldiers. This guard was to receive a tragic baptism of fire on May 6, 1527, during the Sack of Rome ● *36*, and went on to prove value and loyalty the Pope many times. Each year May 6 a sumptuo ceremony commemorates t combat and the of fidelity. The design of their uniform, which h remained unchar for 450 years, is often wrongly attributed to Michelangelo.

Between 1508 and 1512 Michelangelo was to cover the entire ceiling (over 3,000 square feet) with more than three hundred figures. Before starting work, he had all the preparations made by his assistants erased and the scaffolding remade to ensure that he could paint the whole vault single-handedly, without leaving any gaps. He began by painting the frescoes near the door, progressing toward the altar – which explains the more formal style of *The Life of Noah*.

Recent restoration has revived the work's brilliance, which is typical of true fresco painting since the pigments are absorbed by the fresh mortar.

"He brought the blessing of light to the painting, which sufficed to illuminate a world plunged in darkness for centuries."

Vasari

Despite the indisputable grace of the *ignudi* (nudes), opinions differ as to the meaning Michelangelo intended to give them. As can be seen, he used the chapel's strong architectural framework to provide a structure that would unite the work as a whole.

"MOSES AND THE DAUGHTERS OF JETHRO"
When the construction of the Sistine Chapel had been completed, Sixtus IV commissioned various Tuscan and Umbrian painters to decorate the walls with frescoes that would establish a parallel between the life of Moses and that of Jesus. Botticelli painted the events of Moses' early life.

The story runs from right to left. Moses kills an Egyptian (bottom right-hand corner) and takes refuge with the Midianites; he meets Jethro's daughters and puts to flight the shepherds who are preventing them from watering their flock; Jehovah appears to Moses (top left-hand corner) and he leaves Egypt with the Jews (bottom left). In Proust's *Un amour de Swann* Swann falls in love with Odette because of her resemblance to the figure of Zipporah, a daughter of Jethro (see detail, left): "He admired her large eyes, her delicate face which hinted at an imperfect skin, the marvelous strands of hair that clung to her tired cheeks."

"St Benedict"
This portrayal of St Benedict by Perugino (1450–1523) originally formed part of a painting of *The Ascension* that he made for the Church of San Pietro in Perugia in 1495.

The loggias and rooms decorated by Raphael (1483–1520) in the Vatican are among his greatest works. In addition, three key pictures that mark his development as a painter are preserved in the Pinacoteca.

"THE MADONNA DI FOLIGNO"

This work was commissioned around 1512 by Sigismondo dei Conti as an *ex voto* offering. It portrays the Virgin and Child surrounded by St Francis, St John the Baptist and St Jerome, who is introducing the donor of the painting. It is one of the most important works painted by Raphael in the graceful style of his early days in Rome.

"THE TRANSFIGURATION"

The last picture Raphael painted was commissioned by Cardinal Giulio de Medici. The upper part (reproduced here) portrays the divine miracle. Christ rises in a supernatural light, with Moses and Elijah beside him, while three terror-stricken apostles avert their eyes. The lower part shows the other disciples unable to perform a miracle: in the absence of their master, they are seen to be incapable of healing a boy possessed by the devil. By revealing its strong luminous contrasts a recent restoration has retrieved the narrative power of this work, unanimously recognized as a masterpiece of universal art.

THE RAPHAEL LOGGIAS

(These can only be visited by special permission.) They were decorated by Raphael's pupils, following the designs of the master, then Superintendent of Antiquities.

Each of the thirteen bays contains four Old Testament scenes, while the walls and arches are embellished with grotesques inspired by the decorations of the Domus Aurea ▲ *174*, discovered in 1506.

The scenes reproduced here show *The Expulsion from Paradise*, *Isaac Blessing Jacob*, *The Parting of the Red Sea* and *The Building of the Ark*. These works, frequently reproduced in engravings, constitute what has been called "Raphael's Bible". European painting and decorative arts have drawn from it so often for Old Testament subjects that most representations are ultimately derived from it.

"Descent from the Cross"
Painted between 1602 and 1604 for the Oratorians, this picture originally hung in the Chiesa Nuova ▲ *281*. In 1797 it was requisitioned by the French, despite the discredit in which Caravaggio was held during the 18th century. Its dramatic force derives from the contrast between the pale body of Christ and the shadows enveloping the holy women and St John. The emphatic gesture of Mary Magdalene stresses the pain which Nicodemus' expression invites us to share. The dark background heightens the picture's relief. For the body of Christ, Caravaggio came nearer than usual to the classical ideal by choosing a rather beautiful body whose musculature he wished to emphasize.

between 1701 and 1709, it was radically transformed in the mid 19th century by Antonio Cipolla, who designed the façade. The last sovereigns of the Two Sicilies, King Francesco II and Queen Maria Sofia, are buried here. (Continue along Via Giulia, turn right into Via Sant'Eligio).

SANT'ELIGIO DEGLI OREFICI. This building was erected by Raphael in 1509 for the goldsmiths' guild, St Eligius being the patron saint of goldsmiths and blacksmiths. The façade and the frescoes and painting behind the high altar date from the 17th century. (Return to the Spirito Santo dei Napoletani and take the street facing the church; this leads to a small piazza.)

PALAZZO RICCI. The piazza is dominated by the façade of Palazzo Ricci. Traces of the grisaille frescoes painted in the middle of the 16th century by Polidoro da Caravaggio and Maturino da Firenze can still be seen on the façade. (Turn right into Via di Monserrato.)

SANTA MARIA IN MONSERRATO. This church, begun by Antonio Sangallo the Younger in 1518, has been the national church of Spaniards in Rome since 1875. Its façade, built by Francesco da Volterra, is adorned with a relief showing the Virgin and Child sawing a mountain, an allusion to the Catalan shrine of Monserrat. The painting of *San Diego* in the first chapel on the right is attributed to Annibale Caracci; the chapel also contains the mortal remains of Pope Alexander VI and of King Alfonso XIII of Spain, who died in exile in 1941. On the altar of the third chapel on the left stands a beautiful statue of St James by Jacopo Sansovino. (Cross the Piazza di Santa Caterina della Rota.)

SAN GIROLAMO DELLA CARITÀ. Once famous for Domenichino's painting of *The Last Communion of St Jerome* above the high altar – removed by the French in 1797 and now in the picture gallery of the Vatican (a copy has replaced it) – this church was redesigned by Domenico Castelli in the mid 17th century. Two chapels are of particular interest. The first on the right, the SPADA CHAPEL, was long attributed to Borromini but was designed by Virgilio Spada, perhaps under the master's guidance. Medallions portraying previous members of the Spada family adorn the walls of yellow-and-brown marble. The balustrade is formed by two kneeling angels with removable wings holding a marble drape. The other is the elegant ANTAMORO CHAPEL, to the left of the high altar, which is the only work in Rome of the architect Filippo Juvarra (1678–1736). (Return to the Via Giulia.)

"FINESTRE INGINOCCHIATE"
A particularly fine feature of the Palazzo Sacchetti is its "kneeling" ground-floor windows: the frame of each window is supported on consoles.

The façade of Santa Maria in Monserrato.

The *Last Communion of St Jerome* ▲ 231 by Domenichino, now in the Vatican picture gallery.

PALAZZO FALCONIERI. Orazio Falconieri, who had bought two adjacent palazzi, asked Borromini to unite them. The façade on the Via Giulia is composed around two doorways framed in rustic bossage; at the back an ample loggia overlooks the Tiber. At each end of the façade there are two tall pilasters supporting falcons' heads on female busts, the vivid emblem of the originally Tuscan Falconieri family.

SANTA MARIA DELL'ORAZIONE E MORTE. This oratory belonging to the confraternity of the "buona morte", which ensured Christian funerals to the poor of Rome, was rebuilt according to plans by Ferdinando Fuga between 1733 and 1737. Its curved façade with pilasters and columns alternating on two levels is clearly influenced by Borromini and the high cupola is a fine achievement. The small skulls used as a decorative motif throughout, particularly over the main door, recall the purpose of this pious confraternity. The building supports a bridge over the Via Giulia to the gardens of Palazzo Farnese. Another bridge was originally to span the Tiber and connect the Palazzo with the Farnesina ▲ *360*; however, Michelangelo's plans for linking the two palaces were never carried out. Farther down the street is the FONTANA DEL MASCHERONE, built of ancient marble remains, which takes its name from the mask that decorates it. (Take the Via del Mascherone opposite the fountain.)

PALAZZO FARNESE

PIAZZA FARNESE. Somewhat severe in appearance today, the piazza (formerly also known as Piazza del Duca) was at one time animated by frequent celebrations and spectacles, including bullfights. Due to the influence of Renato Nicolini, a member of the municipal council who organized the *estate romana* ("Roman summer") for a few years in the 1980's, it briefly recovered some of its past glory.

THE CONSTRUCTION OF THE PALACE. The Palazzo Farnese is the largest of Rome's patrician palaces. Originally planned by Antonio Sangallo the Younger in 1517 for Cardinal Alessandro Farnese, the project was vastly amplified in 1534

Fontana del Mascherone.

PALAZZO FARNESE
A pair of large twin fountains enliven the piazza. The water runs into Egyptian granite basins brought here from the Baths of Caracalla, surmounted by what are often taken to be *fleur-de-lys.* The flowers are in fact irises, the emblem of the Farnese family.

FAMOUS FRESCOES
After studying Michelangelo's frescoes in the Sistine Chapel, Annibale Carracci (1560–1609), youngest and most brilliant artist of the Carracci family, painted the vaulted ceiling of the great gallery of Palazzo Farnese. Within a framework of *trompe l'oeil* architectural effects, these Baroque frescoes brought mythology to life in joyfully exuberant style.

hen the latter became Pope, taking the name of Paul III. In 546, following Sangallo's death, Michelangelo was entrusted ith its continuation. He was responsible for the design of the econd floor, the cornice and the two upper orders of columns the courtyard. After Michelangelo's death in 1564, iacomo della Porta completed the building, erecting the çade and the splendid loggia that overlooks the Via Giulia. the 18th century the palace was inherited by the Bourbons Naples. Today it houses the French Embassy and the agnificent library of the Ecole française de Rome, a esearch institute for archeologists and historians. The oman nickname for the palace is *il dado* ("the dice").

RCHITECTURE. Some of the materials used for the building ere from ancient ruins: the travertine marble that frames the indows is said to have come from the Coliseum. The façade Piazza Farnese is quite austere. Composed of thirteen ays, it is devoid of decoration save for the window frames nd the bossage of the main entrance, which is surmounted by loggia. The courtyard, which used to contain the Farnese ollection of ancient statuary, is particularly elegant. The ree orders of classical columns (Doric, Ionic and orinthian) are superimposed in a rhythmic accession of windows and open arches. The çade on the garden side of the building choes this use of the three orders. side the palace the most outstanding eatures are the Salotto Dipinto ecorated with frescoes by Francesco alviati and Taddeo Zuccari; the Sala elle Guardie, which is dominated

THE COURTYARD OF PALAZZO FARNESE
"The admirable inner courtyard is the building's masterpiece. Each floor has its own enclosed ambulatory, its portico of columns and each column is engaged in a bold powerfully vaulted arch; but the balustrades, the diversity of the upper floors, one doric, one ionic ... imbue this strict ordering with charming beauty."
    Hippolyte Taine,
    Voyage en Italie

The imposing main entrance of Palazzo Farnese.

The *Triumph of Bacchus and Ariadne*, the central fresco by Annibale Carracci in the gallery of Palazzo Farnese.

PALAZZO SPADA
The façade of Palazzo Spada has niches enclosing eight stucco statues of the great men of ancient Rome, among them Marcellus and Caesar (shown above). The walls of the courtyard are decorated with mythological figures such as Venus, Mars, and Pluto.

BORROMINI'S PERSPECTIVE ★
The impression of depth in this corridor, less than 30 feet long, is mainly achieved by the use of diminishing columns placed ever closer together. The perspective effect, which contracts and extends the space deceptively, gives the illusion of a depth of over 120 feet. The actual height of the seemingly tall statue at the end of the corridor, including the pedestal, is less than that of an average person.

The fountain in front of the Monte di Pietà.

by a copy of the statue of Ercole Farnese ▲ *320* (the original is in Naples); and above all the Galleria, with its superb frescoes depicting the loves of the gods and goddesses painted by Annibale Carracci, with the help of his brother Agostino, between 1597 and 1604. (Take Via dei Venti.)

THE AREA AROUND PALAZZO SPADA ● 8

Cross the minute Piazza della Quercia, where an evergreen oak lends a note of rusticity, and you will come to the front of Palazzo Spada. Its façade, in full splendor after restoration work, is festooned with statues, medallions, garlands, and other decorative moldings by Giulio Mazzoni, providing a startling contrast to Palazzo Farnese.
PALAZZO SPADA. Built for Cardinal Girolamo Capo di Ferro between 1548 and 1550, but modified for the Spada family in the 17th century, this palace has been the seat of the Council of State since 1927. On the left as one enters the courtyard one can view the astonishing *trompe l'oeil* perspective devised by Borromini. The Galleria Spada, one of the most important collections of 17th century paintings in Rome, can also be visited. It contains works by Guercino, Honthorst, Reni and Valentin, among others. A remarkable statue of Pompey stands in the Sala Grande. (Turn right as you come out of the palace.)

ANTISSIMA TRINITÀ DEI PELLEGRINI. The celebration of the jubilee every fifty years attracted crowds of pilgrims to Rome and hostels were created in almost every part of the city. This church was built near one of the hostels between 1603 and 1616. The rendered brick façade, designed by Francesco De Sanctis, was added in 1723. Above the high altar there is Guido Reni's *Holy Trinity* (1625) painted to look like a relief.

AN PAOLO ALLA REGOLA. According to tradition this church was built on the site of the house where St Paul stayed while in Rome. Its plan, in the shape of a Greek cross, and façade were designed in the 18th century by Giacomo Cioli and Giuseppe Sardi. (Continue through Piazza San Paolo alla Regola and Piazza San Salvatore to the Monte di Pietà.)

ONTE DI PIETÀ. This institution was founded by Pope Paul IV to provide Romans with pawnbroking facilities. The financial system of the Pontifical States being largely based upon the fiduciary issue of currency, the Monte di Pietà acquired economic importance in modern times. The present building, erected in the 17th and 18th centuries, was completed by Nicola Salvi (1697–1751), the architect of the Fontana di Trevi ▲ 298. The chapel was decorated in a remarkable Baroque style during the first half of the 18th century. (Take Via dei Specchi, then the first turning on the left.)

ROUND CAMPO DE' FIORI

AN CARLO AI CATINARI. This church belonging to the Barnabites (who took their name from San Barnaba, their original church, in Milan) was built between 1612 and 1620 according to plans by Rosato Rosati. The façade is the work of Giambattista Soria. The interior is rich in ancient marbles and is surmounted by a fine dome with stucco decorations. In the pendentives paintings by Domenichino illustrate the four cardinal virtues; and above the high altar, which is

adorned with ancient columns, hangs Pietro da Cortona's *St Charles Borromeo during the Procession of the Holy Nail* (1650).

VIA DE' GIUBBONARI. This bustling street is famous for the variety of its shops, and the little restaurant in the Largo dei Librari which serves *filetti di baccalà* (cod in batter), with white wine from the Castelli. (Take the second turning on the right, Via dei Chiavari. The houses in the first street to the left Via di Grotta Pinta stand on the site of Pompey's theater ▲ 248.)

CHARLES BORROMEO
Born in 1538 in Arona, he was raised to the rank of cardinal in 1560 and named archbishop of Milan by his uncle Pius IV. He died in 1584 and was canonized in 1610. The Church of San Carlo ai Catinari was dedicated to him in 1611, and Guido Reni painted this portrait of him in 1636.

THE "CATINARI"
The church received its name because of the presence of makers of wooden bowls (*catini*) in the neighborhood. Today there are still a number of craftsmen in the surrounding streets who ply the traditional trades of the area.

This painting of *The Annunciation* in San Carlo ai Catinari, with its remarkable luminosity and chiaroscuro effects, is one of Giovanni Lanfranco's finest works. The face of the Virgin is illuminated by the light of the Holy Spirit.

The Via di Grotta Pinta is a remarkable example of urban continuity: its houses follow the outline of the *cavea* of the Theater of Pompey. Sections of its walls can be seen in the cellars of several of the buildings.

CAMPO DEI FIORI, APPEALING TO ALL THE SENSES ✪
At dawn, Monday to Saturday, fresh fruit and vegetables, flowers, meat and delicacies are set out on the colorful stalls of Rome's most picturesque market. In the early evening the square comes to life again as people meet up at the *Vineria Reggio* or the *Taverna del Campo* to enjoy a glass of white wine from the Castelli Romani region.

POMPEY'S THEATER AND PORTICOS. In 61 BC work began on Rome's first permanent theater. Until then there had only been wooden stages because it was feared that lasting constructions would encourage people to attend entertainments ▲ *172* too often. Heartened by the particularly sumptuous Triumph he received upon his return

from Asia, Pompey cleverly bypassed the law. He had a theater built on his own land and topped it with a temple dedicated to Venus Victrix (the goddess of victory), so he could claim that the hemisphere of seats was an immense flight of steps leading to the temple! The complex, designed to enhance the creator's image, conferred on him the status of a Hellenistic monarch. The theater, which could hold 18,000 spectators, was inaugurated in 55 BC with literary and musical events, and with hunts lasting several days. One hundred lions, twenty elephants and a number of lynxes were massacred during the festivities. Behind the stage a portico of massive dimensions had been erected. It was adorned with numerous statues of women, and at the end of it was a large exedra which became the Curia (meeting place) of the Senate; this was where Julius Caesar was assassinated. Inside the Curia, diametrically opposite the temple of Venus Victrix, there was a statue of Pompey holding a globe in his hand. Today, remains of the Curia can be seen in the Area Sacra dell' Argentina ▲ *250*.

CAMPO DE' FIORI. This piazza owes its name to the fields full of flowers which were here before the erection of buildings in the 15th century. It soon became the site of inns, bookshops and the colorful market still held here

The Renaissance model of a cupola – as conceived by Brunelleschi, then Bramante, Antonio di Sangallo the Younger and finally Michelangelo – was a spherical dome with convergent ribbing resting on a drum and surmounted by a lantern. This eventually gave way to the variations of the Mannerist architects, who replaced the sphere with an ellipse, got rid of the lantern, and used frescoes for effect.

SAN ROCCO
The amazing use of color in the pendentives contrasts with the dark cupola.

SANTA MARIA MAGGIORE ▲ 342
(The Pauline Chapel)
Cigoli's fresco fills the whole cupola.

SANTA MARIA IN CAMPITELLI ▲ 159
An exercise in sobriety, with its monochrome uniformity and even lighting.

SANTI AMBROGIO E CARLO AL CORSO ▲ 309
An option for color in a monochromatic symphony of warm tones.

SAN CARLO AI CATINARI ▲ 247
Diminishing coffers and pictorial foreshortenings enhance the cupola's depth.

SANTA MARIA DELLA VITTORIA ▲ 294
The architecture is little more than support for an orgy of Baroque painting and stucco decoration.

M·AGRIPPA·LF·COS·TERTIVM·FECIT

The Emperor Hadrian had these words inscribed on the architrave: *M(arcus) Agrippa L(ucii) f(ilius) c(on)s(ul) tertium fecit* ("Marcus Agrippa, son of Lucius, third time consul, made [this temple]"). Below, an inscription in smaller lettering refers to restoration work in 202 AD under Septimus Severus and Caracalla.

DONKEY'S EARS
This is how Pasquino described the two bell turrets that Bernini added to the façade of the Pantheon in the 17th century. They were removed in 1883.

Annunciation in 1750. (On leaving the church, turn left into Via del Seminario, which will take you to Piazza della Rotonda.)

THE PANTHEON ★   ● 70

PIAZZA DELLA ROTONDA. The square in which the Pantheon is set was created under Clement XI (1700–21) and involved the demolition of several buildings. At the same time Giacomo della Porta's fountain (1578) was drastically modified: it was given a pedestal decorated with dolphins and the Pope's coat of arms, and an obelisk was added which, like the one in Piazza della Minerva, came from the neighboring Temple of Isis.

AGRIPPA'S TEMPLE. The plan of the Pantheon combines the pronaos (porch) of a temple with a rotunda of the kind found in Roman baths ● 68. A brilliant composite of geometrical forms and contrasting features, its architecture was intended to reflect the terrestrial and cosmic order. This is the best preserved building of ancient Rome – thanks to the Byzantine Emperor Phocas' donation of it to Pope Boniface IV and its transformation into a church, which received the name of Santa Maria dei Martiri (St Mary of the Martyrs) in 609 AD. It was originally built in 27 to 25 BC by Agrippa, who wanted to dedicate it to Augustus, his father-in-law and friend. When Augustus declined the honor, it was dedicated to the major deities venerated by the families of Claudius and Julius Caesar (Mars, Venus and the divine Julius himself) instead. The building was then rectangular and faced south. What we see today dates from the early years of Hadrian's reign, between 118 and 125 AD. The pediment was adorned with a crowned eagle, as witness the sockets. The great portico is supported by eight monolithic granite columns with white marble capitals and bases. It is

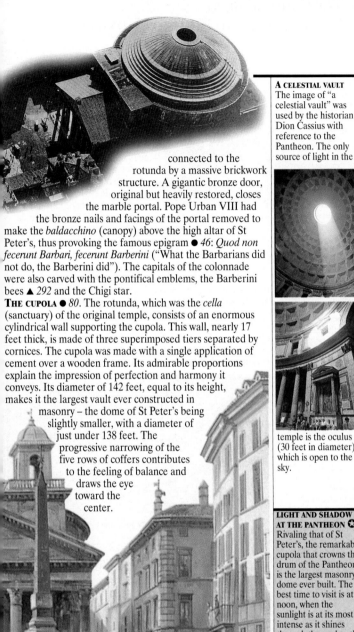

connected to the rotunda by a massive brickwork structure. A gigantic bronze door, original but heavily restored, closes the marble portal. Pope Urban VIII had the bronze nails and facings of the portal removed to make the *baldacchino* (canopy) above the high altar of St Peter's, thus provoking the famous epigram ● *46: Quod non fecerunt Barbari, fecerunt Barberini* ("What the Barbarians did not do, the Barberini did"). The capitals of the colonnade were also carved with the pontifical emblems, the Barberini bees ▲ *292* and the Chigi star.

THE CUPOLA ● *80*. The rotunda, which was the *cella* (sanctuary) of the original temple, consists of an enormous cylindrical wall supporting the cupola. This wall, nearly 17 feet thick, is made of three superimposed tiers separated by cornices. The cupola was made with a single application of cement over a wooden frame. Its admirable proportions explain the impression of perfection and harmony it conveys. Its diameter of 142 feet, equal to its height, makes it the largest vault ever constructed in masonry – the dome of St Peter's being slightly smaller, with a diameter of just under 138 feet. The progressive narrowing of the five rows of coffers contributes to the feeling of balance and draws the eye toward the center.

A CELESTIAL VAULT
The image of "a celestial vault" was used by the historian Dion Cassius with reference to the Pantheon. The only source of light in the

temple is the oculus (30 feet in diameter), which is open to the sky.

LIGHT AND SHADOW AT THE PANTHEON ✪
Rivaling that of St Peter's, the remarkable cupola that crowns the drum of the Pantheon is the largest masonry dome ever built. The best time to visit is at noon, when the sunlight is at its most intense as it shines through the oculus, the temple's only source of light. In the evening, with its colorful lighting and the bustle of life, the piazza has quite another appeal. Those who love good coffee will not miss out on a visit to the Tazza d'Oro (a stone's throw away, on the Piazza Sant'Eustachio), which is famous for its espresso and its frothy cappuccino.

▲ The Campo Marzio
From the Gesù to Palazzo Madama

THE PORTICO OF THE ARGONAUTS
Along the left side of the Pantheon is the back wall of the portico that separated Agrippa's temple from the Saepta, a large square used for electoral meetings under the Republic (under the Empire it became a center for entertainment). A reconstruction of the portico is shown above.

THE NICHES
These were originally decorated with statues of the gods and are now chapels. Beneath the third aedicule on the left is the tomb of Raphael (1483–1520), inscribed with the famous epitaph composed by Cardinal Bembo: *Ille hic est Raffaello Sanzio, timuit quo sospite vinci rerum magna parens et moriente mori.* (Alexander Pope, who borrowed the couplet for another epitaph, translated it as "Living, great nature feared he might outvie Her works; and dying, fears herself to die.") Other artists buried here include Giovanni da Udine, Perin del Vaga, Annibale Carracci, Taddeo Zuccari and Baldassare Peruzzi, as well as two kings of Italy, Vittorio Emanuele II and Umberto I.

THE NICHES. Opposite the door is the main niche, over which there is an arch. Its two fine columns are made of *pavonazzetto*, a beautiful violet-veined marble from Synnada in Asia Minor. The other niches – three on either side, alternating from rectangular to circular in shape – are fronted with monolithic columns made of a Tunisian marble known as *giallo antico*. This use of marbles, which was so important in classical architecture, is carried through in the paving of the floor, where geometrical patterns alternate, and also in the shrines (*aedicoli*) between the niches. Columns of red porphyry, *giallo antico* and granite support either triangular or rounded tympanums. Their alternation is said to have served as a model for many renaissance façades, especially that of Palazzo Farnese ▲ *244*.

THE BASILICA OF NEPTUNE AND BATHS OF AGRIPPA. Behind the Pantheon, along the Via della Palombella, there are columns, a brick wall and a marble frieze which includes dolphins and tridents. These are all that is left of a basilica dedicated to Neptune, erected by Agrippa and rebuilt by Hadrian. A little further on, near the Corso Vittorio

Emanuele, is the site of Rome's most ancient baths, inaugurated in 19 BC with an artificial lake, the Stagnum Agrippae. Both were fed by the Aqua Virgo.

THE TEMPLE OF MATIDIA. Hadrian is surely the only man in the world to have deified his mother-in-law and to have dedicated a temple to her. Situated close to the present-day Piazza Capranica, it can be reached by the Via degli Orfani. A truncated column from it can be seen in the alley called the Vicolo della Spada d'Orlando. (Take Via de' Pastini to the Piazza di Pietra.)

The Temple of Hadrian.

THE TEMPLE OF HADRIAN. After Hadrian's death his son, Antoninus Pius, erected a temple in his honor, which was dedicated in 145 AD. Eleven white-marble columns, now imprisoned within the northern wall of the Borsa (STOCK-EXCHANGE BUILDING) on the Piazza di Pietra, testify to the grandeur of the temple. Reliefs from it portraying allegorical figures, alternating with trophies, are preserved in the courtyard of the Palazzo dei Conservatori and in the National Museum of Naples. (Walk through to the Piazza Colonna, which is nearby.)

PIAZZA COLONNA

The urbanization of this section of the Campo Marzio began under the Antonines in the 2nd century.

THE COLUMN OF MARCUS AURELIUS. In the center of the square rises the column of Marcus Aurelius. Just over 83 feet tall, it was made between 193 AD (the year of the emperor's death) and 196 AD. The lower part of the column commemorates his victories over the Germanic tribes on the Danube frontier, and the upper part his success against the Sarmatians (in the area between the Volga and the Vistula rivers). Its base, originally nearly 30 feet taller, was decorated with festoons and reliefs showing victories and scenes of barbarians being forced to submit: these were destroyed in 1589 by Sixtus V. The column itself has twenty complete rings of reliefs, rather fewer than its model, Trajan's column ▲ *166*.

With its simplification and violent contrasts, it heralds the eminently dramatic 3rd-century style. The facial expressions, for example, are quite remarkable – especially those of the terror-stricken or desperately beseeching barbarians, the soldiers and the emperor-philosopher, who is most

The Bocconi ● *90* department store (now Rinascente) opened in Piazza Colonna in 1885. With its metal and glass structure the building was influenced by the stores that had sprung up in other European capitals, such as La Belle Jardinière and Le Printemps in Paris.

THE COLUMN OF MARCUS AURELIUS Inside the column a spiral staircase with 190 steps leads to the top, where the Emperor's statue originally stood. In 1589, at Sixtus V's request, Domenico Fontana replaced it with a statue of St Paul.

LEGIONARIES CROSSING A RIVER (THE EMPEROR IS TALKING TO TWO OFFICERS).

AUXILIARY TROOPS PROTECTING THE ARMY ON THE MARCH.

BATTLE SCENE, WITH LEGIONARIES MASSACRING BARBARIANS.

Drawings of the reliefs made by Giovanni Guerra when the column was restored in 1589.

THE COLUMN OF ANTONINUS PIUS
The reliefs on the base depict the apotheosis of the Emperor and his wife Faustina, being carried to heaven by a winged *genius*. On the two smaller sides there are equestrian parades.

frequently sculpted face on, no doubt to make him appear more majestic. Ranuccio Bianchi Bandinelli, a specialist in Roman art, emphasizes the artistic originality of the image of Marcus Aurelius: "Among the scenes of death and destruction, the face of the emperor in person emerges ... deeply marked by anguish, exhaustion and age. He must have been about 54 years old: this is certainly not the face of a triumphant conqueror exalted by his victories but that of a man who was 'a total stranger to the habits of the rich' (*The Meditations of Marcus Aurelius*, I, 3), a genuine, suffering lay saint." (The fountain to the right of the column is by Giacomo della Porta. Palazzo Chigi faces it on one side of the square; opposite, on the other side of the Corso, is the Galleria Colonna.)

PALAZZO CHIGI. Carlo Maderno and Felice della Greca both had a hand in the construction of this stark palazzo of the Counter-Reformation period. Building began in 1580 but it was not completed until 1630. The Baroque courtyard is decorated with stucco motifs and a fountain bearing the Chigi arms. The palazzo, acquired by the State in 1917, was the headquarters of the Ministry of Foreign

fairs before it became the seat of the Presidenza del
nsiglio dei Ministri (Prime Minister's office).

LLERIA COLONNA. When the Palazzo Boncompagni
mbino was demolished by the Municipality of Rome in
89 there were lengthy discussions about what should be
ne with the site. In the end it was decided to build a large
vered gallery which could also house the headquarters of
: Istituto Romano dei Beni Stabili. The gallery was
ugurated in 1922. Nearby, on Largo Chigi, the Bocconi
partment store (now Rinascente), completed in 1885–7,
s one of the first buildings in Rome to use modern
terials (metal and glass) while retaining a Neo-Renaissance
le. Its architect, Giulio De Angelis, was one of the principal
ponents of the Roman eclectic trend. (Cross the Corso and
: Piazza Colonna again to get to Piazza di Montecitorio.)

The pictures above
show Palazzo di
Montecitorio (left and
center) and Piazza
Colonna with Palazzo
Chigi (right).

ONTECITORIO

AZZA DI MONTECITORIO. Under the Antonines the site
cupied by the Palazzo di Montecitorio (which houses the
lian Chamber of Deputies) was used for the emperors'
mation ceremonies; the remains of the *ustrina* (logs) found
re can be seen in the National Roman Museum. In 1703 the
se of Antoninus Pius' column, now in the Cortile della
gna at the Vatican, was
o discovered here. Other
gments of the huge
anite column were used
: restoring and stabilizing
: obelisk of Psammetichus
(6th century BC), which
s erected in the middle of
: piazza in 1792.
ansported from Heliopolis
Rome in 10 BC, the
elisk was originally set up
the Campus Martius by
ugustus to serve as the
omon (pointer) of an
ormous sundial. It was
earthed in 1748 between
: Piazza del Parlamento
d San Lorenzo in Lucina.
LAZZO DI MONTECITORIO.
is building has two very
fferent aspects: the
iginal façade by Bernini
d a 20th-century Art
ouveau façade (on the
azza del Parlamento) by
rnesto Basile. The lovely,
rmonious Baroque façade
s begun in 1650 under
pe Innocent X, who

**PALAZZO DI
MONTECITORIO**
Its two façades
contrast in every way.
Whereas Bernini's is

anted to build a palace for the Ludovisi. After being held up
til 1694 the project was completed by Carlo Fontana, and
nocent XII decided to install the Tribunals (the Curia
nocenziana) there. When the Piedmontese entered Rome
1870, they were faced with the problem of finding a suitable

fluid and grandiose,
the façade added by
Ernesto Basile has a
rather cold and stolid
appearance.

The colorful market held in Piazza delle Coppelle presents an irresistible invitation to stop and browse.

The Church of Santa Maria in Campo Marzio.

site for the new parliament. In the end it was decided to use the great courtyard to accommodate the Chamber of Deputies, enclosing it with a glass roof. However, it soon became necessary to enlarge the building. Basile's design for the extension is a fine example of the style known as *floreale* (floral) in Italy because of decorative motifs inspired by exuberant vegetation. Flanking the entrance on the Piazza del Parlamento are two statues by Domenico Trentacoste (1911). The semicircular Chamber, entirely paneled in oak, is decorated with an allegorical frieze on canvas (1908–12) by Giulio Aristide Sartorio, portraying Italian civilization, the virtues of the Italian people and the most significant episodes of the nation's history. There is also a bas-relief by Davide Calandra celebrating the glory of the House of Savoy. (To reach the Church of Santa Maria in Campo Marzio, take Via Ufficio del Vicario, where you will find the *gelateria* Giolitti, which sells some of the best ice cream in Rome.)
SANTA MARIA IN CAMPO MARZIO. This church has existed since the 7th century, but it was rebuilt between 1670 and 1685 by Giovanni Antonio de Rossi. From the street nothing but the walls of the convent can be seen, recently repainted their original color, a very pale blue. Restorers have been returning to the pale colors which were used for painting façades in Rome before the 19th century. The church's portico opens onto a pretty courtyard, and its graceful cupola has a flattened, oval shape. (From here you can make a detour through the picturesque Piazza delle Coppelle, and stop at the fashionable Hemingway bar; then follow Via delle Coppelle and turn right into Via della Maddalena.)
SANTA MARIA MADDALENA. This 14th-century church was rebuilt in the 17th century by Carlo Fontana. But the façade, a combination of Baroque and Rococco surmounted by a circular pediment, was added in 1735 by Giuseppe Sardi who was greatly influenced by Borromini. The interior has the same sense of movement combined with sumptuous decorations: the organ loft is astonishing – with its gilded woodcarvings, statues and cherubs – and the sacristy is one of the most beautiful in Rome. (Continue to Piazza della Rotonda and turn right into Via Giustiniani, which leads to San Luigi dei Francesi.)

THE SANTA CECILIA CHAPEL. In the Church of San Luigi dei Francesi Domeni- chino painted a cycle of frescoes based on the saint's legendary life. The *Glory of Cecilia* is shown here.

SAN LUIGI DEI FRANCESI

This is a particularly French neighborhood. Next to San Luigi dei Francesi, which is the French national church, are the

on this church, which they wished to have under their protection. When Antonio Barberini, a Capuchin friar and Urban VIII's younger brother, became cardinal, he decided to rebuild the church of his Order; the Pope granted him a subsidy. From then on, many of the great figures of the time, including the Emperor Ferdinand II, sought to sponsor the decoration of the side chapels – so much so that the Capuchins had to make repeated appeals or their church not to be too richly decorated. While the Pope seized this opportunity to refuse all help, it did not prevent him and his brother from calling upon some of the greatest painters of the time for the altar paintings. The crypt is definitely worth a visit: it is decorated, in Baroque taste, with the bones of some four thousand Capuchin friars. (Cross Piazza Barberini and take the Via delle Quattro Fontane.)

PALAZZO BARBERINI. The overall plan was entrusted to the architect Carlo Maderno, who had to incorporate a palace that stood on the land bought by the Barberini in 1625. Casting aside the traditional scheme for Roman palaces (built around a square courtyard), he finally adopted that of the villa (a central edifice flanked by two wings). The work, which began in 1627, was continued after Maderno's death in 1629 by Bernini, who retained his predecessor's principal assistant, Francesco Borromini. Bernini designed the façade on the garden side of the building, including the main entrance, and the square staircase in the left wing, which leads to the gallery. Borromini was responsible for the oval staircase in the right wing, as well as the *trompe l'oeil* windows on the second floor ● 87. Inside, most of the rooms of the *piano nobile* have painted ceilings – notably by Andrea Camassei and Andrea Sacchi, including his *Divine Wisdom*, painted between 1629 and 1633. However, the most remarkable of all is the ceiling in the principal salon, painted between 1633 and 1639 by Pietro da Cortona. Its allegorical theme was provided by Francesco Bracciolini, a protégé of Urban VIII and his brother's secretary. In the center Divine Providence triumphs over Time and assigns the Barberini emblem to Immortality, while the lateral scenes portray the virtues of Urban VIII and the achievements of his pontificate. Nowhere else in Rome does a painting so shamelessly exalt a pope and his family.

"ST MICHAEL TRAMPLING ON THE DEVIL"
Great painters of the Bologna school such as Guido Reni, whose famous *St Michael Trampling on the Devil* (first chapel on the right) is pictured here, Lanfranco (second chapel on the right) and Domenichino (third chapel) made their contribution to the Capuchin church, as did painters of the younger generation like Pietro da Cortona (first chapel on the right) and Andrea Sacchi (fifth chapel on the right).

THE CRYPT OF THE CAPUCHIN CHURCH
It took no fewer than three hundred journeys with full cartloads to gather the bones that adorn the crypt of Santa Maria della Concezione.

291

The Barberini family emblem.

To the very rare items remaining from the Barberini collection have been added works from other private collections and State acquisitions and legacies. Thus the museum is able to show paintings by such Italian masters as Filippo Lippi, Lorenzo Lotto, Andrea del Sarto, Perugino, Bronzino and Caravaggio together with works by foreign artists like Quentin Metsys, Holbein and Nicholas Poussin.

Since it became the property of the State in 1949, the Palazzo Barberini has housed the Galleria Nazionale di Arte Antica, created at the end of the 19th century. This museum, which is one of the most important in Rome, takes up practically the whole of the palace's piano nobile. In these rooms one finds works by many of the great Italian and foreign painters of the 13th to the 18th century. The floor above, which was redecorated between 1750 and 1770, offers a fine setting for the collection of 18th-century paintings.

"LA FORNARINA"
This painting, long considered to be the most precious work in the Barberini collection, was purchased by the State when the collection was dispersed. It is commonly thought to be a portrait of La Fornarina, the mistress with whom Raphael was said by Vasari to have indulged in the pleasures of love to such an extent that it caused his death. However, the attribution to Raphael is now disputed.

Reaching Rome around 1591, Caravaggio (1573–1610) worked under the patronage of Cardinal del Monte. He left Rome in 1606.

Piazza del Quirinale
seen from the air.

THE QUIRINAL

PIAZZA DEL QUIRINALE. The piazza was built over several centuries. In the 16th century Sixtus V had the two statues of the Dioscuri and their horses erected in the center – which is why the square is also known as Piazza Montecavallo – moving them from the 4th-century Baths of Constantine. In the early 17th century the square was leveled. In 1783 Pius VI added the obelisk, brought from the Mausoleum of Augustus ▲ *143*; and in 1813 the fountain was completed with the addition of the basin, which came from near the temple of the Dioscuri in the Forum, where it had been used as a drinking trough for cattle. With its various components, the fountain illustrates an essential feature of Roman art: the reuse of ancient materials or architectural elements in new constructions. As a finishing touch, in 1886 the balustrade on the west side of the piazza was added, from which there is a magnificent view over the city, stretched out at the bottom of the hill with St Peter's in the distance.
PALAZZO DEL QUIRINALE. Originally the popes' summer residence, then a papal palace, this building was a royal palace between 1870 and 1944. When the Republic was proclaimed it became the official residence of the President. Construction began in the late 16th century under Gregory XIII and was completed under Clement XII (1730–40); many Roman architects of the Counter-Reformation and Baroque period made some contribution to it, and Bernini built the Loggia of the Benedictions over the main entrance. The palace was gradually surrounded by annexes, among them the PALAZZO DELLA CONSULTA, on the north side of the piazza. Built between 1732 and 1734 by Ferdinando Fuga, it now houses Italy's constitutional court. (Take Via XXIV Maggio.)
THE STABLES The stables were built on the site of the Temple of Serapis by Alessandro Specchi and completed by Ferdinando Fuga in the late 18th century. Since their recent restoration, they have been used for temporary exhibitions. (Take Via XXIV Maggio.)

The Corazzieri (presidential guards) in the hall of honor of the Palazzo del Quirinale

Pictured on the left is the elegant helicoidal staircase designed by Ottaviano Mascherino for Gregory XIII. With its pairs of polished-marble columns, it is one of the finest architectural elements in the Palazzo del Quirinale.

The aqueduct built by Agrippa in 19 BC to supply water for his baths was given the name Aqua Virgo, as the location of the spring feeding it was supposed to have been revealed to some Roman soldiers by a virgin. This bas-relief on the Fontan di Trevi illustrates the legend.

VIA XXIV MAGGIO. Immediately on the left is the side entrance of the Palazzo Rospigliosi built between 1611 and 1616 for Cardinal Scipione Borghese. Its gardens boast the Casino Pallavicini (open to the public the first day of each month), which has a famous fresco by Guido Reni, *Aurora* (1614). On the other side of the street an imposing balustrade marks the entrance to the gardens of the Palazzo Colonna ▲ *299*. Michelangelo is reputed to have frequented them in order to meet his great friend the poetess Vittoria Colonna, whose last breath he witnessed. One can still see there a few remains of Caracalla's temple of Serapis.

SAN SILVESTRO AL QUIRINALE. This richly decorated church (1524) is concealed behind a 19th-century façade. (Return toward the Piazza del Quirinale and go down the Via della Dataria, designed by Paul V as the official access to the papal residence, then take the second street on the right, Via San Vicenzo.)

FONTANA DI TREVI

THE WISHING FOUNTAIN. At the bottom of the street, backed by the façade of the Palazzo Poli, where a museum of printing and journalism is soon to open, looms the most stunning of the fountains of Rome: the central figure, the Ocean (by Pietro Bracci) dominates sea horses guided by Tritons, while in the niches on either side are the figures of Abundance and Health, by Filippo della Valle. Bernini was originally commissioned by Urban VIII to construct a monumental fountain, but the project was abandoned after the Pope's death. Almost a century later, Nicola Salvi built this ensemble on the site of one of Rome's earliest fountains designed to receive the water of the Aqua Virgo. The bliss of returning to the Eternal City is guaranteed to all foreigners who, with their back turned, throw a coin over their shoulder into the fountain. Also in the square is the church of Santi Vincenzo e Anastasio. Cardinal Mazarin, who financed the work, commissioned the ornate Baroque façade (1641–50) from Martino Longhi the Younger.

RIONE TREVI. The neighborhood around the fountain provides one of the most picturesque parts of Rome. This area, once densely populated, remained of the liveliest sections of the city throughout the Middle Ages and the Renaissance. In the 16th century its narrow streets were filled with craftsmen's workshops which attracted many foreigners, and some craftsmen chose to live here. Later, demolition works did not detract from its inherent charm. Whether you take the Via della Panetteria or the Via del Lavatore, which has an open market every morning, you will find that this is still a lively neighborhood. (Take the Via della Stamperia to the right of the fountain.)

ACCADEMIA NAZIONALE DI SAN LUCA. In 1934 this academy, founded in 1577, moved into the ancient building once known as Palazzo Vaini, which was renamed the Palazzo Carpegna in the 17th

THE FONTANA DI TREVI AND THE WATERS OF FORTUNE ✪
In a scene of Fellini's *La Dolce Vita* the voluptuous Anita Ekberg bathes in the Fontana di Trevi before Mastroianni's astonished gaze. This has become an unforgettable moment in Italian cinema. You may not be able to do the same – the fountains of Rome are not public baths! – but with your back to the powerful Neptune, toss a small coin into the water; this, so it is said, will guarantee your return to the Eternal City. But do not even think of diving in after the coins that glisten from the bottom of the fountain: they belong to the city council, which hands out this manna (around 100 € per week) to the municipal street cleaners.

Aurora by Guido Reni, of which the 18th-century French President de Brosses said: "Nothing is better conceived, so graceful, so light, nor better drawn; it is an 'incanto' (a delight)."

...entury when it was modified by Borromini. The original ...urpose of this institution, which brought together famous ...ainters, was to provide an apprenticeship and theoretical ...raining for young painters so as to control the production ...nd distribution of art in keeping with the strict rules of the ...Counter-Reformation. In the 17th century it was truly ...ictatorial: no artist could have a studio in Rome without its ...uthorization. Its picture gallery, containing collections made ...p of gifts from its members and from various popes, includes ...vorks by Raphael, Titian, Bronzino, Poussin and Panini.

CALCOGRAFIA NAZIONALE (6 Via della Stamperia). This ...nuseum of engravings has one of the best collections of its ...ind in the world – comprising more than 23,000 items, ...ncluding 16th-century plates by De Rossi, and a complete set ...f Piranesi's engravings. (Walk back along the Via San ...Vincenzo. Then take its continuation, the Via dei Lucchesi, to ...Piazza della Pilotta – from the Spanish *pelota*, a ball, but ...oday it is the realm of study rather than ball games. Here you ...vill find two great Jesuit institutions: the BIBLICUM, with its ...emarkable orientalist library, and the GREGORIANA, the ...argest Catholic university in Rome. Take Via della Pilotta.)

PALAZZO COLONNA AND ITS GALLERY. You will emerge behind ...he Palazzo Colonna, which is ...inked to its terraced gardens ...by four bridges over the ...oad. (The entrance is in ...Piazza dei Santi ...Apostoli, on the far side ...of the palace from Via ...della Pilotta.) ...Originally

ACCADEMIA NAZIONALE DI SAN LUCA. The name originates in the Christian tradition that attributes the talent of painting to St Luke.

St Luke Painting the Virgin Mary by Raphael.

The Fontana di Trevi.

THE GREAT HALL OF THE PALAZZO COLONNA
Its sumptuous decoration was designed by
Antonio del Grande in the mid 17th century
and completed under the supervision of
Girolamo Fontana after del Grande's death.

Peasant Eating Beans
by Annibale Carracci
(1560–1609), one of
the paintings in the
Galleria Colonna.

built between 1417 and 1431
by Pope Martin V, a member
of the Colonna family, the
building was restructured
several times before the 18th
century. Worthy of note is the
Salone della Colonna Bellica
after the red column it
contains, the family emblem;
its ceiling is decorated with a
fresco glorifying Marcantonio
Colonna, the commander of
the papal fleet at the battle of
Lepanto (1571). The picture
gallery contains a magnificent
collection, largely put
together by Lorenzo Onofrio Colonna under the guidance of
the painter Carlo Maratta. In the 19th century it was enlarged
with the acquisition of paintings by primitives and Renaissance
masters. Both the palace and the gallery still belong to this
ancient Roman family. (Return to Piazza dei Santi Apostoli,
where the Waxwork Museum can be found.)

BASILICA DEI SANTI APOSTOLI. To avoid the risk of it falling
into ruins, despite restoration work carried out in the
Renaissance, the original 6th-century basilica was almost
completely rebuilt between 1701 and 1714 by Carlo Fontana
and his son Francesco. It was then given a neoclassical façade
designed by Valadier in 1827. The portico at the front dates
from the 15th century. This work by Baccio Pontelli (1450–92)
was enclosed with railings in the 17th century by Carlo
Rainaldi, who also added the balustrade and the statues of
the apostles. The interior is decorated with gilt plasterwork,
stuccos and frescoes in the taste of 18th-century Rome. On
the vault Christ is portrayed receiving the saints of the
Franciscan Order (Baciccia, 1707). At the very end of the left

The Basilica of Santi
Apostoli.

ave stands the tomb of Clement
XIV, the first monument Canova
sculpted in Rome (1789).

PALAZZO ODESCALCHI (facing the
Basilica dei Santi Apostoli). The
façade, designed by Bernini in 1664
for Alexander VII's nephew Flavio
Chigi, was a model for a number of
Baroque palaces. Bernini broke with
the tradition of building palace
façades without vertical articulation:
while the ground floor serves as a foundation, on the upper
stories gigantic pilasters divide the seven bays of the central
body of the building, which is framed by two wings set further
back. The balance of this façade was destroyed when in 1745,
at the request of the owner, Prince Odescalchi, Nicola Salvi
enlarged the palace, doubling the width of the central body
and building a second door for the sake of symmetry. A small
detour can be made up a narrow alleyway to the Chapel of the
Madonna del Archetto, built by Virginio Vespignani. In the
same street is one of Rome's few well-known *birrerie* (beer
cellars). (Return to the Via dei Santi Apostoli and proceed to
the Corso.)

SAN MARCELLO AL CORSO. Although founded in the 4th
century, this church was rebuilt after a fire in 1519. It was
designed by Jacopo Sansovino and has a Baroque façade by
Carlo Fontana (1682–86). Parts of the interior, including the
coffered ceiling, go back to the 16th century. The tombs of
Cardinal Giovanni Michiel and Bishop Antonio Orso, to the
left of the entrance, are the work of Jacopo Sansovino. The
third, fourth and fifth chapels on the left are decorated with
frescoes by Francesco Salviati, Perin del Vaga and Federico
Zuccaro respectively. The fourth chapel on the right contains
a 15th-century crucifix which used to be carried in penitential
processions. (On leaving the church, take the first street on
the right, Via dell'Umiltà.)

GALLERIA SCIARRA ● *90*. A fine example of Roman
eclecticism, this gallery, which links Via Minghetti and Via
dell' Umiltà, was built in 1885–6 by Giulio De Angelis. (Go
through the gallery.)

PIAZZA SAN SILVESTRO

Three churches are in or close to this piazza,
which has changed considerably over the past
two centuries.

SANTA MARIA IN VIA. The first, which
stands on the corner of Via del Tritone,
belongs to the Servite Order. It was
rebuilt by Francesco da Volterra in the late 16th
century on the site of a medieval shrine, to plans
by Giacomo Della Porta. The upper section of
the façade is attributed to Carlo Rainaldi
(1670). Inside, the third chapel on the right has
an *Annunciation* by Cavaliere d'Arpino (1596).

SAN ANDREA E CLAUDIO DEI BORGOGNONI.
This church, rebuilt by Antoine Derizet
between 1728 and 1729, had been the church of
the Burgundians of the Franche-Comté.

GALLERIA SCIARRA
This modern (late
19th century)
structure has very
pretty Pompeian-style
decorations painted
by Giuseppe Cellini.
Among other
inscriptions, on the
right is this verse
from Virgil's fourth
*Eclogue: Incipe, parve
puer, risu cognoscere
matrem* ("Little boy,
learn to greet your
mother with a
smile").

The Via della Pilotta,
which leads to the
gardens of Palazzo
Colonna.

**THE MIRACLE OF
SANTA MARIA IN VIA**
A miracle is said to
be at the origin of this
church's foundation.
An image of the
Virgin painted on a
tile fell into a well,
which overflowed, so
that the image
emerged from the
well. Many faithful
still come here to
drink the well's water
and venerate the
"Madonna del Pozzo"
(the Madonna of the
Well).

SAN SILVESTRO IN CAPITE
This church was constructed on the ruins of the Temple of the Sun built by Aurelian. The name "in Capite" refers to the head of St John the Baptist, which has been preserved here as a relic for centuries.

SAN SILVESTRO IN CAPITE. Both the atrium in front of the church and the bell tower date from the 13th century, but the main part of the building was begun in the 16th century by Francesco da Volterra and finished by Carlo Maderno. The façade was erected by Domenico de Rossi who, with his brother Mattia, redecorated the interior at the end of the 17th century. Don't omit to look at the fresco in the nave by Giacinto Brandi (1623–91), as well as the Pomarancio frescoes in the transept crossing (1605). In 1890 Pope Leo XIII gave San Silvestro in Capite to the English Catholics in Rome as their parish church. The former convent buildings next to it now house Rome's central post office.

FROM THE VIA VENETO TO THE PORTA PINCIANA

The Via Vittorio Veneto has been used as a set for numerous films, and especially in the 1960's show-business personalities used to frequent the terraces of its famous bars, cafés and luxury hotels. Going up the Via Veneto, you enter the Ludovisi neighborhood, named after the beautiful villa that once stood here; its grounds were sold and divided into building lots in the 1880's. Leaving to your right the former Ministry of Corporations (now the Ministry of Industry and Trade) – built in 1932, during the Fascist period, by Marcello Piacentini and Giuseppe Vaccaro – you will pass in front of the Banca Nazionale del Lavoro, also built by Piacentini (1036), and will then come to the Palazzo Boncompagni-Piombino (1886–90), which is now the American Embassy. It is also known as the Palazzo Margherita, because it became the residence of Queen Margherita after the assassination of Umberto I in 1900. This building was erected between 1886 and 1890, its architect, Gaetano Koch was inspired by the Palazzo Farnese. If you walk back down the Via Veneto then take Via Bissolati, you will come to Largo Santa Susanna and the Geological Museum built by Raffaele Canevari in 1873. The façade shows the influence of the iron-and-glass construction of the Industrial Revolution.

Paparazzo, the photographer in Fellini's *La Dolce Vita* (played by Walter Santesso), in a night of follies on the Via Veneto.

Il Tridente

306 Piazza del Popolo

308 Via del Corso

309 The Mausoleum of Augustus

310 The Ara Pacis Augustae

313 Piazza di Spagna

314 Trinità dei Monti

315 The Villa Medici

316 The Pincio

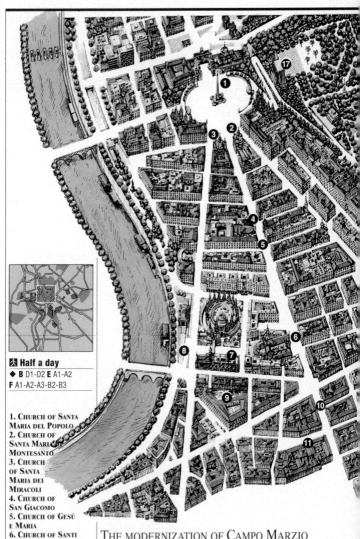

Half a day

◆ **B** D1-D2 **E** A1-A2
F A1-A2-A3-B2-B3

1. CHURCH OF SANTA
MARIA DEL POPOLO
2. CHURCH OF
SANTA MARIA
MONTESANTO
3. CHURCH
OF SANTA
MARIA DEI
MIRACOLI
4. CHURCH OF
SAN GIACOMO
5. CHURCH OF GESÙ
E MARIA
6. CHURCH OF SANTI
AMBROGIO E CARLO
AL CORSO
7. MAUSOLEUM OF
AUGUSTUS
8. ARA PACIS AUGUSTAE
9. PALAZZO BORGHESE
10. PALAZZO RUSPOLI
11. CHURCH OF SAN
LORENZO IN LUCINA
12. PIAZZA DI SPAGNA
13. PALAZZO DI
PROPAGANDA FIDE
14. CHURCH OF
SANT'ANDREA DELLE
FRATTE
15. TRINITÀ DEI
MONTI ✪
16. VILLA MEDICI
17. THE PINCIO

THE MODERNIZATION OF CAMPO MARZIO

The cosmopolitan atmosphere of modern Rome is evident
throughout most of this quarter, which is pleasant for
strolling, a shopper's paradise and full of luxury hotels. Yet
until the middle of the 20th century, it was still the scene of
such typically Roman events as the races of barb horses down
the Via del Corso and the Easter Monday fireworks on the
Pincio. Begun in 1851 and continued until just after the end of
World War II, these firework displays marked the anniversary
of the signing of the Statuto Albertini ▲ *100*. In fact, after the
French occupation the neighborhood underwent radical
changes for a period of 150 years. The Piazza del Popolo
(1809–14) and the gardens of the Pincio (1818) were the first
to be transformed. Then, as the area around Piazza di Spagna
was attracting an increasing number of tourists, more hotels

6. SAN GIOVANNI IN OLEO   7. PORTA LATINA   8. PORTA SAN SEBASTIANO   9. DOMINE QUO VADIS   10. CATACOMBS OF SAN CALLISTO   11. VIA APPIA ANTICA   12. SAN SEBASTIANO   13. MAUSOLEUM OF ROMULUS   14. TOMB OF CECILIA METELLA   15. CIRCUS OF MAXENTIUS

ROADSIDE TOMBS. Since the earliest times the common custom was to bury the dead outside the *pomerium*, the sacred walls of the city. The first few miles of Roman roads were therefore usually flanked by necropolises, distinguished by social status and diversity of funeral rites. Indeed burial and cremation were practiced concurrently, one or the other prevailing according to the fashion. Under the Republic cremation was prevalent so they constructed columbariums (buildings housing thousands of funerary urns) and altars with the ashes of the deceased. Conversely, in the Imperial times

The Via Appia.

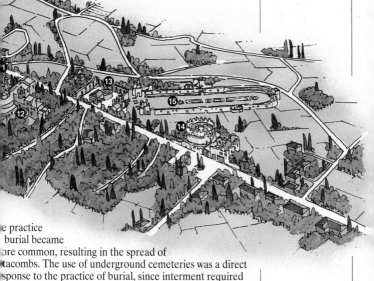

the practice burial became more common, resulting in the spread of catacombs. The use of underground cemeteries was a direct response to the practice of burial, since interment required more space than cremation. From the 4th century the catacombs became almost exclusively Christian, following the conversion of the Roman people.

THE BATHS OF CARACALLA

ROMAN BATHS. From the end of the Republic the Romans frequented public baths, not just for reasons of hygiene and exercise but also for entertainment. The activities offered by the baths and their increasingly important social role led the emperors to build ever larger establishments, accommodating more bathers (the Baths of Caracalla had a capacity of nearly 1600). Progressively, areas for sport were introduced, auditoriums for music, lecture theaters, libraries, gardens, fountains, and porticoes to protect walkers from rain and from the sun. At the same time, the architecture and decoration of these buildings became more sophisticated, richer in mosaics, stucco decorations, colonnades, paintings and sculptures. Eventually premises of a monumental size became indispensable because of the large service staff that was necessary (cloakroom attendants, masseurs, those responsible for depilation, doctors, etc.) and the hordes of entertainers that the bathers came to expect (ranging from itinerant

THE BATHS OF CARACALLA
On either side of the portico there was a huge *exedra* enclosing a *palestra* (gymnasium). At the rear a sort of half stadium concealed the enormous water tanks, each with a capacity of about 20 million gallons.

319

CARACALLA (188–217)
Given access to
power in 198 AD by
his father Septimius
Severus, Caracalla
became Emperor in
211. He continued his
father's initiatives,
and his edict of 212
granting Roman
citizenship to all
inhabitants of the
Empire marked the
fruition of the policy
of "Romanization".
He also pursued an
ambitious foreign
policy, and was
assassinated during a
campaign against
Parthia.

The *Ercole Farnese*
▲ 245. This statue
of Hercules was
found in the
Baths of
Caracalla.

salesmen to musicians, mimics, readers and
orators). Thus, unlike the Greek gymnasiums,
which were limited to the education and
physical development of young men, the
Roman baths were places for social
encounters and leisure activities, where
sport and culture combined in forming, as
the poet Juvenal put it, *mens sana in
corpore sano* ("a healthy mind in a healthy
body"). The baths were open to everyone
until sunset; and it was only from the time of
Hadrian (117–38 AD) that the sexes were
segregated. Today the Baths of Caracalla are
still used for cultural purposes: in summer
there are open-air performances of opera
and ballet.

THE BATHER'S RITUAL. The Baths of
Caracalla (Terme di Caracalla), also known
as the Thermae Antoninianae, are the most
magnificent and best preserved of all the
Imperial baths. Built between 212 and 216
AD, they form an almost perfect square
covering 27 acres and are surrounded by a
wall erected later by Heliogabalus ▲ *151*
and Alexander Severus. The
arrangement of the central block, which
was reserved for sports, is traditional.
Access was through the four gates on

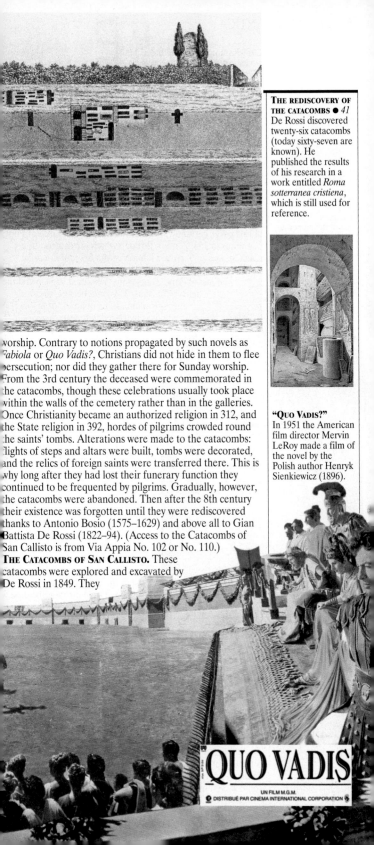

THE REDISCOVERY OF THE CATACOMBS ● 41
De Rossi discovered twenty-six catacombs (today sixty-seven are known). He published the results of his research in a work entitled *Roma sotterranea cristiana*, which is still used for reference.

"QUO VADIS?"
In 1951 the American film director Mervin LeRoy made a film of the novel by the Polish author Henryk Sienkiewicz (1896).

worship. Contrary to notions propagated by such novels as *Fabiola* or *Quo Vadis?*, Christians did not hide in them to flee persecution; nor did they gather there for Sunday worship. From the 3rd century the deceased were commemorated in the catacombs, though these celebrations usually took place within the walls of the cemetery rather than in the galleries. Once Christianity became an authorized religion in 312, and the State religion in 392, hordes of pilgrims crowded round the saints' tombs. Alterations were made to the catacombs: flights of steps and altars were built, tombs were decorated, and the relics of foreign saints were transferred there. This is why long after they had lost their funerary function they continued to be frequented by pilgrims. Gradually, however, the catacombs were abandoned. Then after the 8th century their existence was forgotten until they were rediscovered thanks to Antonio Bosio (1575–1629) and above all to Gian Battista De Rossi (1822–94). (Access to the Catacombs of San Callisto is from Via Appia No. 102 or No. 110.)
THE CATACOMBS OF SAN CALLISTO. These catacombs were explored and excavated by De Rossi in 1849. They

QUO VADIS
UN FILM M.G.M.
Ⓢ DISTRIBUÉ PAR CINEMA INTERNATIONAL CORPORATION Ⓢ

Chi-Rho monogram (the first two letters of Christ's name in Greek). A symbolic praying figure (far right).

The good shepherd, one of the numerous Christian symbols that can be seen on the walls of the catacombs.

are the largest of the Christian burial complexes and were widely used from the 3rd century; at the same time it also became customary for the popes to be buried there. Calixtus, to whom they owe their name, administered these catacombs while he was a deacon and enlarged them after he became Pope in 217. In places they were developed on four levels, and their galleries extend for more than 12 miles. Like many Christian catacombs, they are the result of the 4th-century unification of several earlier nucleuses. The oldest part, the Crypt of Lucina, beside the Via Appia, probably dates from the end of the 2nd century AD. This section is itself composed of two parts, certainly linked at the time of the burial of Pope Cornelius in 253. ZONE I, through which the catacombs are reached, was constructed later. Visitors first enter a *cella trichora* (room with three apses), which originally housed the bodies of Pope Zephyrinus (who died in 217) and the martyr Tarsicius. This *cella* became an underground basilica in honor of Sixtus II, who was martyred with four deacons in the cemetery during Valerian's persecutions in 258. Steps then lead to a vestibule with walls covered in graffiti, which opens on to the CRYPT OF THE POPES, discovered in 1854, where four niches for the sarcophagi may be seen and six *loculi* ("niches for bodies") on each side. It is thought that at least fourteen popes were buried in San Callisto, and it is certain from the inscriptions that five of them reposed in this crypt: namely Pontian (230–5), Anterus (235–6), Fabian (236–50), Lucius I (253–4) and Eutychian (275–83). De Rossi believed that the crypt known as the CRYPT OF ST CECILIA contained her tomb, but this opinion is now rejected. The learned archeologist thought he recognized the figures of

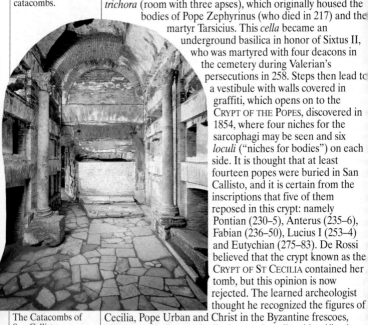

Cecilia, Pope Urban and Christ in the Byzantine frescoes, which were in fact too badly damaged to allow identification. The niche which according to this tradition was destined to contain St Cecilia's sarcophagus now contains a copy of her effigy by Stefano Maderno (the original is in the Church of Santa Cecilia in Trastevere ▲ *353*). Other sections of the catacombs that can be visited include the five *cubicula* ("funeral chambers") known as the Crypt of the Sacraments, which are adorned with 3rd-century frescoes, and the Crypt of Pope Eusebius, who died in 310.

The Catacombs of San Callisto.

IXΘYC

The fish, a symbol of Christ.

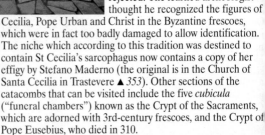

The catechumen struggling with the serpent.

THE BASILICA AND CATACOMBS OF SAN SEBASTIANO

This complex is located just after the crossroads between the Via Appia and the Via delle Sette Chiese. The latter acquired its name from the custom revived in the 16th century of making a pilgrimage to the seven most important churches of Rome ▲ *381*, including San Sebastiano.

THE BASILICA. This basilica-cemetery built in the time of

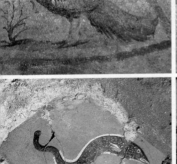

Constantine was originally dedicated to the apostles Peter and Paul. Its shape resembled that of a circus, with three naves separated by masonry pillars surmounted by brick arches. In the 17th century Cardinal Scipio Borghese had it rebuilt, and the edifice was reduced to a single nave. Above the tomb of St Sebastian, whose veneration had overshadowed that of the two apostles after the 9th century, a new chapel was built (the first on the left) in which a statue of the martyr was placed, based on a model by Bernini. The altar now in the Chapel of Relics (the first on the right) once stood in the center of the basilica, above the Triclia (see below) where the apostles were venerated. It also contains some venerable relics, including the famous stone supposed to bear the impression of Christ's footprints ▲ 324. From the apse, where the ambulatory has been transformed into a museum, one reaches the PLATONIA, a richly decorated tomb at the back of the basilica that contains the relics of St Quirinus, Bishop of Pannonia.

THE CATACOMBS. Throughout the period of late antiquity this cemetery was simply referred to by the expression *ad catacumbas*, from the Greek *kata kymbas* ("near the caves", which may possibly have referred to the neighboring stone quarries). Subsequently the name was used for all necropolises of this type. Here the sepulchers of pagans and Christians lie side by side, as they do in almost all the catacombs. The first of the four levels of galleries has been virtually destroyed. The CRYPT OF SAN SEBASTIANO, the first site visited, no longer contains the martyr's remains, as they were removed in the 9th century. Next to be seen are the three pagan hypogeums, which were columbariums ▲ 319 before becoming burial places. Magnificently preserved, they have stucco decorations and frescoes combining pagan motifs (such as the Gorgon's head) with Christian ones (the miracle of the demoniac of Gerasa), some of them as early as the 1st or 2nd century AD. The inscription reveals that Marcus Claudius Hermes was the owner of the tomb on

The frescoes in the Catacombs of Priscilla (on the Via Salaria) and Commodilla (on the Via Ostiense).

The first and last letters of the word "martyr".

The Catacombs of San Sebastiano.

never ceased to intrigue travelers and artists.

The Circus of Maxentius.

the right. One then passes into the MEMORIA APOSTOLORUM, an irregular room remarkable for its red-painted walls covered with about a hundred graffiti, dating from the 3rd and 4th centuries, in honor of the apostles Peter and Paul. This room, known as the Triclia, was formerly an open space where funeral banquets were celebrated in honor of the apostles. No convincing archeological argument has yet made it possible to choose between two interpretations that have puzzled generations of scholars. Were the bodies of the two apostles buried *ad catacumbas* just after their martyrdom, then transferred from the catacombs at a much later date? Or were they merely temporarily buried here at the time of Valerian's persecution in 258? Either way, the Constantinian basilica was built around the Memoria Apostolorum, which was painstakingly preserved as a place of veneration.

THE VILLA AND CIRCUS OF MAXENTIUS

Between the second and third milestones of the Via Appia, on the left, is a complex built by the Emperor Maxentius, whose brief reign lasted from 307 to 312 AD. It included three main buildings: a palatial villa, a circus and a mausoleum.

THE CIRCUS OF MAXENTIUS. This building is the most intact part of the complex, and the two great towers at the western end attract instant attention. Some 1,700 feet long, it had a capacity of at least 10,000 spectators. A long corridor linking the Imperial palace with the circus and the mausoleum gave the Emperor direct access to his box, located above the finishing post. On the south side was a box for the magistrate who oversaw the games. The chariot teams started from twelve *carceres* (stalls) at the western end of the circus. The archway that served as the main entrance was at the center of these stalls, which were flanked by the two towers. On the east side stood another great arch (the triumphal entrance), where in 1825 fragments of a dedication to Maxentius' son Romulus were found, making it possible to identify the monument. As in other circuses, the *spina* ▲ *177–9* around which the chariots raced was surmounted by a variety of ornamental features,

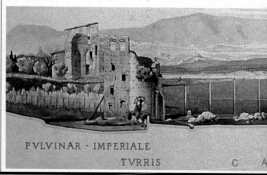

PVLVINAR · IMPERIALE
TVRRIS

including fountains and, in the middle, an obelisk. This was Domitian's obelisk, perhaps taken from the Campus Martius; in 1650 Pope Innocent X had it moved to Piazza Navona ▲ *276* to crown Bernini's Fontana dei Quattro Fiumi.

MAUSOLEUM OF ROMULUS. Maxentius' son Romulus, who died in 309, was certainly buried here, but this was probably a dynastic tomb intended for the whole family. The mausoleum itself, which stands in the middle of a grandiose quadriportico (four-sided portico) facing the Via Appia, is a circular building, about 100 feet in diameter, with a projecting pronaos (porch) similar to that of the Pantheon ▲ *264*. Surrounding it are numerous monumental tombs of the 4th century. Originally there were two floors, of which only the lower one remains, partly buried and half hidden by a modern farmhouse; niches for sarcophagi were hollowed out in the wall. The upper floor has almost entirely disappeared, but it was probably devoted to the funerary cult of Maxentius' son and would have been covered by a vast dome.

THE TRIOPIUS OF HERODES ATTICUS AND VILLA OF MAXENTIUS. Herodes Atticus was a very rich Greek from Athens. A gifted public speaker, he became the tutor of the children of the Emperor Antoninus Pius (138–61) and married Annia Regilla, a Roman aristocrat who owned a villa on the Appian Way. When his young wife died suddenly, her family accused Herodes of murdering her. After his acquittal he dedicated his land to the gods of the underworld and to the funerary cult of his wife. A temple was also built here in honor of the goddess Demeter and Antoninus Pius' wife Faustina. The whole heritage was renamed "Triopius", from the name of the Thessalonian Triopas whose cult in Cnides, in Asia, was associated with that of Demeter. Later, Maxentius' villa was built on this site; hardly anything remains of it, but the few ruins that have survived, particularly those of the great reception hall, give an idea of the sumptuousness of the villa.

AN IMAGINATIVE RECONSTRUCTION
In reconstructing the decoration of the Circus of Maxentius (above), Alfred Recoura, who was awarded the Prix de Rome in 1894, aimed to give an idea of its former splendor. Hence the abundance of marble and ornaments, with *quadrigae* surmounting the twin towers (decorated with bas-reliefs), sculptures of magistrates set in niches in the façade, and a statue of the Emperor in gilded bronze in the center. On the left is the Imperial box, which was connected by the villa by a corridor.

The Circus of Maxentius.

CRIVMPHALIS   TRIBVNAL · IVDICVM
A · PRIMA   PORTA · LIBITINENSIS
E   R   E   S   TVRRIS

At the entrance remains of tombs on the Via Appia excavated in 1836 are set into the walls.

EASTERN INFLUENCES
The form of the Tomb of Cecilia Metella is similar to that of the Mausoleum of Augustus ▲ *309* and other tombs from the same period found in Italy. These buildings provide evidence of the evolution of funerary architecture both in Rome and elsewhere in Italy, and indicate the progressive diffusion of new ideological models influenced by Asian and Hellenistic traditions.

THE TOMB OF CECILIA METELLA   ● 7.

After the Maxentius complex, the Via Appia rises steeply toward a massive tomb (on the left). This is the best known and best preserved of the mausoleums beside the road. Its dedication states that it was the tomb of Cecilia Metella, the daughter of Quintus Metellus Creticus (consul in 69 BC) and wife of Crassus (probably the son of the fabulously wealthy contemporary of Caesar and Pompey). The building consists of a circular tower, about 95 feet in diameter and 36 feet high set on a square cement base that has been stripped of its facing. It leans against the ruins of a fortress built in the 12th century by the Caetani, who used it as a dungeon. The marble frieze is decorated with a relief featuring garlands of flowers, weapons and

bucranes (ox skulls); because of the *bucranes* the locality became known as Capo di Bove. Inside the castle (to the right of the entrance) there is a display of fragments of inscriptions and decorations from tombs on the Via Appia. From here a narrow corridor leads to the funeral chamber, the upper part of which consisted of an enormous cone faced with bricks.
ROMANTIC RUINS. Opposite the mausoleum, on the other side of the road, stands the small church of SAN NICOLA A CAPO DI BOVE built by the Caetani family. This section of the Appian Way has been considerably damaged, and the villas and numerous tombs with which it was lined are now barely identifiable ruins. But if you are traveling by car, go as far as the fifth milestone; near it (on the right) are three tumulus-shaped tombs. In the 19th century it was believed that these were the TOMBS OF THE HORATII AND THE CURIATII who died in the famous duel which ended the war between Rome and Alba Longa. A little further on (on the left) you will come to the picturesque ruins of the VILLA DEI QUINTILI (2nd century AD), part of a huge estate that belonged to one of the great aristocratic families of ancient Rome. The four Quintilii brothers came to an untimely end: under the pretext that they were plotting against him, the Emperor Commodus (180–92) had them assassinated and confiscated their villa, which he wanted for himself.

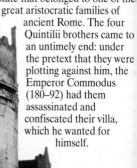

From the baths of Diocletian to San Pietro in Vincoli

333 Piazza della Repubblica

336 National Roman Museum

338 Stazione Termini

339 Via Giovanni Giolitti

339 Porta Maggiore

340 Piazza Vittorio Emanuele II

342 Basilica of Santa Maria Maggiore

344 Santa Pudenziana and Santa Prassede

346 Basilica of San Pietro in Vincoli

347 Toward the Via Nazionale

🚶 **One day**

◆ **E** A3-A4-B3-B4-C3
G B1-B2

1. **PIAZZA DELLA REPUBBLICA**
2. **BATHS OF DIOCLETIEN** AND CHURCH OF **SANTA MARIA DEGLI ANGELI**
3. **MUSEO DELLE TERME**
4. **STAZIONI TERMINI**
5. **CHURCH OF SANTA BIBIANA**
6. **TEMPLE OF MINERVA MEDICA**
7. **PIAZZA VITTORIO EMANUELE II**
8. **THE TROPHIES OF MARIUS**
9. **BASILICA DI SANTA MARIA MAGGIORE**
10. **CHURCH OF SANTA PRASSEDE**
11. **CHURCH OF SAN MARTINO AI MONTI**
12. **CHURCH OF SAN PIETRO IN VINCOLI**
13. **VIA NAZIONALE**
14. **ÉGLISE SANTA PUDENZIANA**

The northern part of Rome underwent a fresh bout of town planning activity in the mid 15th century and again at the time of Sixtus V (1585–90) who concentrated on the reorganization and repopulation of the upper part of the town. Here he moved the cattle market that had traditionally been held on the grounds of the Abbey of Farfà and installed workshops for silk production in his own villa (the Villa Peretti, now vanished), planning to divert water there from the Aniene River. A network of streets was woven around Santa Maria Maggiore, the starting point for pilgrimages to the basilicas outside the walls ▲ *380* and to San Giovanni in Laterano ▲ *198*. The district retained its new features until the 1850's, when Rome's main station was built.

FUNCTIONAL TOWN PLANNING. In modernizing Rome, Pius IX (1846–78) respected the grand design of Sixtus V's plans. The first of the new arterial roads was Via Nazionale, built in 1867 in accordance with the directions of Msgr de Merode, who had acquired part of the area included in the project. After 1870 and the arrival of the Piedmontese ● *33*, who wanted to make "modern Rome" the capital of a united Italy, the government had to decide on the location of the future ministries, and the Ministry of Finance was built along Via XX Settembre. The 1871 general urban plan also provided for the construction of dwellings in the Esquiline, Castro Pretorio and Viminale areas. This was an incentive for particularly aggressive property speculation around Piazza Vittorio Emanuele, Santa Maria Maggiore and Porta San Lorenzo. The whole district between the station and the Piazza Vittorio

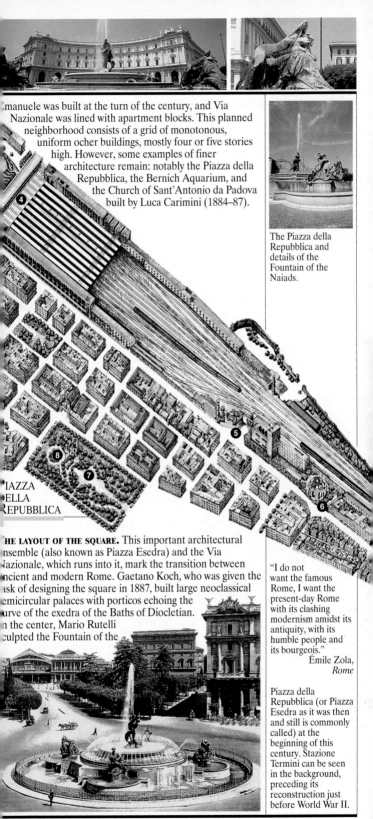

manuele was built at the turn of the century, and Via Nazionale was lined with apartment blocks. This planned neighborhood consists of a grid of monotonous, uniform ocher buildings, mostly four or five stories high. However, some examples of finer architecture remain: notably the Piazza della Repubblica, the Bernich Aquarium, and the Church of Sant'Antonio da Padova built by Luca Carimini (1884–87).

The Piazza della Repubblica and details of the Fountain of the Naiads.

PIAZZA DELLA REPUBBLICA

THE LAYOUT OF THE SQUARE. This important architectural ensemble (also known as Piazza Esedra) and the Via Nazionale, which runs into it, mark the transition between ancient and modern Rome. Gaetano Koch, who was given the task of designing the square in 1887, built large neoclassical semicircular palaces with porticos echoing the curve of the exedra of the Baths of Diocletian. In the center, Mario Rutelli sculpted the Fountain of the

"I do not want the famous Rome, I want the present-day Rome with its clashing modernism amidst its antiquity, with its humble people and its bourgeois."
Émile Zola,
Rome

Piazza della Repubblica (or Piazza Esedra as it was then and still is commonly called) at the beginning of this century. Stazione Termini can be seen in the background, preceding its reconstruction just before World War II.

▲ FROM THE BATHS OF DIOCLETIAN TO SAN PIETRO IN VINCOLI

ST BRUNO
(c. 1030–1101)
This statue of the saint who founded the Carthusian order is in the passage leading to the transept of the Church of Santa Maria degli Angeli. It is the work of the sculptor Jean-Antoine Houdon (1741–1828), who was a "pensionnaire" (art scholar) at the French

Academy's Villa Medici ▲ *315,* from 1766 to 1768.

1. CHURCH OF SANTA BIBIANA
2. TEMPLE OF MINERVA MEDICA
3. PORTA MAGGIORE

THE SUNDIAL OF SANTA MARIA DEGLI ANGELI
This sundial in the floor of the transept was used to regulate the clocks of Rome from 1702 to 1846.

Naiads (1901), which created a furor, the nudity of the lovely bathers outraging local sensibilities. Finally passions cooled, and the central group alone was altered: the marine deity Glaucus now grasps a dolphin.

THE BATHS OF DIOCLETIAN
(Terme di Diocleziano). On his return from Africa in the autumn of 298 AD, the Emperor Maximian undertook the building of a sumptuous complex of baths, designed to enable some three thousand people at a time to engage in a variety of sports and cultural activities. The baths were only completed after the abdication, on May 1, 305, of Maximian and his co-emperor Diocletian. Surrounded by a wall, the complex covered an area measuring about 1,230 x 1,200 feet (the central building alone measured approximately 820 feet x 590 feet). It was constructed according to the usual plan ● *68,* ▲ *319*: a large central hall, a *caldarium-tepidarium natatio* complex along the minor axis, and gymnasiums on either side of the major axis. These central structures are the best preserved, but important vestiges of the outer walls are still standing; some sections of the baths now form part of the National Roman Museum. The façade of the Facoltà di Magistero stands on the site of the northwestern façade of the ancient buildings. On the west corner, toward Via Cernaia, the great octagonal hall (transformed in 1928 into a planetarium and then a movie theater) has since 1991 housed a display of ancient sculptures from various baths in the city. One of the rotundas at the corners of the external walls is now the Church of San Bernardo alle Terme ▲ *295.*

SANTA MARIA DEGLI ANGELI. Responding to the vow of a Sicilian priest who had a vision of a cloud of angels flying round the Baths of Diocletian, in 1561 Pope Pius IV commissioned Michelangelo to build a church here dedicated to the angels and to the Christian martyrs who, according to tradition, had been forced to build the baths. One of the well-preserved apses of the *caldarium* forms the church's entrance (as seen in the picture at the foot of the page). Through it you enters a small circular room with two great square exedras, flanked by the tombs of the painters Salvator Rosa (1615–73) and Carlo Maratta (1625–1713); this is the former *tepidarium.*

The visitor finally reaches the main body of the church, which occupies what was the central hall of the baths. Despite the modifications introduced by Michelangelo and then by Vanvitelli in 1749, the church retains the vast proportions of the ancient building. Its vaults, as well as the eight immense columns of red granite, also belong to the original building. Gigantic paintings – many of which come from St Peter's ▲ *212*, where they were replaced with mosaics – decorate the walls of the transept and the choir. The most remarkable of these paintings are the *Fall of Simon the Magician* by Pompeo Batoni (1755), the *Martyrdom of St Sebastian* by Domenichino (1629) and the *Baptism of Jesus* by Carlo Maratta (c. 1697). Turn left.)

MUSEUM OF THE BATHS. This used to house the National Roman Museum ▲ *336,* whose works have been transferred to the Palazzo Massimo ▲ *338* and the Palazzo Altemps ▲ *284*. It now houses archaeological works from the Baths of Diocletian and other large public buildings such as the Temple of Aurelian. There is in addition an epigraphical section, some which boasts 10,000 inscriptions. A section devoted to the prehistory of the Eternal City is due to open soon on the first floor of the cloister. (Turn into Via Gaeta).

CASTRO PRETORIO (Praetorian barracks). Between 21 and 23 AD the Emperor Tiberius built a huge barracks complex on the northwest boundary of the town for the Praetorian cohorts (the permanent guard for the emperor, originally created by Augustus), who until that time had been billeted in different parts of Rome. The Praetorian guard used the area between the barracks and the Servian Wall for training. As well as containing the guards' dwellings, the barracks included various functional buildings: the commander's headquarters, the treasury, the armory, a hospital and granaries (*horrea*), etc. The perfectly preserved wall of the building is visible to the northeast of Stazione Termini, between Viale Castro Pretorio and Viale del Policlinico. The main national library, the Biblioteca Vittorio Emanuele II, built between 1965 and 1975, now occupies part of the site. (Walk back toward the station, taking the Via San Martino della Battaglia and Via Solferino.)

As the inscription at the entrance of the National Roman Museum indicates, it was necessary to demolish numerous buildings in order to make room for the Baths of Diocletian. It took an army of workmen eight years to build the gigantic baths complex – including, according to medieval tradition, 40,000 Christians.

MUSEUM OF THE BATHS
It is pleasant to walk in the Great Cloister and the old garden of the Baths, which include archeological remains, sarcophagi and ancient inscriptions.

This museum (also known as Museo delle Terme was established in 1889 in the Carthusian conver to house the archeological finds of the perio particularly the stuccos and paintings discovere in the gardens of the Farnesina. It was enriched t numerous acquisitions and became one of the m important museums in the world as regards the a of antiquity. Today some of its treasures, includir the famous collection gathered in the 17th centu by Cardinal Ludovisi, are housed in the Palazzo Altemps and in the former Collegio Massimo (ir Piazza dei Cinquecento).

"THE MAIDEN OF ANZIO"

This young girl is standing, with her head slightly bowed, holding a tray. Her tunic, which is slipping off one shoulder, is gathered at the waist. The vivacity, the freshness and the grace expressed in the motion of the body and the position of her head, freed from classical conventions, date this as a 3rd century BC work.

THE PORTONACCIO SARCOPHAGUS

In the center a Roman general, whose expression is clearly depicted, spurs his horse against the enemy; all around him Roman soldiers with helmets and breastplates are triumphing over barbarians, shown in pathetic attitudes. This theme of the fray, rendered here with splendid relief work, was frequently used in the iconographic repertoire of the Roman sarcophagus workshops in the 2nd century AD.

WALL PAINTING

The "garden" of the villa belonging to Livia, the wife of Augustus, looks like a walled orchard planted with different species of trees and full of birds. The painter's technique gives this mural decoration an idyllic, almost Eden-like, atmosphere.

"THE WOUNDED NIOBID"

Because of its severity of expression, the style of this work is clearly that of the 5th century BC. It is one of the many representations of the famous Greek myth transmitted to Rome by Ovid. Niobe had boasted of being superior to Leto due to the many children she had. Leto's own children, Apollo and Artemis, punished Niobe's impudence by slaughtering her seven sons and seven daughters with arrows.

THE BIRTH OF APHRODITE"

The central panel of the *Ludovisi Triptych*, this relief shows the goddess emerging from the waves with the assistance of the Hours, as in Homer's poem. The quality of the relief and the depiction of the body, almost lifelike beneath the folds of drapery heavy with water, are reminiscent of the work of artists from Magna Graecia in the mid 5th century AD.

STAZIONE TERMINI

The Bernich Aquarium (below right).

ROME'S STATION
The name Stazione Termini was chosen for the station because of the baths (*terme*) nearby.

PIAZZA DEI CINQUECENTO. This square served in the 19th century as a parade ground for the troops stationed in the Praetorian barracks. At the entrance to the Via delle Terme stands an obelisk (fa left) dedicated to the 548 Italian soldiers killed in 1887 during the attempted conquest of Eritrea. The Palazzo Massimo, at No 68, is today one of the annexes of the National Roman Museum ▲ *336*.

THE HISTORY OF THE STATION. Pius IX developed the railways in the Pontifical States. About 1857 the idea was put forward of combining the arrivals and departures, previously divided. The site for the new station was chosen in 1860, but the design of architect Salvatore Bianchi was not accepted until 1867: a building flanked by two wings, with alternating Tuscan, Ionic and Corinthian columns concealing a metal structure. Following the creation of the State Railways, from 1905 proposals were put forward for the general restructuring of Stazione Termini. The Universal Exhibition of 1942 ▲ *386* contributed a new impetus, and in 1938 the old station was partially replaced with buildings designed by Angiolo Mazzoni del Grande. In 1967 the refurbishment was completed with the impressive structure housing the main hall, ticket offices and restaurant. Thus the present station combines the architecture of the Fascist period and that of the 1960's. (Follow the via Giovanni Giolitti, then take Via Cattaneo as far as Piazza Fanti.)

Via Giovanni Giolitti

The Bernich Aquarium. Between the station and Piazza Vittorio Emanuele II, one can now visit a very pretty but long neglected building put up between 1885 and 1887. Designed as the municipal aquarium, it combines travertine marble and cast iron in an extremely original setting entirely focused on the marine environment. It is now used for a variety of cultural activities, including exhibitions and concerts. (Follow Via Rattazi in order to return to Via Giovanni Giolitti.)

Santa Bibiana. Now practically nestling against the railway track, this small 5th-century basilica was originally located in the heart of the country. In 1624 the bodies of St Bibiana, her parents and her sister were exhumed from under the main altar; consequently Urban VIII decided to rebuild the church. Bernini designed the façade as well as the main altar, which he crowned with his first great religious sculpture. The saint's left hand holds carefully worked folds of drapery which give life and movement to the statue. Above the colonnade in the nave, frescoes representing Bibiana's life were painted by Agostino Ciampelli (on the right) and Pietro da Cortona (on the left). This was Cortona's first major work, and henceforth Urban VIII involved these two painters in all the important artistic enterprises of his pontificate.

Temple of Minerva Medica. This large decagonal hall, which once had a circular dome, was originally part of the Gardens of Licinius. It dates from the 4th century AD and was named after a statue of Minerva found close by, now reserved in the Vatican.

Temple of Minerva Medica
The bold architecture of the temple inspired many Renaissance buildings. Today, bordered by railway tracks and ugly

apartment blocks, it has lost much of the charm that Stendhal found in it.

Porta Maggiore

Claudius' aqueduct. The Porta Maggiore, a magnificent archway in travertine marble, was formed from arches belonging to two aqueducts, the Aqua Claudia and the Anio Novus, begun by Caligula in 38 AD and completed by Claudius fourteen years later. It only became a true gateway when it was included in the Aurelian Wall ▲ *323*. In the 5th century Honorius added an external bastion, the demolition of which in 1838 led to the discovery of the tomb of Eurysaces. On the upper part of the structure one can read the inscriptions, repeated on both sides, of Claudius and also of Vespasian and Titus, who restored the arch in 71 and 81 AD respectively.

The tomb of Eurysaces. This tomb was built around 30 BC

Porta Maggiore
The tall attic (upper section) with three superimposed bands corresponds to the conduits of the two aqueducts. The monument was built using the so-called "unfinished" technique typical of the time of Claudius, which merely hinted at many of the architectural elements.

for Marcus Vergilius Eurysaces, a baker who supplied bread to the army, and his wife Atistia, as the inscriptions recall. Its location between the Via Labicana and the Via Prenestina determined its curious trapezoidal design. The cylindrical architectural elements are evocative of the receptacles in which dough was kneaded, and the relief shows the various phases of breadmaking (above). All the decorative motifs of the tomb are designed to exalt the profession of this freed slave who lined his pockets during the civil wars.

THE UNDERGROUND BASILICA OF PORTA MAGGIORE. This intriguing building (closed to the public) was discovered by chance in April 1917. Its function is not known for certain: it may have been a tomb, a funeral basilica, a nymphaeum, or a neo-Pythagorean temple. It comprises a large hall (about 40 30 feet), preceded by a square vestibule divided into three naves; the central one ends in an apse. All the walls are covered with stucco decorations, but the vault and the apse are the most interesting elements; the former consists of three sections featuring mythological and realistic scenes, masks and other decorative elements that are arranged in an evident attempt at symmetry. In the apse one can see Sappho who, pushed by a cupid, is flinging herself into the sea from the cliff of Leucas; under the gaze of Apollo, she is welcomed by a triton and Leucothea, who is raising her veil. The decoration is rich in mysterious metaphysical and symbolical meanings which are not yet fully understood. (Take the Via di Porta Maggiore, then Via Principe Eugenio.)

The tomb of Eurysaces.

The stucco decorations of the vault of the underground basilica.

PIAZZA VITTORIO EMANUELE II

AN ANIMATED CENTER. In building the Esquiline neighborhood, the first large urban project in Italy's new capital ● 33, the vast square dedicated to King Victor Emmanuel II formed the focal point for the streets leading from San Giovanni in Laterano, Santa Croce in Gerusalemm and Porta Maggiore. Its porticos, completed in 1882 and 188 reflect the influence of Piedmontese architecture, as Turi

THE ARCH OF GALLIENUS
(Take Via Merulana, then Via San Vito.) Completely rebuilt by Augustus, this is one of the gateways in the oldest of the city walls; it was originally called the Porta Esquilina. The inscription of Marcus Aurelius Victor to the Emperor Gallienus and his wife Salonina, engraved on the cornice bordering the attic, is a later addition.

Piazza Vittorio Emanuele II in the last century.

340

as the first capital of the new kingdom; and at its center is ne of Rome's most picturesque markets. In the gardens here is a fountain by Mario Rutelli, a mass of tritons, olphins and octopuses originally designed to adorn the ountain of the Naiads in Piazza della Repubblica ▲ *334*. This marine cluster has earned the fountain the nickname of *fritto misto* ("fish fry")!

THE TROPHIES OF MARIUS. The monumental brick structure n the northwest corner of the gardens was, in Renaissance imes, named "I Trofei di Mario" due to the two 1st-century marble reliefs that adorned it before they were moved to the balustrade of the Capitol ▲ *334*. It is in fact the remains of a massive fountain dating from the time of Alexander Severus (3rd century AD), which crowned the water tower of the Aqua Julia. Nearby stands the intriguing Porta Magica, inscribed with an alchemist's ormula for making gold. (Turn eft into Via Leopardi.)

THE AUDITORIUM OF MAECENAS. This was certainly part of the house of Maecenas, Augustus' famous minister who was a patron of many writers and poets. An apsidal hall, partly underground and completely structured in *opus reticulatum*, it may have been designed for public readings of literary works by authors such as Horace or Virgil, who both lived in the neighborhood. There are six deep rectangular niches on either side of the hall, with sumptuous bucolic decorations. The exedra has seven narrow steps, above which there are five niches decorated with garden scenes; under them runs a frieze with a black background showing hunting scenes, which are a continuation of the decorations in the main part of the hall. (Take Via Merulana.)

TROPHIES OF MARIUS
There is no doubt that the fountain resembled the proposed restoration shown on the left; a monumental façade with a central niche flanked by two open arches. These held the two trophies portraying the weapons of the "barbarians" (the Chatti and the Dacians) conquered by Domitian in 89 AD.

TROPHEE · VVLGAIREMENT · APPELE · DE · MARIVS
TROVVE · SVR · LES · RVINES · DV · CHATEAV · DE · L'EAV · IVLES

The Basilica of Santa Maria Maggiore is framed by two squares on which the popes left their mark. To match the obelisk in the Piazza dell'Esquilino, Paul V had the fluted marble column from the Basilica of Maxentius ▲ *145* erected in the Piazza Santa Maria Maggiore. Carlo Maderno set it on a pedestal and crowned it with a statue of the Virgin.

BASILICA OF SANTA MARIA MAGGIORE ★

CHURCH OF MANY NAMES. The Virgin Mary herself is supposed to have shown Pope Liberius (352–66) where this church was to be built by causing snow to fall on the top of the Esquiline on August 5, 356. The church is therefore also known as the Liberian Basilica, but it was built by St Sixtus III (432–40) immediately after the maternity of Mary had been defined at the Council of Ephesus (431). Dedicated to the Virgin Mary, the fourth patriarchal basilica was subsequently given the name of Santa Maria ad Praesepe ("St Mary of the Crib") because of a shrine dedicated to the holy crib situated under the altar of the Sixtus V chapel.

THE FAÇADE. On the Piazza di Santa Maria Maggiore the basilica has a baroque façade enhanced by a loggia, designed by Ferdinando Fuga for Pope Benedict XIV in the mid 18th century. Returning from Avignon in 1377, Gregory XI had the CAMPANILE (bell tower) built; approximately 245 feet high, it is still the tallest in Rome. Under the 12th-century PORTICO, restored by Gregory XIII for the Holy Year of 1575, there is a bronze statue of Philip IV of Spain, the benefactor of the basilica. To the left of the portico a flight of stairs leads to the loggia, where one can admire the fine mosaics with which Filippo Rusuti adorned the original façade at the end of the 13th century. From here the Pope used to bestow his benediction "Urbi et Orbi" upon the crowds.

PAPAL MODIFICATIONS. Despite the numerous alterations introduced by various popes over the centuries, the general appearance of the basilica's interior is still quite similar to

hat it
riginally was.
orty Ionic
olumns, of
vhich 36 are
narble
nonoliths,
ivide the inner
pace into three
aves of majestic proportions. In the 9th century Pascal I
ndertook the restoration of the choir and Benedict III
ehabilitated the baptistery. The beautiful paving that Eugene
II had made by the Cosmati (1145–53) was, however,
adically rearranged when Ferdinando Fuga was
ommissioned to restore the basilica in the 18th century. But
he most important modifications were carried out under
Nicholas IV (1288–92), who had a transept and a new apse
esigned. Rodrigo Borgia, the future Pope Alexander VI
1492–1503), commissioned Giuliano da Sangallo to make the
plendid coffered ceiling with the Borgia arms. The fact that
ts ornamental roses are some 3 feet in diameter gives an idea
f the building's dimensions. This ceiling is said to have been
ilded with the first gold brought from the New World.
THE MOSAICS ★. Thirty-six panels of 5th-century mosaics
rom the central nave above the architrave illustrate scenes
rom the Old Testament; they are
mong the earliest Christian mosaics
n Rome. Those on the chancel arch,
vhich date from the same period and
lisplay Byzantine influence, show

cenes of the birth and childhood of
esus above representations of the
owns of Jerusalem and Bethlehem (below). They proclaim
he glory of the Virgin, who is dressed as an Oriental empress.
The mosaics in the apse, which complete the series in the
nave in a blaze of color, are by Jacopo Torriti (1295), a pupil
f Cavallini. They consist in part of 5th-century elements (the
oliage and the Jordan, for example) and consecrate the
riumph of Mary: between the windows episodes of her life
unfold, and in the arched vault above the apse is Torriti's
nasterpiece *The Coronation of the Virgin* (above).
THE CHAPELS. Two domed chapels stand on either side of the
confessio. On the right is
the richly ornamented
SISTINE CHAPEL, which
Sixtus V commissioned
Domenico Fontana to build
in 1586. It was adorned with
marbles from the
Septizodium ▲ *150* and
decorated with frescoes.
Fontana also designed the
monumental tombs of Sixtus V
and Pius V, each decorated with
five bas-reliefs. When Paul V
asked Flaminio Ponzio to build
the PAULINE CHAPEL to the same
design, Ponzio also used the
form of the Greek cross and for

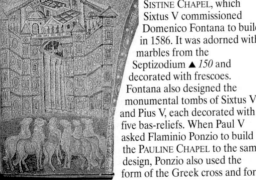

"THE CORONATION OF THE VIRGIN"
In Torriti's
masterpiece, Christ
and the Virgin are
seated on a precious
throne; the Son is
crowning his Mother.
To the right, in the
midst of a procession
of angels and saints
are St Francis and St
Anthony, the
Franciscan saints, as
well as the Order's
former general, Pope
Nicholas IV, kneeling
beside Cardinal
Giacomo Colonna.
In the episode of the
Dormition, the artist
and his assistant are
shown kneeling at the
feet of Our Lady.

THE PAULINE CHAPEL
Between 1611 and
1615 most painters in
Rome worked on the
decorations of this
chapel. One finds the
older generation –
Cigoli (*The Virgin
Mary and the Apostles*,
in the dome) and
Cavaliere d'Arpino
(*Prophets and Sibyls*,
in the pendentives of
the dome and
*Apparition of the
Virgin and St John*,
above the altar) – as
well as younger artists
such as Lanfranco
and Guido Reni, who
painted the figures of
saints above the
tombs.

343

▲ From the baths of Diocletian to San Pietro

THE APSE OF SANTA PUDENZIANA ★
The mosaic in the apse portrays Christ teaching the apostles in a circle around him. In the foreground are Peter and Paul; behind them, holding up crowns, are two women personifying the Church of the Circumcision and the Church of the Gentiles. A portico closes off the scene, beyond which the roofs of a town, no doubt Jerusalem, are visible. In the sky, on each side of a cross encrusted with precious stones, are the four evangelists in their symbolic forms of the eagle, the bull,

the tombs of Paul V and Clement VIII imitated Fontana's arrangement.

PIAZZA DELL'ESQUILINO. Sixtus V transformed this square and re-erected there one of the obelisks that had stood outside the entrance to the Mausoleum of Augustus ▲ *309*. When the twin cupolas of the chapels of Santa Maria Maggiore were completed, it became apparent that they needed to be integrated with the basilica as a whole. Eventually Clement X (1670–76) entrusted the building of the apsidal end to Carlo Rainaldi, and the basilica now appears in its full glory at the top of his magnificent tiers of steps leading from the Piazza dell'Esquilino. (Turn left into Via Urbana.)

Santa Pudenziana and Santa Prassede

the lion and the angel.

•
Santa Pudenziana: the bell tower, the doorway, and a detail of the façade.

A HOLY FAMILY. According to tradition, St Peter was given hospitality by a senator named Pudens who had two daughters, Pudentiana and Praxedes, and two sons, Novatus and Timothy. The latter was probably St Paul's companion. After the death of her parents and husband, Pudentiana is said to have turned her house in Vicus Patricius (now the Via Urbana) into a church. A few years later, after the death of Pudentiana and Praxedes, Pope Pius I (1402–55) is reputed to have built two churches, one in Vicus Patricius dedicated to St Pudentiana and the other dedicated to St Praxedes.

SANTA PUDENZIANA. Excavations below the church have revealed a Roman house over which baths were built in the 2nd century. Although the church itself dates back to the 4th century, a variety of modifications radically altered the appearance of this paleo-Christian building. The bell tower was added at the end of the 12th century, and the lovely doorway in the 16th century (using much older materials); then in 1588 Francesco da Volterra was entrusted with a major refurbishment of the church and the building of an elliptical dome. Santa Pudenziana is best known for the mosaic in the apse (although it suffered some damage during the restoration work of the 16th and early 17th centuries); dating from the end of the 4th or beginning of the 5th century, it is one of the earliest Christian mosaics in Rome. The CAETANI CHAPEL in the left nave – perhaps the first place of worship in Pudens' home – is one of the richest in Rome, embellished with marble and stucco decorations. (Return to Piazza Santa Maria Maggiore and Via di Santa Prassede.)

SANTA PRASSEDE
Mosaic of the
Heavenly City on the
chancel arch (above).

The mosaics in the
apse (left).

SANTA PRASSEDE ★. There is no archeological evidence of a
church here before 489, and the earliest restorations date
from the pontificate of Pope Hadrian I (772–95). The present
building dates from the time of St Pascal I (817–24), who
rebuilt the church completely, changing its orientation and
adding a monastery. The splendor of its Carolingian mosaics
have earned it renown, especially those in the choir and in the
Chapel of St Zeno. The mosaics in the apse, similar to those
in the Church of Santi Cosma e Damiano ▲ *168*, show the
Savior surrounded by six people: to the right, St Peter, St
Pudentiana and St Zeno, or perhaps St Cyriaca; to the
left, St Paul, St Praxedes and Pope Pascal I
holding a model of the church. Two palm
trees (the two Testaments) frame the
composition; a phoenix, the symbol of
the Resurrection, perches on the one
on the left. Above, twelve sheep
representing the Apostles converge
toward the mystical Lamb. On the
chancel arch, the elect proceed
toward the heavenly Jerusalem,
where Christ is flanked by two
angels. Part of the mosaic had to
be sacrificed in order to sink
niches into the piers of the arch:
St Charles Borromeo intended
them to house the martyrs' relics.
The CHAPEL OF ST ZENO ★ opens
off the right-hand nave. It was
built by Pascal I in honor of his
mother Theodora, who was buried
here. The chapel, in the form of a
square, is entirely covered with
mosaics; a matching chapel
dedicated to St John the Baptist
was planned for the opposite

**THE CHAPEL OF ST
ZENO**
The door is flanked
by two columns – the
one of granite, the
other of black
porphyry – and
surmounted by
mosaics showing the
Virgin and Child
between St Praxedes
and St Pudentiana.
On the vault of the
chapel, four angels
are bearing the
Savior's image. The
walls are decorated
with figures of saints
in the heavenly
paradise (Praxedes,
Pudentiana and
Agnes are on the left;
Andrew, James and
John on the right).

FROM THE BATHS OF DIOCLETIAN TO SAN PIETRO IN VINCOLI

PIAZZA SAN PIETRO IN VINCOLI.
This watercolor by Roesler shows the medieval tower of the Margini, which was converted into a bell tower for the national church of the Calabrians, San Francesco di Paola.

A "TRAGEDY"
The construction of the tomb of Julius II took nearly forty years; Michelangelo described it as a "tragedy".

The Salita Borgia, which leads to the Basilica of San Pietro in Vincoli, is lined with medieval houses.

nave. (Take Via di San Martino ai Monti.)

BASILICA OF SAN MARTINO AI MONTI.
Pope Silvester I (314–35) had established an oratory in the house of a priest called Equitius, and a later pope, St Symmachus (498–514), built a basilic there dedicated to St Martin of Tours. From 1636 to 1663 it was radically transformed by Pietro da Cortona. Gaspard Dughet, Poussin's brother-in-law, subsequently painted the lateral naves with frescoes in which the countryside of the Roman Campagna features prominently. Behind the basilica, in the Piazza di San Martino ai Monti, are two crenelated medieval towers, much restored, that belonged to the families Graziani (on the left) and Capocci; both towers were built with bricks from the Baths of Trajan ▲ *174.* (Take Via delle Sette Sale, in front of the church on the right.)

BASILICA OF SAN PIETRO IN VINCOLI

ST PETER'S CHAINS. The basilica owes its name (St Peter in Chains) to the precious relic it guards: the links of the chains used to fetter St Peter during his imprisonment in Jerusalem and in Rome. According to tradition, when the two chains were brought together, they were miraculously united. Preserved in the confessio, they are the object of veneration of pilgrims.

ADDITIONS OVER THE CENTURIES. The original basilica, dedicated to the Apostles and built over a 3rd-century house, first saw the light during the 4th century; it was rebuilt and consecrated under Sixtus III in 439. Cardinal Giuliano della Rovere, the future Julius II, completely transformed the church between 1471 and 1503, and it was further modified in the 18th century. Entered via a portico with five arches, the church is built to the plan of a basilica. The interior is divided by twenty ancient marble columns, and on the ceiling there is a beautiful fresco painted by the Genoese artist Giovanni Battista Parodi in 1706. Of particular note, among the church's numerous works of art are the paleo-Christian sarcophagus in the crypt, paintings by Guercino and Domenichino, a Byzantine mosaic showing a bearded St Sebastian, and the tomb of Nicholas of Cusa (a philosopher and the church's titular cardinal from 1448 until his death in 1464).

THE TOMB OF JULIUS II. Located at the end of the right nave, this work by Michelangelo, although very

(including the Stefaneschi, Papareschi and Alberteschi) lived in the area, but of their homes only those belonging to the Anguillara and the Mattei have survived from that period (both heavily restored). When the papacy returned from Avignon, for a little while Trastevere became the seat of the Studium Urbis university. At that time, there were only two points of communication with the left bank of the Tiber: the Isola Tiberina (Tiber island) and from 1475 the Ponte Sisto, which was intended to give pilgrims access to St Peter's.

ACCESS ROUTES. Until the 14th century no great town planning initiatives affected this district, its population being concentrated close to the Tiber.

Numerous churches were built or renovated during the 16th century, but very few palazzi were constructed. In this period the Via della Lungara took shape, running parallel to the Tiber to provide an easier link with the Borgo (the *rione* of St Peter's ▲ *232*). But it was not until the 19th century that the main avenues were built: the Viale di Trastevere running through the middle of the district, and the Lungotevere skirting the river.

A LIVELY QUARTER. Trastevere remained a predominantly working-class area until the 1960's, when it increasingly came to be seen as a neighborhood of restaurants and nightlife. But in the morning it retrieves some of its traditional character, and the *vicoli* (small streets) around Santa Maria in Trastevere offer a glimpse of the daily life of the past. The true spirit of the district is revealed in the month of July

THE TRASTEVERE, CENTER OF NIGHTLIFE ✪
Having attracted travelers and artists since antiquity, the Trastevere is Rome's bohemian quarter par excellence. Today it is frequented most especially by night owls, rivaling the Via Veneto ▲ *302*, capital of *la dolce vita*, and the Piazza Navona ▲ *276* in the number of establishments that stay open until the early hours. It has lost much of its original character after housing speculation in the 1960s drove out the craftsmen, the small local shops and the ordinary working people. However, something of its old spirit returns in July during the Festa de Noantri ("our own feast"), when restaurant tables invade the sidewalks and processions, concerts, theatrical performances and firework displays fill the small squares and narrow streets.

THE TRASTEVERINI
With their own dialect, the people of Trastevere had always considered themselves the descendants of the ancient Romans. The quarter was frequently a source of uprisings; consequently the popes distrusted the Trasteverini. In 1849 this was the area that continued to defend the short-lived Republic of Rome to the very end.

351

SAN BARTOLOMEO ALL'ISOLA
Only the Romanesque campanile of the old church remains. A well with beautiful medieval statues stands beside the presbytery. The church was completely rebuilt in 1624 by Martino Longhi the Younger but still retains the columns of the pagan temple.

PONTE ROTTO
At the southern tip of the island is the Ponte Rotto (the "broken bridge"). This is all that remains of the Pons Aemilius (2nd century BC), which was rebuilt several times before it finally collapsed in the 15th century. The point of the island is formed by a ship's prow sculpted in travertine in reference to the story of Aesculapius – part of a marble wall that once encircled the island to make it look even more like a ship.

The Tiber.

during the *Festa de' Noantri* ("our own feast") ● *44*. On summer nights in the back streets behind Via Garibaldi it is common to see people bringing chairs out into the street for a convivial improvised meal with neighbors.

ISOLA TIBERINA

THE ORIGIN OF THE ISLAND. According to legend the island in the Tiber was formed when the people flung the wheat harvest of the Campus Martius (which at that time belonged to the Etruscan kings) into the river after the expulsion of Tarquinius Superbus from Rome in the 4th century BC. Another legend has it that in order to end a plague some Romans went to Epidaurus in Greece to fetch Aesculapius, the god of medicine, and brought back a sacred serpent symbolizing the god. The serpent swam ashore to the island, the shape of which is said to be identical to that of the ship. In 293 BC a temple to Aesculapius was built here; its ruins lie beneath the Church of San Bartolomeo all'Isola, erected in the 10th century by the German Emperor Otto III. Until the 19th century this was the church of the millers' corporation, who used to celebrate their feast on the island on December 8.
A SPARSELY POPULATED ISLAND. The Isola Tiberina was barely inhabited until the Middle Ages, when the Pierleoni and Caetani families settled there. A tower that formed part of

eir fortifications remains standing at the head of the Ponte bricio. In the 17th century, especially during the plague of 56, it was used as a place of quarantine for plague victims in der to limit epidemics in the city. The island's medical cation has remained; even today the Fatebenefratelli spital covers almost all of it. The Baroque interior of the tle church of San Giovanni Calibita should not be missed. **RIDGES OVER THE TIBER.** Two bridges span the Tiber from e island. The one, the Ponte Fabricio, links the island with e Campo Marzio; on it is an inscription giving the name of builder (Lucius Fabricius, son of Caius) four times over d the date 62 BC. The two four-headed busts of Janus aming the entrance on the Campo Marzio side have earned he popular nickname of Ponte dei Quattro Capi ("Bridge the Four Heads"). The other bridge, the Ponte Cestio, built the 1st century BC as a link with Trastevere, was partly molished in 1888 and rebuilt in 1892.

The Ponte Rotto (above left) and the Church of Santa Cecilia.

IPAGRANDE

HE PORT OF RIPAGRANDE. Sadly this was destroyed when the ingotevere embankments were built at the d of the 19th century. The river now flows tween high walls (*muraglioni*) and it is not ossible to imagine how colorful and busy it ice was. Barges arriving from Ostia used be hauled from the right bank of the ber by men or buffaloes, which explains e presence near Porta Portese of an area lled the *bufalara*. The port was also known the Ripa Romea (the "bank for pilgrims ing to Rome") because pilgrims bound r St Peter's used to alight there.

Medieval buildings in the vicinity of Santa Cecilia.

IAZZA IN PISCINULA. The piazza's appearance today dates om the end of the 19th century when the palazzo facing alazzo Mattei was demolished. Some rather questionable estorations have attempted to recreate a medieval Roman azza. There are theories that Palazzo Mattei dates back to e time of Gregory IX (1227–41), or even to the time of nocent II (1130–43) and the Papareschi family; but as it w stands it doesn't go back further than the 14th or 15th ntury. SAN BENEDETTO IN PISCINULA is the smallest omanesque basilica in the city and boasts a fine bell tower, a 3th-century fresco of *St Benedict* in the porch and a splendid osmatesque ● 76 paving in the nave. In the area around the quare there are many fine medieval features to be seen, such s the beautiful porches of some of the houses (in Vicolo ell'Atleta, for instance) or the little church of Santa Maria in apella, which you come to after taking Via Anicia and assing SAN GIOVANNI BATTISTA DEI GENOVESI, which has a 5th-century cloister attributed to Baccio Pontelli.

THE MARTYRDOM OF SANTA CECILIA
On her wedding night Cecilia, a devout Christian, revealed to her husband Valerian that her purity was protected by an angel and that he would be able to see it if he converted. Valerian agreed to be baptized on the Via Appia, and was able to see the angel. Their faith was discovered and they were both martyred. When their remains were unearthed in 1600, Stefano Maderno was commissioned to make a statue of the saint in the exact position her body was found in.

The church of the Madonna dell'Orto.

"THE BLESSED LODOVICA ALBERTONI"
As in Santa Maria della Vittoria ▲ 294, in the Church of San Francesco a Ripa Bernini paid careful attention to lighting effects. An indirect light heightens the movement of the copiously draped agonizing figure. Her body rests on a mattress of multicolored marble fringed with gilded bronze. Above the statue a painting by Baciccia (*The Virgin and Child with St Anne*, 1675) reveals the nature of the blessed visionary's apparition.

BASILICA OF SANTA CECILIA. Set aside from the bustle of Piazza dei Mercanti (where the restaurant D meo Patacca aims to provide tourists with the atmosphere of a traditional tavern) and protected by a quadrangle planted with a rose garden, Santa Cecilia offers a haven of silence. It is believed to have been built on the remains of the house of Cecilia and her husband Valerian, and after their martyrdom it became a titular church. As a shrine already documented in the 4th century, it was restored during the pontificate of Pascal I (817–24), who commissioned the mosaics in the apse and donated a precious ciborium. A monastery dedicated to these holy martyrs was founded next to the church (this was rebuilt by Pascal II in 1100). At the end of the 13th century a rich French prelate, Cardinal Cholet, entrusted Pietro Cavallini with the task of decorating the church with frescoes. His amazing *Last Judgment* (a deta of which is shown on the right) was discovered during restorations in 1900 and can be seen today on the first floor, where it is jealously guarded by the Benedictine oblates. Also, Arnolfo di Cambio was commissioned to build a new ciborium in the church choir (1293), which is one of the fines works by this artist in Rome. The church was radically modified several times, most significantly in 1600. A corridor to the right of the entrance leads to the *caldarium* from whic Santa Cecilia is supposed to have emerged unscathed after being tortured by suffocation. Beneath the church, as well as the crypt containing Cecilia's and Valerian's sarcophagi, one can see important remains of Roman buildings from differen periods of antiquity, including pavements, baths, columns an inscriptions. (Take Via di San Michele, on the right, then tur into Via della Madonna dell'Orto.)

SANTA MARIA DELL'ORTO. This church was founded in 1492 b the corporation of market gardeners. Its façade, built betwee 1566 and 1579, was probably designed by Vignola. But its most remarkable features are inside, where an exuberant profusion of garlands, wreaths, flowers and fruit makes a sumptuous display of Baroque decoration. These stuccos, dating from the 18th century, were donated by the local guild (*università*), which included gardeners (*ortolani*), millers (*molinari*) and fruit, poultry and pasta vendors (*fruttaroli*, *pollari* and *vermicellari*). The high altar by Giacomo dell

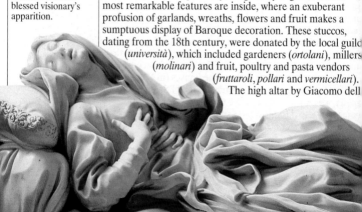

rta has a superb image of the Virgin Mary. (Take Via nicia, on the right.)

N **FRANCESCO A RIPA.** This church is built on the site of the n Biagio Hospice, where St Francis is supposed to have yed, and it still belongs to the Franciscan Order. modeled by Mattia De Rossi around 1682, it contains many pulchers dating from the 17th and 18th centuries. In the st chapel on the left there is a splendid *Birth of the Virgin* by mon Vouet, painted between 1618 and 1620 and clearly fluenced by Caravaggio. Three chapels farther on, you will d *The Blessed Lodovica Albertoni* (1671–5), one of Bernini's

PORTA PORTESE
Rome's famous flea market has been used as a location for many films. In *Bicycle Thieves* (Vittorio de Sica, 1948) the hero takes his son to Porta Portese in the hope of finding his stolen bicycle. In *Mamma Roma* (Pier Paolo Pasolini, 1962) the son of the prostitute Mamma Roma (played by Anna Magnani ● 43) goes there to try to sell a record he has just stolen from his mother.

st and greatest sculptures. The funerary monuments here ing to mind an item mentioned by Stendhal in his *roniques italiennes*: a Roman princess was reported to have d a midnight Requiem Mass celebrated here for the lover e was about to have killed. Skirting the church and taking a Ascianghi, you will come to the PIAZZA DI PORTA PORTESE n ancient times the arsenal of Rome stood near here). On nday mornings the city's famous flea market takes place in is piazza and in the neighboring streets. From the corner e SAN MICHELE A RIPA GRANDE complex, which has a çade more than 1,000 feet long, stretches back along the ber embankment. This gigantic building was erected at the d of the 17th century as a home for the poor, then became institution for juvenile delinquents. Its restoration, which gan in 1972, is almost complete and it now houses a variety departments belonging to the Ministero dei Beni e delle ttività Culturali (the ministry responsible for Italy's cultural d environmental heritage). It contains two magnificent urtyards, the first unfortunately disfigured by a modern aircase. (Return to Viale Trastevere and take Viale Glorioso d Via Dandolo to No. 47.)

HE **SYRIAN TEMPLE ON THE JANICULUM.** From the end of the public the commercial area on the Tiber attracted many aders and freed slaves of oriental origin. It is therefore not rprising that on both sides of the river traces have been found of religions originating in Anatolia (the cult of Cybele), Egypt and Syria. These include inscriptions confirming that a close link existed between slave traders and the goddess of Syria. The

The long façade of San Michele.

AN INTRIGUING ROOM
In the Syrian temple on the Janiculum there is an octagonal room with an apse at the end of it. In a cavity beneath the triangular altar a bronze statuette was found, portraying a human figure entwined in a serpent's coils – probably the Egyptian deity Osiris.

355

temple in Trastevere, discovered in 1906, proves the continuity from the 1st century AD of a Syrian cult, probably dedicated to Hadad (Heliopolis' equivalent of Jupiter), Atargatis (the Syrian goddess most widely worshiped in Rome) and Simios (the equivalent of Mercury). The sanctuary is made up of three parts: a rectangular central courtyard (the entrance), a room to the east containing a triangular altar; and a basilica, on the west side, preceded by a sort of atrium. (Go back down Via Dandolo to Piazza San Cosimato.)

PIAZZA DI SAN COSIMATO. The Benedictine monastery facing the piazza passed into the hands of the Franciscans in the 13th century and is now a hospital. It has two cloisters, one Romanesque and the other dating from the 15 century. (Return to the Viale di Trastevere.)

VIALE DI TRASTEVERE. This wide avenue, originally named Viale del Re, was built between 1880 and 1890 to link Ponte Garibaldi to Stazione Trastevere. Few buildings along it are modern, save for the TOBACCO FACTORY (1863) designed by Antonio Sarti.

THE EXCUBITORIUM. On the corner of Via di Monte Fiore and Via della VIIª Coorte is the entrance of the Excubitorium, a building dating from Imperial times that was the guardhouse of the seventh cohort of the *vigiles* (city guards). This private house, which was turned into a barracks toward the end of th 2nd century AD, provides a valuable insight into the activities of the *vigiles*. These units were formed under Augustus in 6 B and served as a police force for the city as well as a fire brigade.

SAN CRISOGONO. The present building was erected in the 12t century on top of a paleo-Christian church, but on a much greater scale, with three wide naves separated by 22 ancient columns. The campanile (bell tower) dates from 1125; the

mosaics attributed to Pietro Cavallini and the Cosmatesque paving ● 76 are 13th century. The rest of the building was restored by Giambattista Soria in 1620. Bernini designed the CHAPEL OF THE BLESSED SACRAMENT. From the sacristy yo can go down to the church beneath, the Titulus Chrysogonus, built in the 5th century to house the tomb of the holy martyr beheaded in the time of Diocletian. This sanctuary with a single nave was restored and decorated with frescoes durin the pontificate of Gregory III (731–41). Th *Scenes from the Life of St Benedict* were added in the 10th century. (Walk across Piazza Sonnino.)

THE ANGUILLARA PALAZZO AND TOWER. Th name of the Anguillara family, already famous in the 11th and 12th centuries, cam from their feudal domain near Lake racciano. In the 13th century their dwelling in Trastevere resembled an urban fortress. Then in 1464 modifications transformed it into a residential palace, leaving nothing but the tower – the only one today of the many that were erected in Trastevere in the Middle Ages. The Anguillara family died out in the 18th century, and the building was restored in 1887. Today it houses the Casa di Dante, dedicated to the author of the *Divina Commedia*. On the piazza facing the river is a statue of the poet Giuseppe Gioacchino Belli ● *43* by Michele Tripisciano, erected in 1913. (Turn left into Via della Lungaretta; Piazza Santa Maria in Trastevere is at the western end.)

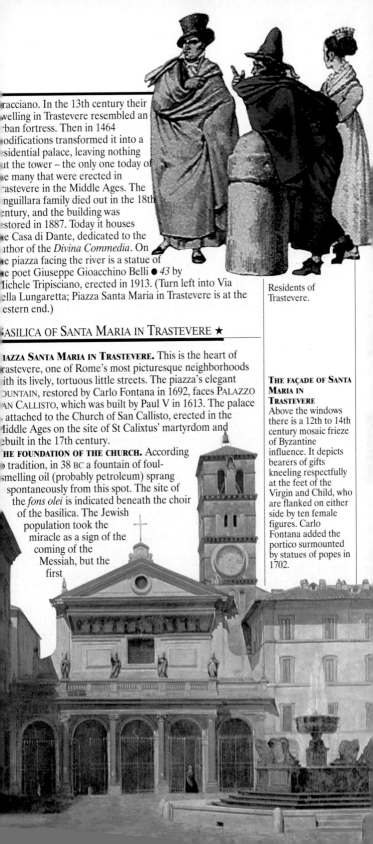

Residents of Trastevere.

BASILICA OF SANTA MARIA IN TRASTEVERE ★

PIAZZA SANTA MARIA IN TRASTEVERE. This is the heart of Trastevere, one of Rome's most picturesque neighborhoods with its lively, tortuous little streets. The piazza's elegant FOUNTAIN, restored by Carlo Fontana in 1692, faces PALAZZO SAN CALLISTO, which was built by Paul V in 1613. The palace is attached to the Church of San Callisto, erected in the Middle Ages on the site of St Calixtus' martyrdom and rebuilt in the 17th century.

THE FOUNDATION OF THE CHURCH. According to tradition, in 38 BC a fountain of foul-smelling oil (probably petroleum) sprang spontaneously from this spot. The site of the *fons olei* is indicated beneath the choir of the basilica. The Jewish population took the miracle as a sign of the coming of the Messiah, but the first

THE FAÇADE OF SANTA MARIA IN TRASTEVERE
Above the windows there is a 12th to 14th century mosaic frieze of Byzantine influence. It depicts bearers of gifts kneeling respectfully at the feet of the Virgin and Child, who are flanked on either side by ten female figures. Carlo Fontana added the portico surmounted by statues of popes in 1702.

"THE DORMITION OF THE VIRGIN"
This depiction of the last episode of Mary's life is one of the six mosaics by Pietro Cavallini in the choir of Santa Maria in Trastevere; the others are *The Birth of the Virgin, The Annunciation, The Birth of Jesus, The Adoration of the Magi* and *The Presentation in the Temple*. To the left, St Paul is weeping at Mary's feet; at the right, together with the Apostles and some bishops, is St Peter, with the Roman pallium and the censer, while kneeling beside the deceased is St John. In the middle, between two angels, is the Redeemer bearing Mary's soul. Cavallini's use of lines in this composition was an innovation in Byzantine iconography.

The mosaic in the choir shows Innocent II offering the church to the Virgin.

Christian shrine commemorating it was not established until the 3rd century. The existence of the shrine led to friction between the Christians and the local innkeepers. The Emperor Alexander Severus was asked to intervene and is said to have sided with the former, preferring the building to be occupied by an unconventional sect rather than by drunkards. The official biography of the popes, the *Liber pontificalis*, gives a different version, stating that Calixtus (who was Pope from 217 to 222) invited the faithful to a Mass in a domestic church (*titulus*) which was later converted into a basilica. Between 772 and 795 Hadrian I added the lateral naves. Then Gregory IV (827–44) made extensive changes. As well as having the choir raised, the altar covered with a ciborium, and a crypt made to accommodate the relics of Saints Calixtus, Calepodius and Cornelius, he had a chapel to the Holy Crib built (in imitation of Santa Maria Maggiore ▲ 342) and added a monastery to serve the basilica.

INNOCENT II'S BASILICA. In the 12th century Innocent II (who belonged to one of the great Trastevere families, the Papareschi) further modified the building, adding the transept and decorating the apse with splendid mosaics. Most of the materials came from the baths of Caracalla ▲ 319. The new

MARIA REGINA THRONVM PREPARAVIT

basilica, still unfinished at the time of Innocent's death, was consecrated by Alexander III (1159-81).

THE INTERIOR. Little has changed in the three naves since the time of Innocent II. The ceiling was designed by Domenichino, who also painted *The Assumption of the Virgin* in the center. The handsome Cosmatesque paving ● 76 was restored in 1870. To the left of the apse, the ALTEMPS CHAPEL (1584) was probably the first Counter-Reformation chapel to

NOC EN PP

be dedicated to an ancient cult of the Virgin.

MOSAICS OF THE CHOIR ★. These mosaics show traces of Byzantine influence, but belong to the Roman tradition. Those on the chancel arch portray the prophets Isaiah and Jeremiah, the symbols of the four evangelists, seven candelabra of the Apocalypse, and the cross with the Alpha and the Omega. In the apse one sees Christ and the Virgin enthroned (above); to the left are St Calixtus, St Lawrence and Pope Innocent II donating the church to the Virgin; to the right are the saints Peter, Cornelius, Julius and Calepodius; below, two rows of sheep are shown emerging from Jerusalem and Bethlehem and converging toward the Lamb of God. These 12th-century mosaics mark a renewal in the devotion to the Virgin, and the theme of the coronation of the Virgin was to recur a century later in Jacopo Torriti's masterpiece in Santa Maria Maggiore ▲ *342*. Lower down is one of the finest works of Pietro Cavallini: six episodes from the life of St Mary (1291). The artist makes an astonishing use of color, treating the mosaic as if it were a fresco. (Follow Via della Paglia, on the left as you come out of the basilica, until you reach Piazza Sant'Egidio, where you will find the 17th-century Church of Sant'Egidio and the Museo del Folklore e dei Poeti Romaneschi. Then take Via della Scala.)

SANTA MARIA DELLA SCALA. This church, which belongs to the Discalced Carmelites, was built by Francesco da Volterra. Although the Superiors of the Order refused *The Death of the Virgin* painted for them by Caravaggio, many of his pupils' works found their place in this church. They include *The Decapitation of St John the Baptist* by Honthorst in the first chapel on the right, and *The Death of the Virgin* by Carlo Saraceni in the second chapel on the left. The monastery's pharmacy has retained its 17th-century furnishings and decoration. (Take the Via Santa Dorotea.)

VIA DELLA LUNGARA

PORTA SETTIMIANA. This triumphal arch was built by Septimius Severus as an entrance to one of his villas; but in the 6th century it was incorporated, as a gateway, into the Aurelian Wall. Its present appearance dates from the modifications to the city made by Alexander VI (1498).

VIA DELLA LUNGARA. This long, straight road was constructed during the pontificate of Pope Julius II. Before the building of the Tiber embankments it was the only road linking

MUSEO DEL FOLKLORE
This small museum is dedicated to the life, customs and traditions of Rome in the 18th and 19th centuries. It is in five sections: the Carnival, aspects of daily life, the watercolors of Franz Ettore Roesler, the Artists' Festival in Cervara and firework displays. As well as engravings of the Piè di Marmo, the Bocca della Verità and Pasquino, there is a reconstruction of the poet Trilussa's study, containing paintings, photographs, documents and other possessions, and manuscripts of some of his poems. (This museum is fascinating, but by no means a substitute for visiting the Museo delle Arte e Tradizioni Popolari in EUR ▲ *387*.)

ACHILLE PINELLI (1809–41)
The son of the painter Bartolomeo Pinelli (1781–1835), Achille began painting at an early age. His best-known works are two hundred watercolors of the churches of Rome, including the one of Santa Maria della Scala, above. They are now in the Museo di Roma.

359

● 88

Trastevere to the Vatican. Along it are the Farnesina, the Palazzo Corsini and the Regina Coeli (Queen of Heaven) prison.

THE FARNESINA

AGOSTINO CHIGI'S VILLA. In 1509 this banker, who was the financier of Pope Julius II and Pope Leo X, commissioned Baldassare Peruzzi to build a sumptuous "country villa" with gardens stretching to the Tiber. Dubbed "il Magnifico" and known for his refined taste, this patron of the arts and man of letters even founded a printing press for the publication of classical texts. Not surprisingly, when it came to decorating the apartments of his villa, Chigi called upon the greatest artists of his time, among them Raphael, who was his friend and protégé. The paintings and frescoes of the young artist and his associates make this residence one of the gems of the Renaissance. After Chigi's death in 1520 the villa was abandoned, and in 1527 it was plundered and overrun by Charles V's troops ● 36. It acquired the name Farnesina when it was purchased by Alessandro Farnese around 1580. With the construction of the Lungotevere embankments at the end of the 19th century, part of its gardens were destroyed (revealing remains of an ancient Roman villa) and part of the loggia overlooking the river was demolished. Purchased by the Italian State in 1927, the Farnesina has been the property of the Accademia dei Lincei ▲ 362 since 1944 and now includes the Gabinetto Nazionale delle Stampe (the national collection of prints and drawings).

THE LOGGIA OF PSYCHE. The main entrance to the villa was situated beneath the loggia overlooking the garden, where theatrical performances were often staged. Two orders of columns are surmounted by a terracotta frieze that masks the third-floor windows. The loggia, is decorated with frescoes depicting Cupid and Psyche; these were painted by pupils of Raphael, following cartoons by the master. Giovanni da Udine is the author of the pergola composed of garlands of fruit and flowers that supports the two *trompe l'oeil* tapestries on the ceiling; these show the council of the gods welcoming Psyche on Mount Olympus and the wedding feast of Cupid and Psyche. Painted *putti* above the arches of the loggia and the false windows bear the attributes of the gods, while the lunettes recount the main episodes of Psyche's story.

THE LOGGIA OF GALATEA. To the right of the loggia of Psyche is the Galatea Room, named after Raphael's fresco *The Triumph of Galatea*; the artist is reputed to have used no models for it apart from ideal beauty as he conceived it.

THE MYTH OF PSYCHE

Psyche was so beautiful that she inspired Cupid himself with love for her. One night, as she was trying to see her lover's face, a drop of boiling oil fell from her lamp onto the god's shoulder. Cupid immediately fled. Persecuted by an infuriated Venus (above), who was jealous of her beauty, Psyche was compelled to wander about the world and undergo a thousand hardships until Cupid finally received permission to marry her.

A HISTORICAL GRAFFITO

Charles V's soldiers (*landsknechte*) left their mark in the Farnesina when they sacked Rome in 1527 ● 36. In the painted sky between two *trompe l'oeil* columns they scratched the fateful date.

...eruzzi painted the ...eiling with ...ythological ...escoes showing the ...onstellations of the ...odiac in their ...osition at the time ...f Agostino Chigi's ...rth. The lunettes ...re decorated with ...escoes based on ...vid's *Metamorphoses* by ...ebastiano del

...iombo, who also painted the fresco on the wall of ...olyphemus, the Cyclops, pining for the nymph Galatea.

...HE SALA DELLE PROSPETTIVE. Also known as the "room of ...e columns", this vast room on the *piano nobile* is famous for ...s imposing *trompe l'oeil* frescoes by Peruzzi. The artist's ...tention was to create the illusion of an open loggia offering ...ews over the Roman countryside and the city's monuments. ...is recognized as one of the masterpieces of the early 16th ...entury. Peruzzi's virtuosity makes this a pictorial *tour de force* ...f the Roman Baroque style. The floor pattern extends into ...e illusory loggia, and the painted scenery is organized ...round the focal point of the doorway through which you ...nter the room.

...HE SALA DI ALESSANDRO. For his bedroom Chigi ...ommissioned Giovanni Antonio dei Bazzi, known ...s Il Sodoma, to adorn the main wall with a fresco ...epicting the marriage of Alexander the Great ...o Roxana. Painted around 1513, this is based ...n an ancient model by Aetion that no longer ...xisted but of which the Greek writer Lucian ...ad provided a description. The wall on

A TROMPE L'OEIL ROOM
The originality of Baldassare Peruzzi's work in the Sala delle Prospettive lies neither in the decorative elements, such as the landscapes and columns, nor in the taste for *trompe l'oeil* perspectives (which was very widespread at the time), but in his ingenious use of traditional motifs to achieve the perfect optical illusion of making the walls of the room "disappear".

"THE TRIUMPH OF GALATEA"
Standing on an ethereal chariot drawn by dolphins, Galatea is no longer the cold figure of the Hellenistic and Roman traditions, but has entered the limpid world of the Muses of Parnassus. In this fresco the formal vitality of the figures is derived from the clarity of Raphael's classicism.

THE ACCADEMIA DEI LINCEI. Founded in 1603 by Federico Cesi and of which Galileo was an eminent member, this society brought together scholars who wished to "read the great book of the true and universal world, to visit its different parts, and to learn to observe and experiment". They chose as their symbol the lynx (*lince*), known for the sharpness of its eyesight.

"VENUS AND ADONIS" By casting a pale light over the whole scene Giuseppe Ribera abandoned the chiaroscuro that was such a prominent feature of his earlier work.

"REBECCA AT THE WELL" In this composition Carlo Maratta (1625-1713) strove to capture Raphael's manner of painting draped figures and Annibale Carracci's gift for portraying facial character.

the right portrays the family of Darius submitting to Alexander. Finally, to the left of the entrance is a fresco of inferior quality showing Alexander taming Bucephalus.

PALAZZO CORSINI

Facing the Farnesina across Via della Lungara, Palazzo Corsini replaced the Palazzo Riario, the residence of Queen Christina of Sweden from 1662 until her death in 1689. It was built between 1736 and 1758 by Ferdinando Fuga for Cardinal Neri Corsini, a nephew of Clement XII. The original conception was much more ambitious than what was built. The long façade is articulated around a central body with three portals leading into three galleries. The middle entrance

was designed to allow vehicles to reach the courtyard and gardens, while the other two lead to two staircases that meet on the *piano nobile*. This building is now the headquarters of the Accademia dei Lincei. **GALLERIA CORSINI.** The main floor now houses part of the collection of the Galleria Nazionale d'Arte Antica, the remainder being in Palazzo Barberini ▲ *291*. Among the most

The Orto Botanico contains a rich variety of Mediterranean trees and plants.

utstanding works are Caravaggio's *St John the Baptist*; *alome Bearing the Head of John the Baptist*, attributed to uido Reni; paintings by the Bologna school and the school f Caravaggio; and a number of Neapolitan Baroque works, cluding Salvator Rosa's *Prometheus*.

HE ORTO BOTANICO. The botanical garden belonging to the niversity of Rome was originally the park of Palazzo Corsini. covers an area of nearly 30 acres and boasts a splendid taircase with a waterfall. (Go back along Via della Lungara nd turn left into Via Santa Dorotea.)

ONTE SISTO

HE HOME OF LA FORNARINA. The house at No. 20 Via Santa Dorotea (now the Romolo restaurant) is supposed to have been the bakery owned by the father of Raphael's mistress, La Fornarina, traditionally identified as the subject of the famous portrait in Palazzo Barberini ▲ 292. It is said that in order to accelerate work on the Farnesina, Agostino Chigi allowed the painter to have her live with him on the premises. (Walk to the end of Via Santa Dorotea.)

PIAZZA TRILUSSA. This piazza bears the name of the Trastevere poet Carlo Alberto Salustri (1871–1950), known as Trilussa. When alterations were made to the piazza during the construction of the Tiber embankments at the end of the 19th century, the fountain commissioned by Paul V from Giovanni Fontana and Giovanni Vasanzio in 1613 was moved here from the end of the Via Giulia. This fountain was designed to distribute the water supplied by the Aqua Paola aqueduct ▲ 364.

PONTE SISTO. This bridge, which nks Trastevere to the left bank of the Tiber, was built in 1475 nder Sixtus IV to replace an ancient Roman bridge which ad been destroyed ▲ 364. Widened in the 19th century, it is ow closed to motor vehicles. The middle of the bridge ffords splendid views: of the dome of St Peter's; of the ventine hill and the Aqua Paola, dominated by the aniculum. (Go back along Via Santa Dorotea, past the hurch of SANTA DOROTEA, which is in the shape of a Greek ross; built in 1475, it was remodeled in the 18th century. hen take Via Garibaldi.)

HE JANICULUM

he name Gianicolo, or Janiculum, is derived from the cult of he god Janus. The hill still bears traces of the fierce fighting hat took place here between French troops and the upporters of the Republic of Rome in 1849 ● 33. The Via

THE TRASTEVERE POETS
The two great bards of Trastevere are Giuseppe Gioachino Belli (whose statue stands near the river in the piazza that bears his name ▲ 357) and Trilussa, to whom the monument in Piazza Trilussa was erected in 1954. Because Belli wrote his sonnets in *Romanesco* (Roman dialect 142–3), he has regrettably not achieved the fame he deserves. And yet the epic and tragic dimensions of his satire and the lucid, sarcastic irony with which he describes the pontifical Rome of the 19th century make him a truly great writer. Trilussa, whose writing is easier and less caustic, gives a vivid picture of the lives of the "little" people of Rome.

The Ponte Sisto fountain.

VIEW OF ROME FROM THE JANICULUM
From left to right Sant'Andrea della Valle, the Gesù, Santa Maria Maggiore, San Carlo ai Catinari and the monument to Victor Emmanuel.

The Fontana Paola.

Garibaldi used to be called Via delle Fornaci because of the brick factories beside it. It leads to the most beautiful panoramic view of the city, which according to one French 18th-century diarist, de Brosses, was in itself sufficient to justify "the journey to Italy".

BOSCO PARRASIO. To the right of Via Garibaldi there is a pa[th] leading to what was once the seat of the Arcadia academy, founded in 1690. With its aim of "exterminating bad taste" and of refining poetry, Arcadia exerted a profound influence on Italian literature. In 1926 it became the Italian Academy [of] Literature.

SANTA MARIA DEI SETTE DOLORI. Built between 1643 and 1667 according to a design by Borromini ● *80*, this church is characterized externally by simple brickwork in an interplay of curves and countercurves. Inside, the 19th-century decoration detracts from the rhythm and balance of Borromini's architecture. (Continue up Via Garibaldi.)

SAN PIETRO IN MONTORIO. This church provides a splendid point from which to view the city, which until the end of the 19th century was clearly divided in two distinct parts: ancient Rome on the right and modern Rome on the left. The church's austere façade was built at the end of the 15th century with funds provided by the Spanish sovereigns Ferdinand of Aragon and Isabella of Castile. Attached to the church is a convent which is now largely occupied by the Spanish Academy. The church contains many 16th-century works of art, including Sebastiano del Piombo's famous fresc[o] *The Flagellation*, based on a drawing by Michelangelo. Bernini worked o[n] the RAYMONDI CHAPEL and the fourth chapel on the left has lunettes painted by David de Haen as well as a *Descent from the Cross* by Dirk van Babure[n]. In the middle of a cloister to the right of the church, on the spot where St Peter is supposed to have been crucified, stands one of the most elegant buildings of the Renaissance, Bramante's TEMPIETTO (1502).

THE TEMPIETTO
Bramante's small circular temple (right) is believed to have been the first Renaissance monument inspired by the architecture of ancient Rome. Modeled on the Sibyl's shrine in Tivoli ▲ *392*, it was based on early Renaissance research.

THE FONTANA PAOLA. This fountain was built by Flaminio Ponzio and Giovanni Fontana to receive the waters of Trajan's ancient aqueduct, rehabilitated by Paul V to supply water to Trastevere, the Via Giulia area and the Vatican. Its three arches, modeled on the Aqua Felice fountain ▲ *295*, stand in front of a charming garden. (The street to the left after the fountain leads to the PORTA SAN PANCRAZIO, rebuilt in 1854.)

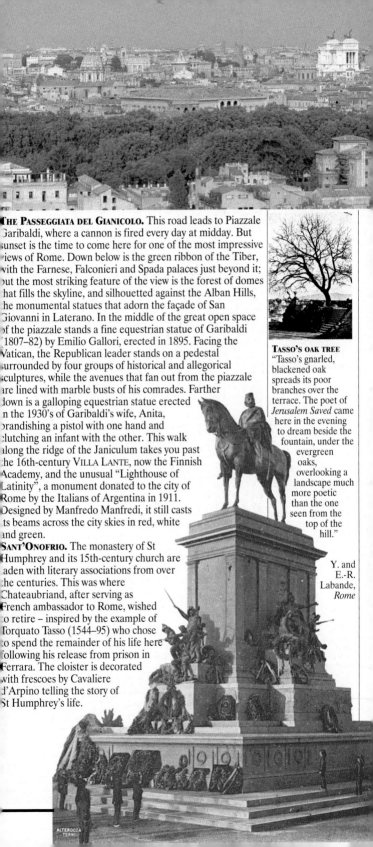

THE PASSEGGIATA DEL GIANICOLO. This road leads to Piazzale Garibaldi, where a cannon is fired every day at midday. But sunset is the time to come here for one of the most impressive views of Rome. Down below is the green ribbon of the Tiber, with the Farnese, Falconieri and Spada palaces just beyond it; but the most striking feature of the view is the forest of domes that fills the skyline, and silhouetted against the Alban Hills, the monumental statues that adorn the façade of San Giovanni in Laterano. In the middle of the great open space of the piazzale stands a fine equestrian statue of Garibaldi (1807–82) by Emilio Gallori, erected in 1895. Facing the Vatican, the Republican leader stands on a pedestal surrounded by four groups of historical and allegorical sculptures, while the avenues that fan out from the piazzale are lined with marble busts of his comrades. Farther down is a galloping equestrian statue erected in the 1930's of Garibaldi's wife, Anita, brandishing a pistol with one hand and clutching an infant with the other. This walk along the ridge of the Janiculum takes you past the 16th-century VILLA LANTE, now the Finnish Academy, and the unusual "Lighthouse of Latinity", a monument donated to the city of Rome by the Italians of Argentina in 1911. Designed by Manfredo Manfredi, it still casts its beams across the city skies in red, white and green.

SANT'ONOFRIO. The monastery of St Humphrey and its 15th-century church are laden with literary associations from over the centuries. This was where Chateaubriand, after serving as French ambassador to Rome, wished to retire – inspired by the example of Torquato Tasso (1544–95) who chose to spend the remainder of his life here following his release from prison in Ferrara. The cloister is decorated with frescoes by Cavaliere d'Arpino telling the story of St Humphrey's life.

TASSO'S OAK TREE
"Tasso's gnarled, blackened oak spreads its poor branches over the terrace. The poet of *Jerusalem Saved* came here in the evening to dream beside the fountain, under the evergreen oaks, overlooking a landscape much more poetic than the one seen from the top of the hill."

Y. and E.-R. Labande, *Rome*

As monuments in piazzas or discreet ornaments in courtyards and on street corners, fountains abound in every part of Rome.

The park is adorned with statues that form a veritable bestiary.

"THE RAPE OF PROSERPINA"
In this work intended to be viewed from all sides, Bernini contrasts the two bodies twisting in opposite directions. Pluto's muscular figure is inspired by Michelangelo's sculptures, but Proserpina's flesh demonstrates the artist's concern with rendering nature rather than seeking to portray "Ideal Beauty".

"APOLLO AND DAPHNE"
This sculpture by Bernini portrays the moment, as described by Ovid, when Daphne turned into a bay tree in order to escape from Apollo's embrace. A masterly use of the marble heightens the contrast between the nymph's lithe body and the bark beginning to cover her and her hair changing into branches. On the pedestal, as well as Ovid's verses, there is an inscription by the future Urban VIII attempting to moralize about the scene, which many had found too libertine.

From Villa Giulia to the Foro Italico
Villa Borghese

"Sacred and profane love"
This early work by Titian was painted in 1514 for N. Aurelio, a collector linked to the humanist movement in Venice. It expresses the abstract theme of the "two Venuses": one being the symbol of universal and eternal beauty, while the other symbolizes the progenitive force. But it is the quality of the artist's painting that is striking, rather than the complexity of the theme.

"The Madonna of the Serpent"
Painted by Caravaggio in 1605 for the Chapel of Sant'Anna dei Palafrenieri in the Vatican, this picture found its way into the Borghese collection either because it was deemed too irreverent by the Corporation of Palafrenieri, who commissioned it, or because the cardinal exerted the necessary pressure. Under the eye of St Anne (the patron of the Corporation), the Virgin Mary and Jesus are shown crushing the serpent under foot. This was a way of affirming, in opposition to Protestant denials, that Mary actually participated in the salvation of humanity. The very natural appearance of Christ and the portrayal of Mary as a woman of the common people make the fusion of the human and the divine almost tangible. The novelty of such a representation might well have shocked certain people in those days.

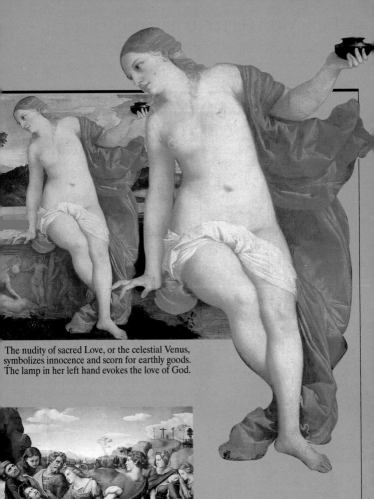

The nudity of sacred Love, or the celestial Venus, symbolizes innocence and scorn for earthly goods. The lamp in her left hand evokes the love of God.

"THE DEPOSITION"

This was one of the last works Raphael painted before he left for Rome. It was commissioned by Atlanta Baglioni of Perugia in memory of her son, who had been murdered a few years previously. Raphael borrowed the composition from a sarcophagus of the classical period and made every effort to convey pathos by a careful study of expressions of grief in the figures portrayed.

"DANAË"

This is one of four erotic paintings Federico II di Gonzaga ordered from Correggio in 1530 as a gift for Charles V. Correggio's graceful style earned him a reputation equal to that of Raphael and Titian. Until the 19th century it was essential for great collections to include an example of his work.

"Universal exhibitions transfigure the exchange value of merchandise. They inaugurate a world of fantasy to which humanity lends itself for its entertainment. The entertainment industry helps in this process by elevating humanity itself to the level of merchandise."

Walter Benjamin

Galleria Nazionale d'Arte Moderna

THE EXHIBITION OF 1911. To commemorate the fiftieth anniversary of the Unification of Italy, a huge exhibition was organized in the northern part of the city. It included an ethnographic and regional section, set up on the right bank of the Tiber, and an exhibition of fine arts in the Valle Giulia (on the site of the Villa Cartoni, on the left bank). In addition, major archeological discoveries were displayed in the Baths of Diocletian; and celebrations in the honor of Garibaldi, the "Father of the Nation", were held in the Vittoriano ▲ *160*, which was inaugurated at the same time. The two main centers of the exhibition were linked by a new bridge, the Ponte Risorgimento, built in reinforced concrete by the French architect François Hennebique. The numerous foreign pavilions brought together an amazing profusion of architectural styles. The BRITISH PAVILION, designed by Edwin Landseer Lutyens in neoclassical style, was built to last and is now the British Academy of Rome. One of the most interesting pavilions was the Austrian one, devised by Josef Hoffmann, which has a room decorated by Gustav Klimt. This lush green valley has been chosen as the site for many academies and research institutes, including the Belgian, Danish, Dutch, Swedish, Rumanian, and Egyptian academies.

GALLERIA NAZIONALE D'ARTE MODERNA. Another building that remained, the Palazzo delle Belle Arti designed by Cesare Bazzani, became Rome's museum of modern art. The same architect was responsible for landscaping the Valle Giulia, with its avenues, shady piazzas, and fountains approached by flights of steps. The gallery contains the most important collections of 19th- and 20th-century Italian paintings and sculptures:

not until 1816, however, that it completely lost its autonomy (until 1870), becoming a small town like so many others in the Papal States.

VIA TIBURTINA

Whereas today's Via Tiburtina winds its way to Tivoli through olive groves, the old road, after Ponte Lucano, used to lead straight to the town. It passed close to a large domed circular hall, the Tempio della Tosse (Temple of the Tosse), which was turned into a church in the Middle Ages. Then it ran alongside the sanctuary of Hercules Victor, the god of war, assimilated with Mars, and also the god of commerce. The temple, which contained an oracle, was at the end of an enormous square surrounded by a portico reached by two great stairways on either side; between these rose the steps of a theater. This combination of temple and theater was typical of sanctuaries in central and southern Italy, such as Praeneste ▲ *398*, Pietrabondante and the Teatro Pompeo in Rome ▲ *248*.

A WALK IN THE TOWN

Starting with Piazza Trento, one can discover numerous medieval houses in the streets of this little town, which is dominated by the Rocca Pia fortress built by Pius II 1458–64).

SANTA MARIA MAGGIORE. This church, founded in the 5th century but rebuilt in the 13th century, has a Romanesque façade and a Gothic portal. Its atrium has a fine 13th-century fresco of *The Virgin and Child*. (Proceed to Piazza del Duomo, part of which is built on the site of the ancient forum.)

THE DUOMO. The cathedral dedicated to St Lawrence was rebuilt in 1650. However, its Romanesque campanile dates from the 12th century. Inside, one should see the famous 13th-century sculpture of *The Deposition* in the fourth chapel on the right; and the *Triptych of the Saviour* (12th–14th century) in the third chapel on the left, opened on request.

VILLA GREGORIANA. This was created by Pope Gregory XVI at the beginning of the 19th century. The park extends along both banks of the Aniene, which the pontiff had partly channeled. Go to the belvedere halfway up the great waterfall and you will appreciate the force with which the river roars down this 350-foot cataract.

TEMPLE OF THE SIBYL. Two temples (reached through the La Sibilla restaurant) stand on the edge of the Aniene falls. The rectangular one, the older of the two (2nd century BC), is dedicated to Tiburnus, the legendary founder of the town. The round temple, built in the Corinthian style, is that of the sibyl Albunea. Surrounded by columns and built of great slabs of travertine, it stands on a podium, the steps of which have disappeared. (Go along Via del Colle as far as the CHURCH OF SAN SILVESTRO, which is Romanesque and has very

A CURIOUS AEDICULE
Between the portal and the great rose window of Santa Maria Maggiore there is a small Gothic aedicule.

THE TEMPLE OF HERCULES VICTOR
The cult of Hercules Victor, which had a major following in Latium, certainly started in Tibur, reaching Rome by the end of Republican times. The opulence of this temple was so well known that Octavian, the future Augustus, attempted to gain possession of it in 41 BC. Subsequently, the Emperor's cult was linked to this deity.

IPPOLITO D'ESTE
A favorite retreat of the ancient Romans, Tivoli was bound to appeal to this cardinal who was a patron of the arts, friend of the humanists and avid reader of classical texts. The richest of all the Italian cardinals, after his hopes of becoming pope were dashed he lavished his wealth on the Villa d'Este.

"The green, blue or almost black waters of these vast pools add their tranquil tones to the insistent, impassioned song of the cascades. On all sides, water jets and

cypresses compete, thrusting skyward in bold rivalry."
Gabriel Fauré

fine 13th-century frescoes. A little further on is the old entrance of the Villa d'Este. The perspective of the gardens was originally designed to be seen from this spot. Finally, return to Piazza Trento.)

VILLA D'ESTE ● 8

In 1550 Cardinal Ippolito d'Este was appointed Governor of Tivoli. He immediately took possession of the Governor's palace, located in a former Benedictine monastery which he asked Pirro Ligorio to remodel to his taste. The Villa d'Este's fame, however, is due more to its gardens than to the building itself. Each alley, path or avenue reveals a new mossy fountain in a carefully landscaped vista: there are supposed to be five hundred fountains altogether. This most famous of Italian-style gardens, which has been widely imitated, reverberates with the sound of so many fountains that it inspired the Romantic composer Franz Liszt to write a piano suite called *Fountains of the Villa d'Este*.

THE LAYOUT OF THE GARDENS. To clear space for the gardens a whole area of the town had to be demolished, many inhabitants being forced to sell or face expropriation. Due to the steepness of the terrain, enormous earth-moving works were undertaken in order to create alternating terraces and slopes. In addition, the site had an irregular shape. The overall layout, designed to be seen from the original entrance at the foot of the hill, had to achieve two main purposes: to create the illusion that the villa was centrally placed (it is in fact slightly off-center) and to set it back by visually increasing the depth of the property. The means chosen to achieve this were unusual for the time. A central alley prolonging the loggia, known as the Avenue of Perspectives, was made to intersect with five paths linking the monumental fountains;

these were mostly positioned toward the sides to give the effect of an enclosure in relation to the surrounding landscape.
DECAY AND RENEWED SPLENDOR. When the cardinal died, the gardens were unfinished despite the speed with which the project had been implemented, and the work was continued by his descendants. This was followed by a period of decay, when the Habsburgs inherited the property. The contents of the villa were sold and, since the upkeep of the gardens proved too costly, they were left to grow wild, forming the unkempt thickets painted by Fragonard and Hubert Robert in the 18th century. After being confiscated by the Italian State during the First World War, the villa was completely restored and opened to the public in the 1920s. Further restoration work is now being done.

A SOBER AND MAJESTIC BUILDING. The *cortile*, surrounded by a portico and adorned with a fountain, took the place of the former cloister of the Benedictine monastery. Passing through it, you come to the Appartamento Vecchio. This apartment is at ground level on the courtyard

dorned the Temple of Artemis in Ephesus and a copy
f Praxiteles' renowned *Venus of Cnidus*). The
rchitectural complex at the bottom of the lake is seen
s symbolizing Egypt; at least that is what one may
educe from the three sculptured groups that
ecorated it, the layout of which is reconstructed in
ne Vatican's Egyptian Museum. Its composition
onsisted of Osiris-Apis in the center, Isis-Demeter at
ne back and, on the walls, several repetitions of
ntinoüs ▲ *395*, Hadrian's young favorite who, after
is premature death in Egypt in 130 AD, was deified
y the Emperor. (Allow time to visit the small
useum beside Canopus to see the items discovered
uring the excavations of the 1950's.)

ORRE DI ROCCABRUNA AND THE ACADEMY. On the
ill overlooking the valley of Canopus from the southwest,
ne can see a number of places of long-standing fame. The
rst is the Torre di Roccabruna, an octagonal building with
vo floors covered by a dome, probably erected as a sort of
anoramic observatory. One then reaches the Academy, a
ast square surrounded by a portico. The best-preserved
uildings in this area are the TEMPLE OF APOLLO, a large
rcular hall surmounted by a cupola, and to the south the
DEON, a small theater of which the stage front remains. The
nest works of art discovered in the Villa Adriana came from
ne Academy, including the *Mosaic of the Doves* ▲ *135*.
Returning to the entrance of the archeological site, one can
valk down a pleasant avenue lined with cypresses to reach the
Greek theater and the nymphaeum,
vhich are at the northern end of
ne villa.

THE CARYATIDS OF CANOPUS
In the middle the
columns are replaced
by six caryatids, four
of which are copies of
those supporting the
roof of the
Erechtheion, one of
the temples of the
Acropolis in Athens;
the other two are
Sileni. The original
statues are now in the
museum.

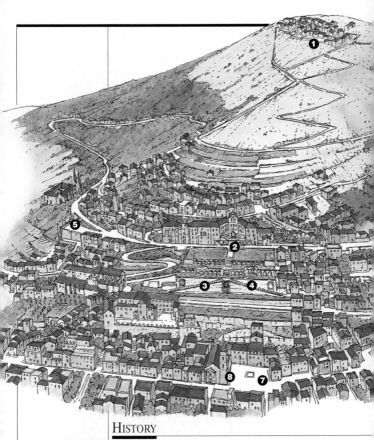

HISTORY

📷 23 miles
⏱ One day

The exedra on the right of the Terrace of the Hemicycles.

A STRATEGIC POSITION. Situated to the east of Rome, near the twenty-fifth milestone on the Via Prenestina, in ancient times Palestrina was called Praeneste. Built on the slopes of Mount Ginestro, the southernmost bastion of the Praenestine Hills, the town overlooks the gorge separating them from the Alba Hills and also dominated the Via Labicana and Via Latina, which lay at the bottom of the valley. This geographical location explains the importance the town acquired from the 7th century BC. Legends abound as to its origins. Some link its foundation to Praenestos, the son of King Latinos; others to Teleganos, the putative son of Ulysses and Circe, or to Caeculus, the son of the god Vulcan.

REBELLION AND SUBMISSION. The earliest references by historians to Praeneste concern its fraught relations with Rome: conquered in 380 BC, it rebelled several times, formed an alliance with the Gauls in 358, and took part in the last Latin War. At the end of the 2nd century BC the town seems to have enjoyed great prosperity – presumably due to its trade with the East – and grandiose constructions, including the shrine to Fortuna, transformed its appearance. In the following century Praeneste sided with Marius, thus earning the hatred of Sulla, who massacred the Praenestines in reprisal. At the beginning of the Empire the town's importance diminished. However, the oracle that had ensure

TYPICAL PRICES
One entry
to a museum
€6–8
One postcard,
with stamp
€0.71
One espresso
€0.60
Breakfast for one
€2
Saltimbocca alla
romana for one
€12
One tiramisù
€2.50
One glass of
amaretto
€2.10

ELECTRICITY
220-volts alternating
current. Electrical
appliances such as
hairdryers and
razors will need an
adaptor. Plugs
are of the round
two-pin type.

STUDENTS
→ CARDS AND CONCESSIONS
■ ISIC Card
The international
student's card gives
reductions in
museums and
hotels, as well as air
and train tickets.
Otherwise, foreign
students may join
the CTS (Centro
Turistico
Studentesco e
Giovanile) and
obtain an ISIC card
for €10.
■ Youth Card
Foreign visitors
under 26 years who
are not students may
join the CTS and
obtain a "youth
card" which entitles
the bearer to
concessions similar
to those of the
ISIC card.
■ Membership Card
For foreign visitors
aged over 26 years,
€26; this entitles
bearers to similar
concessions to those
of the ISIC card.
■ FUAJ Card
For those under 18.
The card gives access
to 4,200 youth
hostels worldwide.

→ INFORMATION
■ UK:
Youth Hostels
Association
8 St Stephen's House
St Albans, Herts
Tel. 01727 855215
www.hosteleurope.
com
■ US:
www.eurotrip.com/
hostels
Also consult the
international
hostelling website
www.iyhf.org
The Italian youth
hostel association is
known as AIG. The
minimum age for
access to youth
hostels is 8 years.

FORMALITIES
Both EU and non EU
nationals need a
passport. (For EU
nationals a passport
that is out of date by
no more than 5 years
is acceptable.)
Written
authorization is
always required
for minors traveling
without their
parents.

TIME ZONE
Italy is in one 1 hour
ahead of Greenwich
Mean Time. When
it is noon in Rome,
it is 11am in London,
and 6am in New
York.

WHEN TO GO
In the early fall,
so as to avoid the
peak of the tourist
season. Then,
temperatures are
pleasantly warm
and suitable for
sightseeing.

→ INFORMATION
■ Information
center for pilgrims
and tourists
Piazza San Pietro
Tel. 06 69 88 44 66
Fax 06 69 88 51 00
■ Accommodation
From July through
September, almost
all hotels are fully
booked. You are
therefore strongly
advised to book a
hotel in advance
through a travel
agent or tour
operator, or by
contacting
Hotel Reservation,
a central bureau
in touch with
200 hotels in all
price ranges.
Tel. (39) 06 699 10 00
7am–10pm daily.
Warning:
During the winter
months, remember
to pack warm
clothing.
The temperature
rarely drops below
zero, but it can still
feel chilly.

→TEMPERATURES °F		
	min./max.	
Jan.	41	52
Feb.	43	54/55
Mar.	45	59
April	50	64
May	56	72
June	63	86
July	68	86
Aug.	63	81
Sept.	55	70
Oct.	48	61
Nov.	48	61
Dec.	43	54

■ Avoiding
the crowds
Holy Week should
be avoided because
of the vast number
of pilgrims in
Rome, not only
around the Vatican
but all over the
city. In August Rome
is deserted as
Romans flee to
escape the heat.

TELEPHONE
→ CALLING ROME FROM THE UK
■ Dial 00 + 39 +
the number you
wish to call,
beginning 06 (the
code for Rome).

→ CALLING ROME FROM THE US
■ Dial 011 39 +
the number you
wish to call,
beginning 06 (the
code for Rome).

HEALTH
→ MEMBERS OF THE EUROPEAN UNION
Form E111, issued by
Health Authorities
of EU countries,
entitles members to
emergency medical
treatment.

→ OTHER COUNTRIES
Non-EU members
must take out
personal medical
insurance. Contact
your travel agent or
insurance broker for
details.

→ VACCINATIONS
None required,
but take adequate
prescription
medication.

ACCOMMODATION
→ HOTELS
Italy classifies its hotels using the European star system (from 1 to 5).

■ **Reservations**
Hotel Reservations
Tel. 06 699 10 00
7am–10pm. Central reservation agency, with 200 hotels in all price ranges. There is no real low season in Rome. It is advisable to book in advance for Holy Week and from July through September.

■ **Prices**
Hoteliers are obliged to display their tarifs in each room. In the 4-star and 5-star bracket, prices vary according to location and season. The following prices are for one night for two people in a double room, without breakfast.
Luxury hotel (*****): from €350
Comfortable hotel (****): from €240
Standard hotel (*** and **): from €100
Budget hotel (*): from €50

→ YOUTH HOSTELS
■ **Ostello per la Gioventù**
A.F. Pessina
Viale delle Olimpiadi, 61
Tel. 06 323 62 67
■ **Information**
Associazione Italiana Alberghi per la Gioventù,
Via Cavour, 44
Tel. 06 487 11 52
■ **YWCA**
Via Cesare Balbo, 4
Tel. 06 488 04 60
For women.
■ **Centro Accoglienza Giovanni XXIII**
Via del Conservatorio, 1
Tel. 06 686 44 60
For foreign students.

→ CONVENTS
A good way of lodging in Rome. But men and women are often segregated and the doors are locked at 10pm, or 11pm at the latest.
■ **Pastoral Advice Center**
Via Santa Giovanna d'Arco, 10
Tel. 06 68 80 38 15

→ ROOMS IN PRIVATE HOUSES
■ **Bed & Breakfast Italia**
Palazzo Sforza Cesarini
Corso Vittorio Emanuele II, 282
Tel. 06 687 86 18
Fax 06 687 86 19
www.bbitalia.it
■ **Dolce Casa**
Tel. 02 331 18 14
or 02 331 18 20
Fax 02 331 30 09
■ **Latte e Miele**
Tel. 06 321 17 83
■ **Guest in Italy**
Largo Antonello 8
Tel. 0765 444 054
www.guestinitaly.com

→ APARTMENTS
■ **Family house**
Via Bixio, 72
Tel. 06 700 07 70
www.family-house.it

AIRLINES
→ BRITISH AIRWAYS
Italian Distribution Center, Viale Citta Europa, 681
Tel. 14 78 2266

→ ALITALIA
Via Bissolati, 3
Tel. 06 656 21
■ **Flight information**
Tel. 06 65643

AIRPORTS
Rome has two international airports.

→ LEONARDO DA VINCI-FIUMICINO AIRPORT
Located 17 miles southwest of Rome and 15 miles from the EUR suburb.
■ **Information**
www.adr.it
Tel. 06 659 51
Open 24 hours daily.
■ **Airport services**
LUGGAGE
Tel. 06 65 95 42 52
Open 24 hours daily.
POST OFFICE
International terminal
Tel. 06 65 01 02 17
Open Mon.–Fri. 8am–12.50pm, 1.50–6.50pm;
Sat. 8am–12.50pm.
National terminal
Tel. 06 65 01 06 12
(same opening times).
TOURIST OFFICE
Tel. 06 65 95 60 74
Open Mon–Sat. 8.15am–7.15pm.
■ **Car rental**
AVIS
Tel. 06 65 01 15 31
www.avis.com
Open daily 7am–midnight.
EUROPCAR
Tel. 06 65 01 08 79
or 06 65 01 09 77
www.europcar.com
Open daily 7am–11pm.
HERTZ
Tel. 06 650 15 53
www.hertz.com
Open Mon–Fri. 7am–midnight; Sat. and Sun. 7am–11pm.
MAGGIORE BUDGET
Tel. 06 65 01 15 08
or 06 65 01 16 78
www.maggiore.it
Open daily 7am–midnight.
SIXT
Tel. 06 65 95 35 47
www.e-sixt.com
Open daily 7am–11pm.
■ **Airport transfer Fiumicino-Rome**
BY TRAIN
To Termini Station
Journey time about 30 mins. Service every 30 mins 6.37am–11.37pm.
Fare: €8.78
To Ostiense, Tuscolana and Tiburtina stations
Journey time about 40 mins. Service every 15 mins 5.57am–11.27pm.
Fare: €4.65

BY BUS (COTRAL)
On the international arrivals level Fiumicino-Lepanto (metro line A)
Journey time about 90 mins.
Service every 40–60 mins 5.30am–7.10pm. Fare: €3.60
Ticket office located in the terminal (open daily 7am–6.40pm).
■ **Night buses** run between the airport and Roma Tiburtina Station. Connections with the *ferrovia metropolitana* FM2 and subway line B. Hourly service, 1.15am–5am.
Fare: €3.60

BY SUBWAY
Fiumicino-subway EUR Magliana Connection with line B. Journey time 15 mins.
Hourly service 5.57am–11.27pm.
Fare: €1.29

BY TAXI
Journey time around 45 mins. Fare: about €40 to Termini station (additional pick-up charge and supplements for luggage, nighttime and public holidays).

→ G.B. PASTINE-CIAMPINO AIRPORT
Located at the foot of the Castelli Romani, about 9 miles southeast of the city center. Used for charter flights.
■ **Information**
Tel. 06 79 49 42 25
Open daily 7am–11pm.
■ **Airport services**
LUGGAGE
Tel. 06 79 49 42 25
Open daily 7am–11pm.
POST OFFICE
Tel. 06 79 34 01 04
Open Mon–Fri. 8am–11.50pm;
Sat. 8–11.50am.
■ **Car rental**
AVIS
Tel. 06 79 34 01 95
www.avis.com
Open Mon.–Fri. 8am–8pm; Sat. 10am–6pm; Sun. 1–8pm.
EUROPCAR
Tel. 06 79 34 03 87
www.europcar.com
Open Mon.–Fri. 8am–1pm, 2–6pm;
Sat. 8am–noon.

formation:
www.festivalroma.it
**Open-air concerts
and theater**
June–Aug, Teatro di
Marcello, Villa Ada,
Piazza di Siena and
Ostia Antica.
Photography
May-June,
International
Photography
Festival. Information:
www.fotografia.
festivalroma.org
Roma live festival
June–July, Foro
Italico, EUR.
Roma Europa
July 15–30, concerts,
dance and drama,
Villa Medici and
Teatro Valle.
Roma Alta Moda
July, presentation of
haute couture,
Piazza di Spagna.

◆ **EVENTS**
Conferences and
other events take
place throughout
the year; they
include a festival
of youth (August),
of the family
(September) and
of the performing
arts (December).

FOOD AND DRINK
Roman cuisine has
a southern character,
deeply rooted in
local country
tradition. Pasta,
of course,
predominates.
Everything about the
history and making
of pasta can be seen
in the Museo
Nazionale delle
Paste Alimentari
Piazza Scanderbeg,
17
Tel. 06 699 11 20

→ **SOME SPECIALTIES**
Abbacchio: baked
suckling lamb in a
chasseur sauce.
Coda alla vaccinara:
oxtail cooked with
tomatoes and white
wine, served with a
celery, pine kernel,
raisin and dark
chocolate sauce.
Coratella: fried lamb
offal.

Fave al guanciale:
fried broad beans,
onions and ham.
**Gran misto di
cervelli, ricotta,
carciofi e zucchine**:
brains with ricotta,
artichokes and
zucchini.
**Saltimbocca alla
romana**: escalope of
veal wrapped in ham
and flavored with
sage.
**Pasta all'
amatriciana**:
pasta with lard,
onion and lardon
sauce.
Pasta alla carbonara:
pasta with egg and
lardons.
Pecorino romano:
ewe's milk cheese.
Trippa alla romana:
tripe in a tomato
and mint sauce
served with cheese,
a specialty of the
Testaccio slaughter-
house area.
Risotto alla romano:
rice with liver,
sweetbreads and
pecorino cheese.

→ **JEWISH CUISINE**
To be found in the
old Ghetto (near the
Portico d'Ottavia).
Fried food is the
principal specialty;
for example
**filetti di baccalà alla
giudea** (cod fillets
deep-fried in batter
or sage in batter).
Be sure to try
carciofi alla giudea
(artichokes with
olive oil and lemon
juice).

→ **SNACKS**
Spuntini: "casse-
croûte" or
sandwiches, sold in
rosticcerie and
friggitorie.
Pizza bianca:
"white" pizza,
without tomatoes,
served with olive oil
and salt.
Supplì: rice
croquettes stuffed
with meat and
mozzarella.
Tramezzini:
small white-bread
sandwiches.

→ **WINES**
In the province
of Rome, white
wine reigns
supreme. Sample
castelli romani, colli
albani and marino
in an enoteca (wine
bar).

GUIDED TOURS
→ **OFFICIAL GUIDES**
■ **Centro guide CISL**
Tel. 06 639 04 09
www.centroguiderom.
org
■ **Centro guide CAFT**
Tel. 06 488 08 48
www.caft-turismo.it

→ **CULTURAL
ORGANIZATIONS**
■ **Percorsi e Dettagli**
Tel. 06 58 33 34 51
For visiting places
that are closed to
individual sightseers
(telephone the
Palazzo Colonna).

→ **ROME BY BUS**
■ **Bus 110**
Departures: daily
10.30am, 2pm,
3pm, 5pm, 6pm.
Sightseeing tours
of Rome taking
in the city's major
historic monuments.
■ **Basilicas tour**
Departures: daily
10.30am, 2pm,
3pm, 5pm, 6pm.
Sightseeing tours of
the basilicas of Santa
Maria Maggiore, San
Giovanni, San Paolo
and St Peter's.
■ **Information**
ATAC sales booths.
Tel. 06 46 95 22 52
or 06 46 95 46 95
Duration: 2 hrs
Price: €7.75

HEALTH
→ **INTERNATIONAL
MEDICAL CENTER**
Via Firenze, 47
Tel. 06 488 23 71
Mon.–Fri. 8am –
8pm; Sat. 8am–1pm

→ **HOSPITALS**
■ **Fatebenefratelli**
Piazza
Fatebenefratelli, 2
Tel. 06 683 71
■ **San Giacomo**
Via Canova, 29
Tel. 06 362 61

■ **San Giovanni**
Via Amba Aradam
Tel. 06 770 51
■ **Policlinico
Umberto i**
Viale del Policlinico,
155
Tel. 06 446 5027

→ **PHARMACIES**
For those open
24 hours see the list
of night pharmacies
published in the
local press or call
06 22 89 41
■ **Farmacia
Internazionale
Antonucci**
Piazza Barberini, 49
Tel. 06 482 54 56
or 06 487 38 61
■ **Farmacia Grieco**
Piazza della
Repubblica, 67
Tel. 06 488 04 10
or 06 448 38 61
■ **Farmacia Piram**
Via Nazionale, 228
Tel. 06 488 07 54
■ **Farmacia
Argenteria**
Via Arenula, 73
Open midnight–7am

→ **EMERGENCIES**
■ **Emergency
medical assistance
(Guardia medica)**
Tel. 06 58 20 10 30
See also under
'Emergency
numbers'.

THE JUBILEE
For the Jubilee (Year
2000), Rome had a
facelift: many
piazzas were
repaved and
pedestrianized;
palazzi and historic
houses were
restored; churches
closed for years for
restoration were
reopened and
archeological areas
are now floodlit. In
short, Rome is now
even more beautiful!

MAIL
Italian mail boxes
are red. Those in the
Vatican are blue. The
Vatican post costs
the same as the
regular Italian mail
service, and it has
the advantage of

being quicker. Stamp your letters and post cards with a "Poste Vaticane" stamp and post in a blue mail box.

→ POST OFFICES
Open Mon.–Fri. 8 .30am–1.50pm; Sat. 8.30am–noon. Post offices close at 11.50am on the last day of the month.
■ **Main post office**
Via Sicilia, 191/197 Open Mon.–Fri. 8am–6pm, Sat. and the last day of the month 8am–2pm.
■ **Vatican post office**
Piazza San Pietro Open Mon.–Fri. 8.30am–7pm; Sat. until 6pm.

→ POSTE RESTANTE
You can have your mail sent to:
c/o Palazzo delle Poste, Fermo Posta, Roma
Your name should be printed in bold, clear letters. Take your passport with you when claiming your mail. A small fee will be charged for the service.

→ EMAIL
Check your email at the **Internet café**
Via dei Marrucini, 12 Tel. 06 445 4953 Mon.–Fri. 9am–2am; Sat.–Sun. 5pm–2am.
Spaceweb
Piazza Barberini 2/16 Open 24 hrs daily. Easyinternet's first store in Italy. 320 PCs on line. Access from €0.50

MARKETS
→ FOOD MARKETS
These markets are often very picturesque and colorful. They play such an important part in Rome that food stores are relatively scarce in the historic city center.
■ **Mercato di Campo dei Fiori**
Mon.–Sat. 6am–2pm.

The quality of the produce and the sheer beauty of this market are some compensation for rather steep prices.
■ **Mercato di Piazza Vittorio Emanuele II**
Mon.–Sat. 7am–2pm. This general market has the lowest prices.

→ BROCANTE
Small *brocantes* (second-hand goods/flea markets) can be found in many parts of the city on weekends. Details are given in *Trovaroma* magazine (the supplement of *La Repubblica*)

■ **Mercatino dell'Antiquariato**
Piazza Verdi (Parioli) Tel. 06 855 27 73 4th Sun. in the month. Open 6am–8pm. 180 exhibitors.
■ **Fiera Antiquaria**
Hotel Parco dei Principi Via Frescobaldi, 8 Tel. 06 841 99 86 Second week in the month. Open 10.30am–8pm.
■ **Mercatino di Ponte Milvio**
Lungotevere Capoprati Tel. 06 907 73 12 1st weekend in the month. Open Nov.–Feb. Sun. 8.30am–7pm; March–Oct. Sat. 1–7pm and Sun. 8.30am–7pm.
■ **L'Antico in Terrazza Peroni**
Via Mantova, 24 3rd Sun. in the month. Open 10am–8pm. 50 exhibitors in

the underground parking lot of the old Peroni brewery.
■ **Underground**
V. Francesco Crispi, 96 1st weekend in the month. Open Sat. 3–8pm, Sun. 10.30am–7.30pm. Closed July–Sept. 140 exhibitors.

→ FLOWER MARKET
■ **Mercato dei Fiori**
Via Trionfale Tue. 10.30am–1pm.

→ BOOKS AND PRINTS
■ **Mercato delle Stampe**
Largo della Fontanella di Borghese Mon.–Sat. 7am–1pm.

→ FLEA MARKET
■ **Mercato di Porta Portese**
Via di Porta Portese Sun. 5am–2pm. Most business is done early in the morning and just before the market closes, around 1.30pm.

→ CLOTHES
■ **Mercato di Testaccio**
Piazza Testaccio Mon.–Sat. 7.30am–1.30pm.

MEDIA
→ ROME
■ **Daily newspapers**
The main Roman daily newspapers are *Il Messaggero* and *La Repubblica* (with its weekly cultural supplement Trovaroma). Both devote a few pages to local news.
■ **Foreign newspapers**
Available from

kiosks in the city center, especially those on the Via Veneto.
■ **Radio**
RFI broadcasts on satellite Astra 1C.
■ **Television**
National networks: *Rai Uno, Due* and *Tre*. Thanks to cable, many European networks, as well as *CNN International*, can be received.

→ VATICAN
■ **Press**
L'Osservatore Romano
■ **Radio Vatican**
93.3 MHz and 105 MHz FM
■ **Television**
The main purpose of CTV, the Vatican television center, is to spread the Gospel.
■ **Papal website**
www.vatican.va

METRO
The Roman metro, which consists of two lines intersecting at Termini station, is the quickest and cheapest means of traveling around the city. Metro stations are marked by a white M on a red background.

→ LINES
A (red): northwest to southeast.
B (blue): northeast to southwest.

→ INFORMATION
■ **Call free**
800 43 17 84 (Italian) 8am–8pm.
■ **Lost property**
Line A Tel. 06 487 43 09 Line B Tel. 06 57 53 22 64

→ SCHEDULES
5.30am–11.30pm (12.30am on Sat.).

→ FARES
See p.421, under Buses and trams: day and weekly tickets are the same for buses, trams and metro.

○ *The editor's choice.*

Cisterna*** ◆ **E** C1
Via d. Cisterna, 7–9
Tel. 06 581 72 12
Fax 06 581 00 91
In a quiet street not
very far from the
Ponte Garibaldi.
Though it has all
the basic comforts,
this is a modest hotel
with modest prices.
The rooms, recently
modernized, are
plain but agreeable,
and the bathrooms
are simple and
adequately
equipped. Breakfast
included.
◼◻▣◆⬛▢

VILLA BORGHESE – VILLA GIULIA

**Aldrovandi
Palace Hotel*******
◆ **B** C2-C3
Via Aldrovandi, 15
Tel. 06 322 39 93
Fax 06 322 14 35
This smart hotel is
located in a park
opposite the gardens
of the Villa
Borghese. Crystal
chandeliers and
paneled ceilings,
elegant carpets and
antique furniture.
Buffet breakfast
included.
◼◻▣◆⬛

**Hotel Cavalieri
Hilton*******
◆ **A** B2
Via Cadlolo, 101 (at
the foot of Monte
Mario)
Tel. 06 350 91
Fax 06 509 22 41
www.cavalieri-hilton.it
After its recent
renovation this may
be the most
luxurious of the
Hilton hotels. It
commands stunning
views over Rome:
the city seems to
spread out at its
feet. It boasts a
superb fitness center
and a park where
guests may lounge
by the poolside or
seek solitude under
the shade of the
great maritime pines
and silvery olive
trees. But best of all,
it houses one of

the best restaurants
in Rome (see
Restaurans section)
◼◻▣◆⬛▢

○ **Lord Byron*******
◆ **B** C2
Via Giuseppe
de Notaris, 5
Tel. 06 322 04 04
Fax 06 322 04 05
In the residential
district of Parioli,
near the Villa Giulia
and the Galleria
d'Arte Moderna,
the Lord Byron is
a refined and
luxurious small hotel

favored by guests
seeking privacy,
peace and quiet as
well as all creature
comforts. Highly
attentive service, a
good restaurant and
piano bar have also
helped to establish
this hotel's well-
deserved reputation.
◼◻▣◆⬛▢

**Parco dei
Principi****** ◆ **B** C3
Via Frescobaldi, 5
Tel. 06 85 44 21
Fax 06 884 51 04
Extensive
refurbishment has
restored this hotel to
its rightful rank. It
was designed in the
1960's by the
architect Giò Ponti.
The rooms have very

high standards of
comfort, and some
of them have lovely
views. There are
long vistas over the
park, and the upper
floor commands a
view as far as St
Peter's.
◼◻▣◆⬛▢

**Shangri–
La Corsetti******
Viale Algeria, 141
Tel. 06 591 64 41
Fax 06 541 38 13
The hotel blends
into a natural setting
like the pretty villas

dotted round about.
Located in the EUR,
it has all the
comfort, service
and facilities that
one would expect of
an international
hotel. Glamorous
young people
lounge around the
pool: it could almost
be Beverly Hills.
This is a haven,
easily reached yet
comfortably distant
from the dust and
bustle of the city.
◼◻▣◆⬛▢

Villa Borghese***
◆ **B** D3
Via Pinciana, 31
Tel. 06 85 30 09 19
Fax 06 841 41 00
The comfortable
rooms here are small

but well furnished,
and a friendly
atmosphere prevails.
On the other side
of the road are the
gardens of the Villa
Borghese.
◼▣◆⬛

Villa Mangili***
◆ **B** B2-C2
Via Mangili, 31
Tel. 06 321 71 30
Fax 06 322 43 13
This has all necessary
comforts and a
pleasant garden
where breakfast is
served at any time.
Reasonably priced.
Breakfast included.
▣◆⬛

OUTSIDE THE WALLS

Turner*** ◆ **C** D1
Via Nomentana, 29
Tel. 06 44 25 00 77
Fax 06 44 25 01 65
Close to the Porta
Pia, in a 19th-century
palazzo. Antique
furniture and stucco,
and marble or
parquet flooring.
There is a different
color scheme for
each room. The
single rooms have
unusually wide beds.
Breakfast included.
▣⬛

TIVOLI – PALESTRINA

Albergo Stella***
Piazzale della
Liberazione, 3
Palestrina
Tel. 06 953 81 72
Fax 06 957 33 60
Hotel-restaurant.
◼▣⬛

Hotel Sirene****
Piazza Massimo, 4
Tel. 0774 33 06 05
Fax 0774 33 06 08
In a 19th-century
villa. Good location.
◼▣⬛

OSTIA

**Albergo
Bellavista****
Piazzale Magellano,
16, Ostie
Tel. 06 562 43 93
Fax 06 562 16 67
Hotel-restaurant.
◼⬛

◆ RESTAURANTS
CAPITOL, FORUM

Places recommended by Paul Betts are preceded by ✪

→ The restaurants are listed by district, then by alphabetical order. The references (e.g. ◆ E B2) allows them to be located in the map section ◆ 502.

Paul Betts on eating in Rome

Rome does not escape the general Italian rule when it comes to eating out: in a country characterized by fine regional cuisines, the best restaurants in Italy tend to be found in the provinces. Metropolitan cities, especially large tourist centers such as the capital, tend to disappoint when it comes to finding good or exceptional restaurants.

Nevertheless, all Italian cities have a vast array of trattorias and restaurants offering the entire range of Italian regional specialties, with ample facilities to dine outside in courtyards, on terraces with good views and on street pavements.

There is only one restaurant that stands out among the rest in Rome and competes with the very best world gastronomic stars: La Pergola Restaurant, in the Hotel Cavalieri Hilton (see p. 443).

Italians like to show off and be seen in what they consider to be the fashionable spots, at times making allowances for food that is not always up to the standard expected from the high prices charged. These days there are three particularly trendy spots worth a detour if one wants to join in with the Rome "in crowd": Reef (see p. 442), Café Romano (see p. 441), and Celestina (see p. 443).

But for a pleasant dining experience in Rome, the traditional family-run restaurant or trattoria remains the safest bet. Some are favored by business people at lunch but offer the visitor good, reliable and consistent food, often in a lovely setting provided by the city itself. The ones I have recommended (indicated by the symbol ✪) provide a range of Roman and regional cuisine in pleasant settings, and you will also find Italians eating there.

Rome has many Chinese, Indian and other ethnic restaurants but they are nothing to write home about. If you want a change from Italian food, Hamasei (see p. 440), the city's oldest Japanese restaurant, is a stylish place in the heart of the old city which attracts a Japanese and Italian crowd. The food is excellent but not cheap.

Opening days:
You will have little problem finding restaurants and bars open on Sundays, a day on which Italians tend to eat out both at lunch and dinner. Restaurants tend to close one day during the week. But beware of the month of August: most restaurants close during the Italian summer holiday exodus. If you decide to visit in August, it is worth checking out which restaurants have decided to stay open.

Outdoor eating:
Virtually every restaurant in Rome will have tables outside, but for a special evening the following are recommended: the garden restaurant at the Hotel de Russie (see p. 435); and the rooftop restaurants of the Hilton (p. 443), Eden (La Terraza, p.443) and Hassler hotels (p. 434).

CAPITOL FORUM

Crab
◆ E C4
Via Capo d'Africa, 2
Tel. 06 77 20 36 36
Closed Sun. dinner, Mon., and variable days in summer.
One of the best fish and seafood restaurants in Rome, with daily deliveries of oysters, shrimp and squid. Courteous and attentive staff.
▣ ✪

Gigetto al Portico d'Ottavia
◆ E C1-C2
Via del Portico d'Ottavia, 21/a
Tel. 06 686 11 05
Open Tue.–Sun. 12.30–3pm and 7.30–11pm.
Closed last week in July and first week in Aug.
In the heart of the Ghetto, and for Jewish cuisine one of the most famous restaurants in Rome. Be sure to sample such deep-fried delicacies as artichokes, cod fillets and stuffed zucchini flowers, and the excellent homemade desserts. Ideal for an evening with friends. Reserve in advance.
▣ ✪

✪ Vecchia Roma
◆ E B2
Piazza Campitelli, 18
Tel. 06 686 46 04
Closed Wed. and for 2 weeks in Aug.
Vecchia Roma has had its ups and downs but it is on the up again. In the summer, you can eat outside on a quiet and elegant piazza just steps away from the Campidoglio. Unlike many other outdoor restaurants, this piazza is quiet and not infested with peddlers and buskers. The food is varied and good, especially the pastas and fish, and a delicious granita made with whatever fruits are in season.
▣ ⊞

AVENTINE

Agustarello
◆ H A3
Via G. Branca, 98
Tel. 06 574 65 85
Closed Sun. and Aug.10–Sept.10.
Offal dishes a specialty.
✪

Cecchino dal 1887
◆ H C3
Via di Monte Testaccio, 30
Tel. 06 574 63 18
Open Tue.–Sat. 12.30–3pm and 8–11pm; Sun. 12.30–3pm. Closed Aug. and Christmas.
A classic restaurant in the slaughterhouse area. For over a century it has been run by a family who approach Roman cuisine with the rigor of archeologists, not only with regard to their recipes but also in their careful choice of ingredients and the revival of the culinary styles and cooking methods of times gone by. Wonderful wine list: visit the wine cellar dug into the Monte dei Cocci. The remains of amphorae that have built up over the centuries form an artificial hill known as Monte Testaccio.
▣ ⊞

♻ *The editor's choice.*

una Piena
◆ H A3
a Luca della
obbia, 15/17
el. 06 575 02 79
*oman specialties
nd homemade
esserts.*
🔲 ✦

CELIO

lfredo a via Gabi
◆ I A4
a Gabi, 36
el. 06 77 20 67 92
osed Tue. and Aug.
*little beyond San
iovanni di
aterano, this
estaurant offers
me of the very
est artichoke dishes
Rome.*
🔲 ✦

annavota
◆ E C4
azza San Giovanni
Latero, 22-24
el. 06 77 20 50 07
losed Wed. and
ug.
raditional cuisine.
✦

**a Taverna del
uaranta**
◆ E C3
ia Claudia, 24
el. 06 700 05 50
losed Christmas
ay.
*easonable prices.
eserve in advance.*
✦

VATICAN

Dal Toscano
◆ A D3
ia Germanico, 58
el. 06 39 72 57 17
losed Mon.
*Vhen it comes to
eat, it is difficult
beat this noisy
estaurant close to
he Vatican in the
rati neighborhood,
un by the Bruni
amily for three
enerations. As its
ame implies, it
pecializes in Tuscan
ood and the
iorentina steak is
nagnificent, as is the
imply grilled filet de
oeuf. It prepares its
rench fries: either in
he traditional finger
hape or in large*

CECCHINO DAL 1887

*circles – crisp and
delicious, as are the
fried zucchini
flowers. Classic
pastas and cold cuts.
You may have to
queue to get a table
if you have not
booked.*
🔲 ✦

Mimi
◆ A D4
Via G. G. Belli, 59/61
Tel. 06 321 09 92
Open Mon.–Sat.
10am–3pm and
7.30pm–11pm.
Closed 3 weeks in
Aug. and 10 days at
Christmas.
*Run by a family of
sailors from the
island of Ponza, this
restaurant is devoted
exclusively to the
sea. The owners
celebrate their
origins, so that every
dish is enhanced by
the flavors of
popular Neapolitan
cooking.*
✦

Osteria dell' Angelo
◆ A D3
Via G. Bettolo, 24
Tel. 06 372 94 70
Open Mon.–Sat.
evenings, and Tue.–
Fri. lunchtime.
Closed Sun., on
public holidays and
in Aug.
*This osteria, run by
an ex-rugby player, is
a short distance from
the main tourist
areas. Here you are
guaranteed to find
genuine traditional
Roman dishes,
such as wild boar
sausages with
rigattoni alla pajata
(tripe), minestra di
arzilla (skate soup),*

coda alla vaccinara
*(oxtail in tomatoes
and white wine), at
moderate prices. This
is now a well-known
restaurant, so it is
necessary to book a
few days in advance.*
🔲 ✦

Taverna Angelica
◆ D A3
Piazza delle
Vaschette, 14/a
Tel. 06 687 45 14
*Small, friendly and
cozy. Imaginative,
not to say surprising,
dishes, with
excellent desserts.
Reservation advised.*
🔲 ✦

CAMPO MARZIO

Al Pompiere
◆ E B1
Via Santa Maria
dei Calderari, 38
Tel. 06 686 83 77
Closed Sun. and Aug.
*At the entrance to
the old Ghetto.
Good cuisine – try
the ravioli di ricotta
e spinaci and the
Jewish specialties –
nice wines, friendly
staff and a pleasant
setting. Meals served
indoors in a large
building.*
🔲 ✦

**L'Antiquario
di Giorgio Nisti**
◆ E A1
Piazzetta San
Simeone, 26/27
Tel. 06 687 96 94
Closed Mon.
lunchtime and Sun;
mid-Aug. and late
Dec. to mid-Jan.
*In a quiet and
charming piazza.
Fish a specialty.*
✦

Camponeschi
♻ E B1
Piazza Farnese, 50/a
Tel. 06 687 49 27
Open evenings only,
7.30pm–12.30am.
Closed Sun.
*An elegant interior,
a large enclosed
terrace, exquisitely
decorated tables.
Refined Italian
cuisine, and fine
service, with a
celebrity clientele
drawn by one of
most varied menus;
it features some
highly creative fish
dishes (a specialty),
Roman cuisine and
such international
classics as soufflés
and game in season.
The wine list is
equally impressive.
Several charming
little rooms are
available for clients
who desire a
measure of privacy.*
🔲 ⊞

Cul de Sac
◆ E B1
Piazza Pasquino, 73
Tel. 06 68 80 10 94
Closed Mon. lunch
*A long dining room,
with limited seating
outside, in a piazza
frequented by
pedestrians. Various
types of hot dishes,
plates of cheese or
ham. The cellar, with
more than 1,200
Italian wines, is also
noteworthy.*
🔲 ✦

Da Baffetto
◆ D B4
Via del Governo
Vecchio, 114
Tel. 06 686 16 17
Open evenings only.
*Da Baffetto is one
of the most famous
Roman pizzerias, a
charming, informal
place with paper
tablecloths and old
photographs on the
walls, in a
pedestrianized
street. Variety,
quality and price
justify the long wait
for a table.*
◼

◆ RESTAURANTS
CAMPO MARZIO

Key to symbols on page 417.

RESTAURANTS
- ■ < €20
- ■ €20–€30
- ■ €30–€50
- ■ > €50

✪ Hamasei
◆ F B3
Via della Mercede, 35-36
Tel. 06 679 21 34
Open Tue.–Sun. noon–2.30pm, 7–10.30pm
Elegant restaurant serving high-quality Japanese cooking.
■ ■

Il Bacaro
◆ E A2
Via degli Spagnoli, 27
Tel. 06 686 41 10
Closed Sun. and the last 3 weeks in Aug.
Not many tables, but good-quality cuisine (with imaginative ideas) for a place that stays open late. Very friendly staff. Reserve in advance.
■ ■

Il Buco
◆ E B2
Via Ignazio, 8
Tel. 06 679 32 98
Closed Mon. and 2 weeks in Aug.
In a quiet little street very near the Piazza del Collegio Romano. Tuscan cuisine at reasonable prices.
■ ■ ■

Il Convivio
◆ F B1
Vicolo dei Soldati, 31
Tel. 06 686 94 32
Closed Mon. lunchtime and Sun.
Very near the Piazza Navona and the Ponte Umberto I. The entrance is on a tiny side street. The restaurant is also very small but quite delightful. The chef describes his cooking as "cucina creativa" (creative cuisine).
■

Il Drappo
◆ D B4
Vicolo del Malpasso, 9
Tel. 06 687 73 65
Open evenings only, until midnight.
Closed Sun. and Aug.
Sardinian cuisine. The restaurant is

located between the Via Giulia and the Via dei Banchi Vecchi (the tiny vicolo, which is not even marked on most maps, joins up with the Vicolo della Moretta).
■ ■

La Campana
◆ E A1
Vicolo della Campana, 18
Tel. 06 687 52 73 or 06 686 78 20
Open Mon.–Sat. 7.30pm–12.30am.
Closed Mon. and Aug.
A classic Italian restaurant. Impeccably clean and smart, with good service. Quiet and air-conditioned. All meals are served indoors. Food of an excellent quality – try the antipasti and the ice cream. Typical Roman cuisine, with an unmistakable touch of elegance. Discreet, unobtrusive décor. An ideal

restaurant for business dinners.
■ ■

✪ La Rosetta
◆ F B2
Via della Rosetta, 8
Tel. 06 68 30 88 41
Open Mon.–Sat. 8–11pm, and Thur. and Fri. 1–3pm.
Closed Sun. and for 2 weeks in Aug.
Expensive and Michelin-starred. There are few restaurants to match La Rosetta when it comes to fish.
■ ■

✪ L'Eau Vive
◆ E B1
Via Monteroni, 85
Tel. 06 68 80 10 95
Closed Sun. and Aug.
For a religious gastronomic experience… This restaurant near the Pantheon is run by French nuns who serve good French food and wine and serenade diners with the Ave Maria. Booking advised.
■ ■

Les Étoiles
◆ D A3
Via Vitelleschi, 34
Tel. 06 687 32 33
Open daily 12.30–2.30pm, 7.30–10.30pm.
A private elevator whisks you up: step out and before you is one of the most remarkable views of the city – it is almost as if you could reach out and touch the dome of St Peter's. Elegant and sophisticated. The cuisine, strongly Mediterranean in character, is no less impressive than the panorama. The menu changes each day, according to what is available in the market and the chef's inspiration.
■ ■ ■ ■

Osteria dell'Ingegno
◆ F C2
Piazza di Pietra, 45
Tel. 06 678 06 62
Closed Sun. and 10 days around Aug. 15
A gorgeous establishment on one of Rome's most charming squares. Service is courteous and attentive, the cuisine always updated. Those with a sweet tooth will appreciate the glorious apricot and cream tarte tatin.
■ ■

Papà Giovanni
◆ F C1
Via dei Sediari, 4
Tel. 06 686 53 08
Open Mon.–Sat. 1–3pm and 8–11pm
A restaurant with a firmly established reputation, located between the Piazza Navona and the Pantheon. Light and tasty regional dishes. Excellent Italian and French wines. Specialties: zucchini dishes, profiteroles with Nemi strawberries. Reservation advised.
■ ■

Castroni ◆ A D4
Via Cola di Rienzo,
196
Tridente
Tel. 06 687 43 83
*The finest
delicatessen in
Rome: exotic spices,
herbs, sauces and
flavorings from all
over the world.*

**G. Giuliani Marrons
Glacés ◆ A** D3-D4
Via Paolo Emilio, 67
Vatican
Tel. 06 324 35 48
*Melt-in-the-mouth
marrons glacés.*

Said ◆ G B2
Via Tiburtina, 135
Baths of Diocletian
Tel. 06 446 92 04
*Sugared almonds,
nougats, chocolates
and other
homemade sweets.*

FASHION

Bacillario ◆ B D1
Via Laurina, 41/43
Tridente
Tel. 06 36 00 18 28
*Ready-to-wear for
teenagers. Some of
the clothes could be
exhibits in an art
gallery!*

Boutique Miss V ◆ F A3
Via Bocca di Leone, 15
Tel. 06 679 58 62
*Haute couture
in a 1960s setting.*

Davide Cenci ◆ F B1-B2
Via di Campo
Marzio, 1/7
Campo Marzio
Tel. 06 699 06 81
*Ready-to-wear.
From clothes by
leading couturiers to
creations signed
Davide Cenci, in a
shop laid out on
traditional lines.*

Fellini ◆ A D4
Via Cola di Rienzo,
281
Vatican
Tel. 06 321 06 29
Men's ready-to-wear.

Fendi ◆ E A2
Via Borgognona, 38
Tridente
Tel. 06 69 66 61
Haute couture.

Laura Biagiotti ◆ E A2
Via Borgognona, 43
Tridente
Tel. 06 679 12 05
Haute couture.

Loco ◆ F D1
Via dei Baullari, 22
Campo Marzio
Tel. 06 68 80 82 16
*The last word
in avant-garde
footwear.*

**Massimo Maria Melis
◆ F** B1
Via dell'Orso, 57
Campo Marzio
Tel. 06 686 91 88
*Jewelry made with
antique materials
and precious metals.*

Nia ◆ B D2
Via Vittoria, 48
Tridente
Tel. 06 679 51 98
*Ready-to-wear for
women. Stocks a
good selection of
suits, accessories and
other items.*

BUCCONE

MISCELLANEOUS

Rome is full of
lively street markets
where you can buy
fresh vegetables,
fruit and flowers
but the one in
Campo dei Fiori is
not only historic but
particularly colorful
and attractive.
If you want to buy
flowers, go to the
Mercato dei Fiori
in Via Trionfale, 45
on a Tuesday
(10am–1pm), when
this wholesale
market is also open
to the public. There
you will find an
incredible selection
of plants and flowers
at wholesale market
prices.

**Atmosphères
◆ B** B2
Via Manfredi 4/a
Villa Borghese – Villa
Giulia
Tel. 06 807 81 85
*Small furniture,
glassware, bibelots,
Liberty lamps (Italian
Art Nouveau).*

Azi ◆ D C4-D4
Via di San Francesco
a Ripa, 170
Trastevere
Tel. 06 588 33 03
*Vast range of
unusual though
handy designer
objects, all at
reasonable prices.*

Bagagli ◆ E A1
Via Campo Marzio,
42
Campo Marzio
Tel. 06 687 14 06
*Dinner services, pots
and pans and cutlery.*

Berté ◆ E B1
Piazza Navona, 108
Campo Marzio
Tel. 06 687 50 11
*From traditional toys
to the latest
electronic games.*

**Casidea
◆ B** B3
Via G. Antonelli, 22
Villa Borghese – Villa
Giulia
Tel. 06 807 92 77
*A home-lover's
paradise in the
Parioli district with
all the well-known
makes of furniture.*

**Contemporanea
◆ D** B4
Via dei Banchi
Vecchi, 143
Campo Marzio
Tel. 06 323 34 65
Decorative furniture

**Disfunzioni Musicali
◆ G** B2
Via degli Etruschi, 4
Baths of Diocletian
Tel. 06 44 619 84
*Absolutely essential
for music fanatics.*

**Drogheria Innocenzi
◆ D** C4
Piazza di San
Cosimato, 66
Trastevere
Tel. 06 581 27 25
*Dried vegetables in
large sacks stacked
behind the counter,
regional produce and
imported goods
often unobtainable
elsewhere.*

**Laboratorio Ilaria
Miani ◆ D** B3
Via degli Orti
d'Alibert, 13/a
Trastevere
Tel. 06 686 13 66
*Workshop devoted
to meticulously
executed woodwork.*

Mode e Materie ◆ E C1
Vicolo del Cinque, 4
Trastevere
Tel. 06 588 52 80
*Exhibition of
prototypes to be
toured as if one were
visiting an art gallery.*

**Romana Stucchi
◆ D** A1
Via Aurelia, 181
Vatican
Tel. 06 39 36 65 42
*One of the last
workshops in Rome
where decorative
stucco is still
produced.*

Taba ◆ E B1
Piazza Campo
de' Fiori, 13
Campo Marzio
Tel. 06 68 80 64 78
*Candles, jewelry,
novelties and
accessories.*

Tad ◆ B D2
Via del Babuino,
155/a
Tridente
Tel. 06 32 60 01 75
*Japan takes the
honors in furniture
and accessories.
Clothes, shoes,
fabrics and perfume.*

◆ PLACES TO VISIT

The symbol ▲ refers to the Itineraries section. The symbol ◆ refers to the Map section.

CAPRAROLA

VILLA CAPRAROLA Palazzo Farnese Tel. 0761 64 60 52	*Open 9am–4pm.* *Closed Mon.*	● *88*

OSTIA

ARCHEOLOGICAL AREA Viale dei Romagnoli, 717 Tel. 06 56 35 80 36	*Dyer's workshop, basilica, Christian basilica, capitolium, Caseggiato dei Dipinti, Caseggiato del Larario, Caserma dei Vigili, Caesareum, curia, Domus Fulminata, Horrea Hortensius, Horrea Epagathiana, Horrea Epaphrodisiana, Serapeum, Insula dei Dipinti, Insula dei Auriges, Meat Market, House of Cupid and Psyche, House of Apuleius, Casa di Diana, Mithraeum of the Seven Spheres, Piazzale delle Corporazioni, Republican Sanctuary, Schola del Traiano, synagogue, Temple of Rome and Augustus, Temple of the Shipwrights and Carpenters, round temple, Republican temples, theater, Baths of Buticocus, Baths of Neptune, Baths of the Seven Sages, Tomb of Cartilius Poplicola.* *Open 9am–5pm in winter; 9am–7pm in summer.* *Closed Mon.*	▲ *411*
CHURCH OF SANTA AUREA Piazza della Rocca, 13 Tel. 06 565 00 18	*Open 7.30am–noon, 4–6.30pm.*	▲ *416*
MUSEO OSTIENSE (ARCHEOLOGICAL MUSEUM) Viale dei Romagnoli, 717 Tel. 06 56 35 80 36	*Closed for building work.*	
MUSEO PORTA SAN PAOLO Via Raffaele Persichetti, 3 Tel. 06 574 31 93	*Open Mon., Wed., Fri. 9am–1.30pm, 2.30–4.30pm; Tue. and Thur. 2.30–4.30pm.*	

PALESTRINA

CATHEDRAL OF SANT'AGAPITO Piazza Regina Margherita Tel. 06 953 44 28	*Open 7am–noon, 4–7pm.*	▲ *402*
NATIONAL ARCHEOLOGICAL MUSEUM Palazzo Barberini Piazza della Cortina Tel. 06 953 81 00	*Open 9am–4pm; public holidays 9am–7pm (Jan.–Feb.), 9am–5pm (Mar.), 9am–6pm (May), 9am–7.30pm (June–Aug.), 9am–5.30pm (Sep.), 9am–5pm (Oct.), 9am–4pm (Nov.–Dec.).*	▲ *402*
TEMPLE OF FORTUNA Piazza della Cortina	*Open 9am–1pm until 1 hour before sunset.* *Closed May 1, Christmas Day and Jan. 1.*	▲ *399*

ROME

		▲ *305* ◆ F A1
ACADEMY OF FINE ARTS Via Ripetta, 222 Tel. 06 322 70 25	*Open Mon.–Fri. 10am–noon.*	
ACADEMY OF PHYSICAL EDUCATION Foro Italico Piazzale L. de Bosis Tel. 06 323 00 10	*Visits on request (fax 06 36 61 30 65).*	▲ *378* ◆ A A3
ACCADEMIA DI SAN LUCA Palazzo Carpegna Piazza Accademia di San Luca, 77 Tel. 06 679 88 50 or 06 678 88 49	*Archives: Mon. 10am–12.30pm.* *Library: Mon., Wed., Fri. 9am–1pm;* *Tue., Thur. 9am–1pm.* *Museum closed.*	▲ *299* ◆ F B3
ARA PACIS AUGUSTAE Lungotevere in Augusta Tel. 06 68 80 68 46	*Restoration work in progress.*	▲ *310* ◆ F A1
AREA SACRA DELL'ARGENTINA – TEMPLE A – TEMPLE B – TEMPLE C – TEMPLE D Piazza Augusto Imperatore	*To visit the temples: tel. 06 67 10 38 19*	▲ *250* ◆ E A1
– TORRE DEL PAPITO Via San Nicola de' Cesarini	*Not open to the public.*	

ARSENAL PONTIFICIO Via Portuense, 11	*Closed for building work.*	◆ H B2
ASTRONOMY AND COPERNICAN MUSEUM Viale Parco Mellini, 84 Tel. 06 35 45 21 47	*Closed for building work*	▲ 377 ◆ A A2- B2
AUDITORIUM OF MAECENAS Largo Leopardi, 2 Tel. 06 487 32 62	*Open Mon.–Wed., Fri. 8.35am–1.35pm, 2.35–4.15pm; Thur. 8.30am–6pm.*	▲ 341 ◆ E B4
BANCA NAZIONALE DEL LAVORO Via Vittorio Veneto, 119 Tel. 06 470 21	*Visits on request.*	▲ 302 ◆ B D3
BANK OF ITALY Via Nazionale, 91 Tel. 06 479 21	*Open Tue.–Sat. 9am–7pm; Sun. and public holidays 10am–7pm.*	▲ 348 ◆ F D4 E B3
BARRACCO MUSEUM Corso V. Emmanuel II, 1 Tel. 06 880 68 48	*Closed for building work until end of 2002.*	▲ 249 ◆ F D1
BARRACKS OF THE 5TH COHORT Church of S. Maria in Dominica Via della Navicella, 10 Tel. 06 7 00 15 19	*Visits on request.*	▲ 186 ◆ E D3
BARRACKS OF THE CASTRA PERIGRINA Excavation of San Giovanni in Laterano Piazza San Giovanni in Laterano Tel. 06 69 88 49 47	*Visits on request.*	▲ 186 ◆ G D1
BARRACKS OF EQUITES SINGULARES Excavation of San Giovanni in Laterano Piazza San Giovanni in Laterano	*Not open to the public.*	▲ 186 ◆ G D1
BASILICA OF SAN PAOLO FUORI LE MURA Via Ostiense, 190 Tel. 06 541 03 41	*Visits on request.*	▲ 382 ◆ H D3
BASILICA OF SAN BENEDETTO IN PISCINULA Piazza in Piscinula, 40 Tel. 06 581 82 97	*Open 9am–12.30pm, 3–7pm.*	▲ 353 ◆ E C1
BASILICA OF SAN CLEMENTE Via San Giovanni in Laterano Tel. 06 70 45 10 18	*Open 7.30am–1pm, 3–7.30pm.*	▲ 193 ◆ E C4
BASILICA OF SAN MARCO Piazza San Marco, 48 Tel. 06 679 52 05	*Open 7am–12.30pm, 3.30–6pm.*	▲ 162 ◆ F D3
BASILICA OF SAN PIETRO IN VINCOLI Piazza San Pietro in Vincoli Tel. 06 488 28 65	*Open 8.30am–noon, 2.30–5.30pm.*	▲ 346 ◆ E C3- B3
BASILICA OF SAN SEBASTIANO Via Appia Antica, 136 Tel 06 780 88 47	*Open 8am–12.30pm, 3–7pm.*	▲ 326 ◆ I D4
BASILICA OF S. CECILIA IN TRASTEVERE Piazza Santa Cecilia, 22 Tel. 06 589 92 89	*Open 7am–7pm.*	▲ 353 ◆ E C1
BASILICA OF SANTA CROCE IN GERUSALEMME Piazza S. Croce in Gerusalemme, 12 Tel. 06 701 47 69	*Open 7.30am–8pm.*	▲ 200 ◆ G C2
BASILICA OF S. MARIA IN TRAVESTERE Piazza Santa Maria in Trastevere Tel. 06 581 94 43	*Open 7am–7pm.*	▲ 357 ◆ D C4
BASILICA OF SANTA MARIA MAGGIORE Piazza Santa Maria Maggiore Tel. 06 581 48 02	*Open 8am–1pm, 4–6pm.*	▲ 342 ◆ E B4
BASILICA OF SANTI APOSTOLI Piazza Santa Maria Maggiore Tel. 06 679 40 85	*Open 8am–1pm, 4–7pm.*	▲ 300 ◆ F C3
BATHS OF CARACALLA Via delle Terme di Caracalla Tel. 06 575 86 26	*Open Tue–Sat. 9am–3pm (winter), 9am–6pm (summer); Mon. 9am–1pm.*	▲ 319 ◆ I A1

◆ PLACES TO VISIT

BATHS OF DIOCLETIAN Piazza della Repubblica Tel. 06 488 05 30	*Open 9am–7pm.* *Only the octagonal hall and the museum* *are open to the public.*	▲ 334 ◆ E A4
BATHS OF TRAJAN Parco del Colle Oppio	*Not open to the public.*	▲ 174 ◆ E B2
BERNICH AQUARIUM Piazza Fanti Tel. 06 446 74 07	*Open only during exhibitions.*	▲ 339 ◆ G B1
BIBLICUM (INSTITUTE OF BIBLICAL STUDIES) Piazza della Pilotta Tel. 06 69 52 61	*Guided tour on request (fax 06 695 26 61 51).*	▲ 299 ◆ F C3
BONCOMPAGNI LUDOVISI MUSEUM (MUSEO DELLE ARTI DECORATIVE) Via Boncompagni, 18 Tel. 06 42 82 40 74	*Open Tue.–Sun. 9am–7pm.* *Group visits on request.*	◆ B D3- D4
BRITISH PAVILION Via Gramsci, 61	*British Academy of Rome.* *Visit by request (tel. 06 326 49 39).*	▲ 376 ◆ B C2
CALCOGRAFIA NAZIONALE Via della Stamperia, 6 Tel. 06 69 98 01	*Open 9am–3.30pm.*	▲ 299 ◆ F B3
CAPITOL Piazza del Campidoglio Tel. 06 6 71 01		▲ 128 ◆ E B2- C2
CAPITOLINE MUSEUMS – PIAZZA DEL CAMPIDOGLIO, 1 Tel. 06 67 10 20 71	*Open Tue.–Sun. 9am–8pm.*	▲ 132 ◆ E B2- C2
– CENTRALE MONTEMARTINI Via Ostiense, 106	*Open Tue.–Sun. 9am–7pm, by appointment* *(06 328 10).*	
CASA DEI CRESCENZI Via Petroselli, 54	*Not open to the public.*	● 72 ◆ E C2
CASA DEI MUTILATI Piazza Adriana, 3	*Visit by appointment only.* *Tel. 06 687 53 52*	▲ 236 ◆ A C2
CASINA DELLA CIVETTE Via Nomentana, 70 Tel. 06 44 25 00 72	*Museum of stained glass. In the Villa Torlonia.* *Open Oct.–March: 9am–4pm;* *Apr.– Sep.: 9am–6pm. Closed Mon.*	◆ C C2
CASINA ROSSA Piazza di Spagna	*Keats-Shelley Museum.*	▲ 313 ◆ E A2
CASINA VALADIER Viale Mickiewicz Pincio Villa Borghese	*Closed.*	▲ 316 ◆ B C2- C3
CASTEL SANT'ANGELO Lungotevere Castello, 50 Tel. 06 681 91 11	*Open Tue.-Sun. 9am–7pm.*	▲ 233 ◆ D A4
CASTRO PRETORIO Viale Castro Pretorio, 105 Tel. 06 498 92 49	*Houses the Biblioteca Vittorio Emanuele II.* *Open 8.30am–7pm, Sat. until 1.30pm.* *Closed Sun.*	▲ 335 ◆ G A1
CATACOMBS OF SAN CALLISTO Via Appia, 102–110 Tel. 06 51 30 15 80	*Open 8.30am–noon, 2.30–5pm.* *Closed Wed.*	▲ 326 ◆ I D3
CATACOMBS OF SAN SEBASTIANO Via Appia Antica, 136 Tel. 06 69 88 64 33	*Open 8.30am–noon, 2.30–5pm.* *Closed Sun.*	▲ 326 ◆ I D4
CHAPEL OF SAN TOMMASO DEI CENCI Via Monte dei Cenci, 14 Tel. 06 68 30 00 55	*Guided tours on 2nd Sun. in the month at* *10.30am. Other days on request.*	▲ 254 ◆ E C1
CHURCH DEI MADONNA DELL'ORTO Via S. Maria dei Calderari, 29 Tel. 06 5 88 32 50	*Open Sun. 9am–noon.*	▲ 354 ◆ E C1
CHURCH OF GESÙ E MARIA Via del Corso, 45 Tel. 06 361 37 17	*Open 7.30am–1pm, 3–7pm.*	▲ 309 ◆ E A2- B2
CHURCH OF NOSTRA SIGNORA DEL SACRO CUORE Piazza Navona Tel. 06 844 01 31	*Open 7am–noon, 5–8pm.*	▲ 278 ◆ F C1
CHURCH OF SAN BARTOLOMEO Isola Tiberina, 22 Tel. 06 687 79 73	*Open 9.30am–12.30pm, 4.30–6.30pm.*	▲ 352 ◆ E C1

CHURCH OF SANTA MARIA SOPRA MINERVA Via Beato Angelico, 35 Tel. 06 679 39 26	Open 7am–7pm.	▲ 260 ◆ F C2
CHURCH OF SANTA PRASSEDE Via Santa Prassede, 9/a Tel. 06 488 24 56	Open 7.30am–noon, 4–6.30pm.	▲ 344 ◆ E B4
CHURCH OF SANTA PRISCA Via di Santa Prisca, 11 Tel. 06 574 37 98	Open 8am–noon, 3–6.30pm.	▲ 181 ◆ E D2
CHURCH OFSANTA PUDENZIANA AL VIMINALE Via Urbana, 160 Tel. 06 481 46 22	Open 8am–6pm.	▲ 344 ◆ E B4
CHURCH OF S. SABINA ALL'AVENTINO Piazza Pietro d'Illiria, 1 Tel. 06 579 41	Open 6.30am–12.30pm, 4–6pm.	▲ 179 ◆ E D2
CHURCH OF SANTA SUSANNA Via XX Settembre, 15 Tel. 06 488 27 48	Open 9am–noon, 4–7pm.	▲ 294 ◆ E A3
CHURCH OF SANTI AMBROGIO E CARLO AL CORSO Via del Corso, 437 Tel. 06 687 83 35	Open 7am–7pm.	▲ 309 ◆ E A2
CHURCH OF SS BONIFACIO E ALESSIO Piazza di Sant'Alessio, 23 Tel. 06 574 34 46	Open 8.30am–12.30pm, 3.30–5pm.	▲ 180 ◆ E D2
CHURCH OF SANTI COSMA E DAMIANO IN VIA SACRA Via dei Fori Imperiali, 1 Tel. 06 69 91 5 40	Open 9am–1pm, 3–7pm.	▲ 168 ◆ E C3
CHURCH OF SANTI DOMENICO E SISTO Largo Angelicum, 1 Tel. 06 670 21	Visit on request.	▲ 347 ◆ F D4
CHURCH OF SANTI GIOVANNI E PAOLO Piazza dei SS. Giovanni e Paolo, 13 Tel. 06 700 57 45	Open 8.30am–noon, 3.30–6pm.	▲ 188 ◆ E C3
CHURCH OF SANTI LUCA E MARTINA Via della Curia, 2 Tel. 06 679 52 05	Closed for restoration.	▲ 131 ◆ E B2- C2-
CHURCH OF SANTI NEREO E ACHILLEO ALLE TERME DI CARACALLA Via Appia Antica Tel. 06 575 79 96	Open Easter–Oct. 10am–noon, 4–6pm. Closed Tue.	▲ 321 ◆ I A2
CHURCH OFSANTI VINCENZO E ANASTASIO Vicolo dei Modelli, 73 Tel. 06 678 30 98	Open 7–11.30am, 4–7.30pm.	▲ 388 ◆ F C3
CHURCH OF THE SANTISSIMO NOME DI MARIA Via del Foro Traiano, 89 Tel. 06 679 80 13	Open Mon.–Thur. 4–6pm; Sun. 9.30am–1pm, 4–6pm.	▲ 167 ◆ F D3
CHURCH OF SANTO STEFANO DEL CACCO Via Santo Stefano del Cacco, 26 Tel. 06 679 38 60	Visit on request.	▲ 260 ◆ F D2
CHURCH OF SANTO STEFANO ROTONDO Via Santo Stefano Rotondo, 7 Tel. 06 70 49 37 17	Open 9am–12.30pm in winter; 3.30–6pm in summer. Closed Mon.	▲ 191 ◆ E D4
CHURCH OF THE ANNUNZIATA Via del Gonfalone, 34 Tel. 06 68 80 24 01	In course of restoration.	▲ 233 ◆ E B1
CHURCH OF THE GESÙ Piazza del Gesù Tel. 06 69 70 01	Open 6.30am–noon, 4–7pm.	▲ 257 ◆ E B2
CHURCH OF THE SACRED HEART Lungotevere Prati, 12 Tel. 06 68 80 65 17	Open 4.30–7.30pm.	▲ 236 ◆ E A1

CHURCH OF THE SANTI QUATTRO CORONATI Via dei Santi Quattro Coronati, 20 Tel. 06 70 47 54 27	*Open 9.30am–noon, 4.30–6pm.*	▲ 192 ◆ E C4
CHURCH OF THE SPIRITO SANTO DEI NAPOLETANI Via Giulia, 34 Tel. 06 69 88 62 17	*Open 10.30am–12.15pm.*	▲ 242 ◆ D B4
CHURCH OF THE TRINITÀ DEI MONTI Piazza della Trinità dei Monti, 3 Tel. 06 679 41 79	*Open 9am–1pm, 4–7pm.*	▲ 314 ◆ F A3
CHURCH OF THE TRINITÀ DEI PELLEGRINI AI CATINARI Via dei Pettinari, 36/A Tel. 06 69 88 63 32	*Visits on request.*	▲ 246 ◆ E B1
CINETECA NAZIONALE Via Tuscolana, 1520 Tel. 06 72 29 41	*Open Mon.–Fri. 9am–4pm.* *Library 9am–6pm. Closed Sat.–Sun.*	
CIRCUS OF MAXENTIUS Via Appia Antica, 153 Tel. 06 780 13 24	*Open Tue–Sat. 9am–7pm; Sun. and public holidays* *9am–1pm.*	▲ 328 ◆ I C3- D4
CIRCUS MAXIMUS Via del Circo Massimo	*Visits on request. Contact the Sovrintendenza* *Comunale (tel. 06 67 10 38 19).*	▲ 177 ◆ E D1- D2
COLISEUM Piazza del Colosseo Tel. 06 700 42 61	*Open 9am–3.30pm in winter; 9am–6pm in summer.*	▲ 170 ◆ E C3
COLLEGIO ROMANO Piazza del Collegio Romano Tel. 06 6 89 28 11	*Not open to the public.*	▲ 258 ◆ F C2
CRIMINOLOGY MUSEUM Via del Gonfalone, 29 Tel. 06 688 99 41	*Open Wed, Fri.–Sat. 9am–1pm; Tue., Thur.* *9am–1pm, 2.30–6.30pm. Closed Sun.–Mon.*	◆ D B4
DOMINE QUO VADIS (CHURCH) Via Appia Antica, 51 Tel. 06 512 04 41	*Open 8am–6.30pm.*	▲ 324 ◆ I C3
DOMUS AUREA Via della Domus Aurea Parco Oppio Tel. 06 47 82 47 58	*Visit on request 9am–7.45pm.*	▲ 174 ◆ E C3- C4
EPISCOPALIAN CHURCH OF SAN PAOLO ENTRO LE MURA Via Napoli, 58 Tel. 06 47 35 69	*Visits by appointment 9am–6pm (last entry).*	▲ 348 ◆ E A3
ETRUSCAN MUSEUM Villa Giulia Piazza di Villa Giulia, 9 Tel. 06 322 65 71	*Open Tue.–Sat. 9am–7pm; Sun. 9am–2pm.* *Closed Mon.*	▲ 370 ◆ B C2
EXCUBITORIUM Via della VII Corte, 9 Tel. 06 67 10 38 19	*Visits on request. Contact the corporation of Rome* *(tel. 06 67 10 38 19).*	▲ 356 ◆ E C1
FARNESINA Via della Lungara, 230 Tel. 06 68 02 71	*Open Mon.–Sat. 9am–1pm.*	▲ 360 ◆ D B4
FORO ITALICO Piazzale L. De Bosis	*Open access.*	▲ 377 ◆ A A3
FRENCH ACADEMY Viale Trinità dei Monti, 1 Tel. 06 676 11	*Visits on request.*	▲ 315 ◆ F A3
GABINETTO NAZIONALE DEI DISEGNI E DELLE STAMPE Via della Lungara, 230 Tel. 06 69 98 01	*Open 9am–1pm. Closed Sun.*	▲ 360 ◆ D B4
GALLERIA BORGHESE Via Scipione Borghese, 5 Tel. 06 841 76 45 or 06 841 39 79	*Villa Borghese.* *Open Tue.–Sat. 9am–7pm;* *Sun. and public holidays 9am–1pm.* *Reservation compulsory (tel. 06 32 81 01).*	▲ 372 ◆ B C3
GALLERIA COLONNA Piazza dei SS. Apostoli, 66 Tel. 06 678 43 50	*Open Sat. 9am–1pm. Closed in Aug.* *Public entrance at Via della Pilotta, 17.*	▲ 300 ◆ E B2

GALLERIA NAZIONALE D'ARTE MODERNA E CONTEMPORANEA – CARMELITE CONVENT OF SAN GIUSEPPE A CAPO LE CASE Via Francesco Crispi, 24 Tel. 06 474 29 04	*Open Tue.–Sat. 9am–2pm, 2.30–5.30pm; Sun. 9am–12.30 pm.*	▲ 376 ◆ F A4-B4
– OLD PERON BREWERY Villa Reggio Emilia, 54 Tel. 06 67 10 79 32	*Open Tue.–Sat. 9am–7pm; Sun. 9am–12.30pm.*	
GALLERIA DELL'ACCADEMIA DI S. LUCA Largo Accademia San Luca, 77 Tel. 06 679 88 50	*Open Mon.–Sat. 10am–12.30pm.*	▲ 299 ◆ F B3
GALLERIA DORIA-PAMPHILJ Piazza del Collegio Romano, 2 Tel. 06 679 73 23	*Open 10am–5pm. Closed Thur.*	▲ 258 ◆ F D3-C3
GALLERIA NAZIONALE D'ARTE ANTICA – PALAZZO BARBERINI Via delle Quattro Fontane, 13 Tel. 06 482 41 84	*Open 9am–7pm; closed Mon.*	▲ 291-292 ◆ E A3
– PALAZZO CORSINI Via della Lungara, 10 Tel. 06 68 80 23 23	*Open Tue.–Sat. 8.30am–2pm; Sun. 8.30am–7pm.*	▲ 362 ◆ D B3-C3
GALLERIA NAZIONALE D'ARTE MODERNA Viale delle Belle Arti, 131 Tel. 06 32 29 81	*Open Tue.–Sun. 9am–7pm.*	▲ 376 ◆ B C2
GALLERIA SPADA Piazza Capo di Ferro, 13 Tel. 06 686 11 58	*Open Tue.–Sat. 9am–7pm; Sun. and public holidays 9am–1pm.*	▲ 246 ◆ E B1
GALLERIA SCIARRA Via dell'Umiltà		▲ 301 ◆ F C3
GEOLOGICAL MUSEUM Largo di Santa Susanna,13	*Closed for building works.*	▲ 302 ◆ E A3
GREGORIANA (PONTIFICIA UNIVERSITÀ GREGORIANA) Piazza della Pilotta, 4 Tel. 06 670 11	*Visit by arrangment. (tel. 06 67 01 52 95).* *Library: open 8.30am–6pm. Visit by arrangment (tel. 06 67 01 51 22). Closed Sun.*	▲ 299 ◆ E A2-A3
HANS CHRISTIAN ANDERSEN MUSEUM Via Mancini, 18/24 Tel. 06 321 90 89	*Open 9am–7pm. Closed Mon.*	▲ 369 ◆ B C1
HOSTARIA DELL'ORSO Via dei Soldati, 25	*Closed.*	▲ 284 ◆ F B1
HOTEL QUIRINALE Via Nazionale, 7 Tel. 06 47 07		▲ 348 ◆ E A3
HOTEL INGHILTERRA Via Bocca di Leone, 14 Tel. 06 699 81		▲ 305 ◆ F A2-A3
HOTEL PLAZA Via del Corso, 126 Tel. 06 69 92 11 11		▲ 309 ◆ E A2-B2
HOUSE OF THE KNIGHTS OF RHODES Salita del Grillo Tel. 06 671 02 63	*Visits on request (fax 06 67 10 42 91).*	▲ 168 ◆ F D4
HOUSE OF ST JOHN AND ST PAUL Piazzale Santi Giovanni e Paolo, 13 Tel. 06 700 57 45	*Visits by appointment. Tel. 06 70 45 45 44*	▲ 188 ◆ E C3-D3
HOUSE OF GIACOMO DI BARTOLOMEO DA BRESCIA Via Rusticucci, 14	*Not open to the public.*	▲ 233 ◆ D A3
KEATS–SHELLEY MEMORIAL HOUSE Piazza di Spagna, 26 Tel. 06 678 42 35	*Open Mon.–Fri. 9am–1pm, 3–6pm; Sat. 11am–2pm, 3–6pm. Closed Sun.*	▲ 313 ◆ E A2
LATERAN BASILICA Piazza S. Giovanni in Laterano, 4 Tel. 06 69 88 64 33	*Open 7am–7pm.*	▲ 198 ◆ G D1
LATERAN PALACE Piazza San Giovanni in Laterano	*Headquarters of the Vicariate of Rome (tel. 06 69 82). Open Sat., 1st Sun. in the month 9am–12.30pm. Open Sun. 8.30am–12.30pm.*	▲ 196 ◆ G D1

◆ PLACES TO VISIT

MATTATOIO (OLD SLAUGHTERHOUSES) Villagio Globale del Mattatoio Lungotevere Testaccio Tel. 06 575 72 33	*Open for exhibitions and other cultural events.* *Closed Mon. and in Aug.*	▲ 184 ◆ H A2- A3
MAUSOLEUM OF AUGUSTUS Piazza Augusto Imperatore	*Open 9am–7pm in winter; 9am–8pm in summer.*	▲ 309 ◆ E A1
MAUSOLEUM OF CECILIA METELLA Via Appia Antica, 161 Tel. 06 780 24 65	*Open Tue.–Sun. 9am until 1 hr before sunset.*	▲ 330 ◆ I D4
MAUSOLEUM OF ROMULUS Via Appia Antica Tel. 06 780 13 24	*Circus of Maxentius and Mausoleum of Romulus.* *Open Tue.–Sat. 9am–7pm.*	▲ 329 ◆ I D4
MEDIEVAL HOUSE IN TRASTEVERE Vicolo dell'Atleta, 14	*Not open to the public.*	● 73 ◆ E C1
MEMMO FOUNDATION Via del Corso, 418/a Tel. 06 683 21 79 or 06 68 30 73 44	*Open Tue.–Fri., Sun. 9.30am–7pm;* *Sat. 9.30am–8pm.*	▲ 312 ◆ E A2- B2
MINISTRY OF INDUSTRY AND TRADE Via Molise, 2 Tel. 06 470 51	*Visit by permission of the bursar's office* *(tel. 06 47 88 78 95).*	▲ 302 ◆ E A2
MINISTRY OF MAIL Palazzo Malvezzi Piazza San Silvestro Tel. 06 679 84 95	*Headquarters of the mail service.*	◆ E A3
MONASTERY OF SAN COSIMATO Piazza San Cosimato	*To arrange a visit, contact the hospital* *management (tel. 06 5 84 41).*	▲ 356 ◆ D C4
MONASTERY OF SAN GREGORIO Piazza Certaldo, 85 Tel. 06 55 26 16 17	*Open 9.30am–12.30pm, 2.30–6.30pm.*	▲ 187 ◆ E D3
MONASTERY OF SANT'ONOFRIO Piazza Sant'Onofrio, 2 Tel. 06 686 44 98	*Open 7am–noon.*	▲ 365 ◆ D B3
MONTE DE PIETA Piazza del Monte di Pietà, 33	*Headquarters of the Bank of Rome* *(tel. 06 67 07 65 17).*	▲247 ◆ E B1
MONTE MARIO ASTRONOMICAL AND **METEOROLOGICAL OBSERVATORY** Viale Parco Mellini, 84 Tel. 35 34 70 56	*Not open to the public.*	▲ 377 ◆ A B2
MUSEO CANONICA Via P. Canonica, 2 Tel. 06 884 22 79	*Open Tue–Sat. 9am–7pm;* *Sun. 9am–1.30pm.*	◆ B C2- C3
MUSEO CASA DI DANTE Palazzo Anguillara Piazza Sonnino	*Private museum.* *Library: Mon., Wed., Fri. 4–6pm.*	▲ 357 ◆ E C1
MUSEO CENTRALE DEL RISORGIMENTO Palazzo del Vittoriano Via San Pietro in Carcere Tel. 06 678 06 64	*Open Mon.–Fri. 9.30am–7.30pm.* *Sat.–Sun. 9.30am–8.30pm.*	▲ 161 ◆ E B2
MUSEO CIVICO DI ZOOLOGIA Via Aldrovandi, 18 Tel. 06 322 11 93 or 06 322 10 31	*Open Tue.–Sun. 9am–5pm.*	▲ 369 ◆ B C3
MUSEO DELL'ALTO MEDIOEVO Via Lincoln, 3 Tel. 06 542 28 11	*Open Tue.–Sat. 9am–7pm;* *Sun. and public holidays 9am–1pm.* *Closed Mon.*	▲ 387
MUSEO DELLA CIVILTÀ ROMANA Piazza G. Agnelli, 1 Tel. 06 592 60 41	*Open Tue.–Sat. 9am–6.45pm;* *public holidays 9am–1.30pm.*	▲ 388
MUSEO DELLE CERE Piazza Santi Apostoli, 67 Tel. 06 679 64 82	*Open 9am–8pm.*	◆ F C3
MUSEO DELLE MURA Via di Porta San Sebastiano, 8 Tel. 06 70 47 52 84	*Open Tue.–Sat. 9am–7pm.*	◆ I A2
MUSEO DEI CALCHI E DEI GESSI Piazzale Aldo Moro, 5 Tel. 06 499 13 96 or 06 499 13 82 70	*University of Rome La Sapienza, Faculty of* *Literature and Philosophy, Institute of Archeology.* *Open Mon.–Fri. 9am–5.30pm (Nov.–June).* *Closed Sat.–Sun.*	◆ G A2

ROMAN FORUM AND PALATINE Piazza S. Maria Nova, 53 or Via dei Fori Imperiali or Via di San Gregorio, 30 Tel. 06 699 01 10	*Open 9am–3.30pm in winter; 9am–6pm in summer.*	▲ *136* ◆ E C2- C3
SAN MICHELE Via di San Michele, 17	*Headquarters of the Ministry of Culture (tel. 06 584 31).*	▲ *355* ◆ E D1
SAN CLEMENTE ARCHEOLOGICAL SITE Piazza San Clemente Tel. 06 70 45 10 18	*Open to the public during cultural events. Open 10am–12.30pm; public holidays 10am–12.30pm, 3–6pm (lower levels).*	▲ *193* ◆ E C4
ST PETER'S Piazza San Pietro Tel. 06 69 88 37 12	*Open 7am–6pm in winter; 7am–7pm in summer.*	▲ *210* ◆ D A3
SOVEREIGN ORDER OF THE KNIGHTS OF MALTA Via dei Condotti, 68 Tel. 06 6 75 81	*The order's headquarters are not open to the public.*	● *50* ◆ E A2-
STADIO DEI MARMI Foro Italico Viale dello Stadio dei Marmi	*Free access.*	▲ *378* ◆ A A3
STADIO OLIMPICO Foro Italico Tel. 06 368 51	*Free access.*	▲ *378* ◆ A A3
SYNAGOGUE (PONTE SANT'ANGELO) Lungotevere dei Cenci Tel. 06 684 00 61	*Open Tue.–Thur. 9am–4.30pm in winter; 9am–7pm in summer.*	▲ *254* ◆ E C2
TABULARIUM AND TEMPIO DI VEIO Piazza del Campidoglio Tel. 06 67 10 24 75	*Visits on request.*	● *64* ◆ E B2- C2
TEATRO ARGENTINA Via dei Barbieri, 22 Tel. 06 68 80 46 01/2	*Visits on request.*	▲ *251* ◆ F D1
TEATRO ARGENTINA MUSEUM Largo del Teatro Argentina Tel. 06 68 40 00 11	*Visits on request.*	▲ *251* ◆ D C4
TEATRO ELISEO Via Nazionale, 183/d Tel. 06 474 34 31		▲ *348* ◆ F C4
TEMPLE OF HADRIAN Palazzo della Borsa Piazza di Pietra	*See Palazzo della Borsa.*	▲ *267* ◆ F C2
TEMPLE OF HERCULES VICTOR (CIRCULAR TEMPLE) Forum Boario Piazza Bocca della Verità		▲ *155* ◆ E C2
TEMPLE OF JUPITER CAPITOLINUS Palazzo Caffarelli Piazza del Campidoglio Tel. 06 67 10 24 75	*Recently renovated. Telephone for opening hours.* *Visit by permission of the Sovrintendenza Archeologica (tel. 06 70 45 16 90).*	● *70* ◆ E C2
TEMPLE OF MINERVA MEDICA Via Giovanni Giolitti (corner of Via Pietro Micca)	*Undergoing building work.*	▲ *339* ◆ G D1
TEMPLE OF PORTUNUS Forum Boario Piazza Bocca della Verità		▲ *155* ◆ E C2
STAZIONE TERMINI Piazza dei Cinquecento Tel. 06 473 01		▲ *338* ◆ G A1- B1
THEATER OF MARCELLUS Via del Portico d'Ottavia, 29 Tel. 06 67 10 38 19	*In course of restoration.*	▲ *157* ◆ E C2
THEATRO DELL'OPERA Via Firenze, 72	*Visit by appointment, tel. 06 48 16 01.*	◆ E A3
TEATRO DI POMPEI Via di Grottapinte	*Not open to the public.*	▲ *248* ◆ F D1
TOBACCO FACTORY Piazza Mastai, 11	*Visits on request (tel. 06 58 57 26 22 or 06 585 71).*	▲ *356* ◆ E C1
TOMB OF EURYSACES Piazza di Porta Maggiore Tel. 06 67 10 20 70		▲ *339* ◆ G C2

◆ PLACES TO VISIT

TOMB OF THE SCIPIOS AND COLUMBARIUM Parco degli Scipioni Via di Porta Latina 06 67 10 38 19	Access from 9am until sunset.	▲ 322 ◆ I A2
TORRE ANGUILLARA Piazza Sonnino Palazzo Anguillara	Not open to the public.	▲ 356 ◆ E C1
TORRE DEI ANNIBALDI Via degli Annibaldi	Not open to the public.	▲ 168 ◆ E C3
TORRE DEI ARCIONI Salita dei Borgia	Not open to the public.	▲ 168 ◆ F D4
TORRE BONIFACE IX Piazza del Campidoglio	Not open to the public.	▲ 130 ◆ E B-C2
TORRE DEI CAPOCCI Piazza di San Martino ai Monti	Not open to the public.	▲ 168 ◆ E B4
TORRE CENTRALE DE LONGHI Torre Campanaria Piazza del Campidoglio	Not open to the public.	▲ 130 ◆ E B2-C2
TORRE DE' CONTI Largo Ricci	Visits to the underground section only, by permission.	▲ 168 ◆ E B3
TORRE DEI FRANGIPANI/ DELA SCIMMIA Palazzo Scapucci Via dei Portoghesi	Not open to the public.	▲ 168 ◆ F D4
TORRE DEI MARGANI Piazza Margana, 49/A	Not open to the public.	▲ 159 ◆ F D2
TORRE MARTIN V Piazza del Campidoglio	Not open to the public.	▲ 130 ◆ E B2-C
TORRE DELLE MILIZIE Via IV Novembre, 94	For information tel. 06 69 94 10 20.	▲ 168 ◆ F D4
TORRE MILLINA Piazza Navona	Not open to the public.	▲ 279 ◆ F C1
TORRE DEI ORSINI/ TORRE ARPACATA Campo dei Fiori	Not open to the public.	▲ 168 ◆ E B1
TORRE SANTA FRANCESCA IN TOR DE' SPECCHI Via del Teatro di Marcello Specchi	Not open to the public.	▲ 159 ◆ E B2-C2
TRAJAN'S MARKETS AND IMPERIAL FORUMS Via IV Novembre, 94 Tel. 06 679 00 48	Open Tue.–Sat. 9am–7pm; Sun. and public holidays 9am–7pm.	▲ 167 ◆ F D4
TULLANIUM/MAMERTINE PRISON Church of San Giuseppe dei Falegnami Clivo Argentario, 1 Tel. 06 679 29 02	Open 9am–noon, 2–5pm in winter; 9am–12.30pm, 2.30–6pm in summer.	▲ 131 ◆ E C2
UNDERGROUND BASILICA OF PORTA MAGGIORE Piazza di Porta Maggiore Tel. 06 702 30 64	Not open to the public.	▲ 340 ◆ G C2
VICTOR EMMANUEL II MONUMENT Piazza Venezia		▲ 160 ◆ F D3
VILLA ALBANI Via Salaria	Visits by request from the wardens of the Villa Torlonia (tel. 06 686 10 44).	▲ 368 ◆ B C4-D4
VILLA ALDOBRANDINI Via Mazzarino, 11 Tel. 06 678 78 57	Visits on request.	▲ F D4 ◆ B D4
VILLA BONAPARTE Via Piave, 23	French Embassy near the Holy See. Visit by permission (fax 06 42 03 09 68).	
VILLA BORGHESE (GARDENS)	Access on the Piazzale San Paolo del Brasile, Piazzale Flaminio, Via di Porta Pinciana, Via de Mercadante, Via Aldovrandi, or Viale delle Arti. Open all day.	▲ 372 ◆ B C2-C3
VILLA CELIMONTANA (GARDENS) Piazza della Navicella, 12	Open from sunrise to sunset.	▲ 190 ◆ E D3
VILLA DORIA-PAMPHILJ (GARDENS)	Access on the Via Aurelia Antica, Via San Pancrazio, Via della Nocetta or Via Leone XIII. Open from sunrise to sunset.	▲ 369 ◆ D C2

VILLA FARNESINA Via della Lungara, 230 Tel. 06 68 80 17 67	*Gardens open Mon.–Sat. 9am–1pm.*	▲ *360* ◆ **D** B4
VILLA GIULIA Viale di Villa Giulia, 9 Tel. 06 322 65 71	*Houses the Etruscan Museum.*	▲ *370* ◆ **B** C2
VILLA LANTE Passegiata del Gianicolo, 9	*Finnish Embassy (tel. 06 68 80 46 04).*	▲*365* ◆ **D** B3- C3
VILLA MADAMA Via di Villa Madama	*Closed for building work.*	▲ *378* ◆ **A** A2
VILLA MEDICI Via della Trinità dei Monti, 1	*French Academy (tel. 06 676 11).* *Open Mon., Wed.–Sat.10.30am.–2pm,* *3.30–8pm.*	▲ *315* ◆ **B** D2
VILLA TORLONIA (GARDENS) Via Nomenta, 70	*Open from sunrise to sunset.*	▲ *381* ◆ **C** C2- D2

TIVOLI

CHURCH OF SAN SILVESTRO Via del Colle Tel. 07 74 33 56 27	*Open 8am–12.30pm, 3.30–7pm.*	▲ *391*
CHURCH OF SANTA MARIA MAGGIORE Piazza Trento Tel. 07 74 31 13 29	*Open 8.30am–noon, 4–6pm.*	▲ *391*
DUOMO Piazza del Duomo Tel. 07 74 33 52 27	*Open 8am–noon, 4.30–5.30pm.*	▲ *391*
VILLA ADRIANA Via di Villa Adriana, 204 Tel 07 74 53 02 03	*Open 9am–4pm (winter); 9am–6pm (summer).*	▲ *394*
TEMPLE OF THE SIBYL Via della Sibilla, 50	*The temple is in the gardens of the restaurant* *La Sibilla (tel. 07 74 33 52 81).* *Closed Mon.*	▲ *391*
VILLA D'ESTE Piazza Trento, 5 Tel. 07 74 31 20 70	*Open 8.30am–4pm (winter); 8.30am–6.45pm* *(summer). Closed Mon.*	▲ *392*
VILLA GREGORIANA Piazza Massimo	*Open 9am–4pm.*	▲ *391*

VATICAN

BELVEDERE GARDENS	*Not open to the public.*	▲ *214*
CASINA OF PIUS IV **OR PONTIFICAL SCIENCE ACADEMY** Piazza del San Uffizio Tel. 06 69 88 31 95	*Visits on request Mon.–Fri. 9am–2pm.*	▲ *214* ◆ **D** A2
VATICAN LIBRARY Via di Pora Angelico Tel. 06 698 79 11	*Visits Mon.–Fri. 9am–5.30pm.*	▲ *214* ◆ **D** A2
VATICAN MUSEUMS Viale Vaticano Tel. 06 69 88 33 33	*Open Mon.–Fri. 8.45am–3.30pm;* *Sat. 8.45am–12.30pm.* *Borgia Apartments, Biblioteca Apostolica,* *Chapel of Nicolas V, Chapel of Pius V, Pauline* *Chapel, Sistine Chapel, Galleria Clementina,* *Galleria dei Candelabri, Map Gallery, Galleria* *Lapidaria, Galleria degli Arazzi, Urban VIII Gallery,* *the Raphael Loggias, Museo Chiaramonti, Christian* *Museum, Belvedere Museum, Egyptian Museum,* *Etruscan Museum, Gregorian Museum, Museum of* *Ethnology, Museo Pio-Clementino, Museo Sacro,* *Pinacoteca, Sala Ducale, Sala Regia, Sala* *Alessandrina, Sala dell'Immacolata, Sala della Biga,* *Sala Sobieski, Raphael Rooms.*	▲ *216-* *231* ◆ **D** A3

◆ BIBLIOGRAPHY

ESSENTIAL READING

◆ GREGOROVIUS (F.): History of the City of Rome in the Middle Ages, English tr., London, 1906; reprinted New York, 1967
◆ MASSON (G.): Companion Guide to Rome, London, 1965
◆ NASH (E.): Pictorial Dictionary of Ancient Rome, London, 1966
◆ Michelin Guide to Rome, London (many editions)
◆ SHOWERMAN (G.): Monuments and Men of Ancient Rome, New York, 1935
◆ STORTI (A.): Rome, A Practical Guide, Venice, 1980
◆ VARRIANO (J.): Rome, A Literary Companion, London, 1991

GENERAL

◆ ARMELLINI (M.), CECCHILLI (C.): Le Chiese di Roma dal secolo IV al XIX, 2 vol., Rome, 1942
◆ Attraverso l'Italia, Roma, Touring Club Italiano, Milan, 1986
◆ BENTLEY (J.): Rome: Architecture, History, Art, London, 1991
◆ CIPRIANI (G.B.): Architecture of Rome, originally Rome 1835–7, reprinted New York, 1986
◆ Civiltà del Lazio primitivo (exhibition catalogue), Rome, 1976
◆ DE TOMMASSO (F.): Le Cupole di Roma, Rome, 1991
◆ D'ONOFRIO (C.): Castel Sant'Angelo, Rome, 1972
◆ Fontana di Trevi, Fratelli Palombi Editori, Rome, 1992
◆ GALASSI PALUZZI (C.): Chiese romane, Ente provinciale per il turismo di Roma
◆ Guida al Quirinale, Fratelli Palombi Editori, Rome, 1985
◆ HAUSER (E.D.): Italy, a Cultural Guide, New York, 1981
◆ Hutton (E.): Rome, London, 1950
◆ LANCIANI (R.): New Tales of Old Rome, London, 1901
◆ LANCIANI (R.): Wandering through Ancient Roman Churches, New York, 1924
◆ Lazio, Touring Club Italiano, Milan, 1967
◆ MENEN (A.): Rome

Revealed, London, 1960
◆ MORETTI (U.): Artists in Rome, Tales of the Babuino, (tr. W. Weaner), London and New York, 1958
◆ PARTNER (P.):The Lands of St. Peter, London, 1972
◆ PEREIRA (A.): Rome, London, 1990
◆ PIETRANGELI (C.), PERICOLI (C.): Guide rionali di Roma, Fratelli Palombi Editori, Rome 1971–80
◆ POTTER, (O.M.): The Colour of Rome, London and Philadelphia, 1909
◆ RAVAGLIOLI (A.): La Storia in piazza. Breve profilo della storia urbanistica della citta di Roma, Edizioni di "Roma Centro Storico", 1987
◆ RAVAGLIOLI (A.): Tutta Roma, Rome, 1983
◆ ROMA, Touring Club Italiano, Milan, 3 1992
◆ SHARP (M.): A Guide to the Churches of Rome, Philadelphia, 1966
◆ VENTRIGLIA (U.): La Geologia della citta di Roma, Rome, 1971
◆ WILLEY (D. AND M. C.): Welcome to Rome, Glasgow, 1981

GENERAL HISTORY

◆ DURUY (V.): History of Rome and the Roman Peoples, Boston, 1890
◆ GIBBON (E.): The Decline and Fall of the Roman Empire (many editions)
◆ HIBBERT (C.): Rome – the Biography of a City, London, 1985
◆ MOMMSEN (T.): The History of Rome (many editions)
◆ NIEBUHR (B.C.): The History of Rome, London, 1855-60

ANCIENT ROME

◆ ASBY (TH.): The Roman Campagna in Classical Times, E. Benn, London, 1927
◆ BAKER (G.B.): Twelve Centuries of Rome, 753 BC–AD 476, London, 1936
◆ BALSDON (J.P.V.D.): Julius Caesar and Rome, Harmondsworth, 1967
◆ BARROW (R.H.): The Romans, Harmondsworth, 1949
◆ BARTON (I.M.) (ED.): Roman Public Buildings, Exeter, 1989
◆ BERTOLOTTI, IOPPOLO, SARTORIO: La Residenza Imperiale di Massenzio,

Itinerari d'Arte di Cultura, Rome, 1989
◆ BIRLEY (A.): Marcus Aurelius, London, 1966
◆ BORTOLOTTI (L.): Roma fuori le mura, Laterza, Rome-Bari, 1988
◆ CAPRINO (C.), COLINI (A.M.), GATTI (G.), PALLOTTINO (M.), ROMANELLI (P.): La Colonna di Marco Aurelio, Rome, 1955
◆ CARCOPINO (J.): Daily Life in Ancient Rome, Harmondsworth, 1941
◆ CARY (M.): History of Rome down to the Reign of Constantine, London and New York, 1935
◆ CASTAGNOLI (F.): Il Campo Marzio nell'antichita, Mem. Acc. Lincei, 7,1, 1946, p.93
◆ CASTAGNOLI (F.):Il Circo di Nerone in Vaticano, Rendic Pont. Acc. 32, 1959–60, pp. 97 sqq.
◆ CASTAGNOLI (F.): Topografia e urbanistica di Roma antica, Società Editrice Internazionale, Turin, 1969
◆ CASTAGNOLI (F.), CECCHELLI (C.), GIOVANNONI (G.), ZOCCA (M.): Topografia e urbanistica di Roma, Bologna, 1958 (Storia di Roma, 22)
◆ COARELLI (F.): Il Campo Marzio occidentale, storia e topografia, in Mélanges de l'Ecole française de Rome, 89, 1977, pp.807 sqq.
◆ COARELLI (F.): L'"Ara di Domizio Enobarbo" e la Cultura artistica in Roma nell'il secolo a. C., in Dialoghi di Archeologia, 2, 1968, pp.302 sqq.
◆ COARELLI (P.): Public Building in Rome between the Second Punic War and Sulla, in Papers of the British School at Rome, 45, 1977, pp. 1 sqq.
◆ COARELLI (F.): Il Complesso pompeiano del Campo Marzio e la sua decorazione scultorea, Rendic. Pont. Acc. 44, 1971–72, pp. 99 sqq.
◆ COARELLI (F.): Il Foro romano, 2 vol., Quasar, 1985
◆ COARELLI (F.): Il Sepolcro degli Scipioni a Roma, Itinerari d'Arte e di Cultura, Rome, 1989
◆ COARELLI (F.): Italia centrale,Laterza, Rome-

Bari, 1985
◆ COARELLI (F.): L'Identificazione dell'Area Sacra dell'Argentina, in Palatino, 12, 4, 1968, pp. 365 sqq.
◆ COARELLI (F.): Roma sepolta, Curcio, Rome, 1984
◆ COLINI (A.M.): Il Campidoglio nell'antichita, in Capitolium, 40, 4, 1965, pp. 175 sqq.
◆ COLINI (A.M.), COZZA (L.): Ludus Magnus, Rome, 1962
◆ DE ROSSI (G.B.): La Roma sotterranea cristiana, 3 vol., Rome, 1864–77
◆ DILL (S.): Roman Society from Nerito Marcus Aurelius, London, 1925
◆ DIXON (S.): The Roman Family, London and Baltimore, 1992
◆ D'ONOFRIO (C.):Gli Obelischi di Roma, Rome, 1965
◆ FRANK (T.): Roman Buildings of the Republic, Rome, 1924
◆ GIULIANI (C.F.): Domus Flavia: una nuova lettura, in Römische Mitteilungen, 84, 1977, pp.91 sqq.
◆ GARDNER (J.F.) AND WIEDEMANN (T.): The Roman Household, A Sourcebook, London, 1991
◆ GRANT (M.): The World of Rome, London, 1960
◆ GRANT (M.): The Roman Emperors, 31 BC–476 AD, London
◆ GREENIDGE (A.H.J.): Roman Public Life, New York, 1901
◆ GREENIDGE (A.H.J.) AND CLAY (A.M.): Sources for Roman History, Oxford, 1903
◆ GUARDUCCI (M.): L'Isola Tiberina e la sua tradizione ospitaliera, Rendic. Acc. Lincei, 26, 3–4,1971, pp.26 sqq.
◆ GUIDOLBALDI (F.): Complesso archeologico di San Clemente. Risultati degli scavi piu recenti e nesame dei resti architettonici, Rome, 1978
◆ GUZZO (P.G.): Antico e archeologia. Scienza e politica delle diverse antichità, Nuova Alfa Editoriale, Bologna, 1993
◆ HANFMAN (C.M.P.): Roman Art, A Modern Survey of the Art of Imperial Rome, New York, 1975

46–7 The Bocca della Verità, cl. M. Marzot.
47 *Cagliostro and Lorenza*, fan, 1786, musée Carnavalet © Giraudon.
Madama Lucrezia, marble bust, cl. A. Idini.
48 Figures for *Il Carnevale romano*, Goethe's description. G. M. Kraus, after J.G. Schütz, watercolored engraving on wood, 1788–9 © Goethe-Museum, Düsseldorf.
48–9 *October Festival outside the walls of Rome*, W. Marstrand, oil on canvas, 1839 © Thorsvaldsens Museum, Copenhagen.
49 *Feast of St Joseph*, A. Pinelli, watercolor, 1852, Museo di Roma, cl. B. Brizzi.
Moccoletti in Via del Corso, detail, 1833, *idem*.
Spring festival at Trinità dei Monti, cl. S. Bottani.
50 Cross of the Order of Malta, all rights reserved.
The Knight of Malta, H. Baldung Grien, oil on canvas, early 16th century, Nouvelle Résidence, Bambreg © Giraudon.
Siege of Rhodes by the Turks, Latin manuscript 60067 © Bibl. nat., Paris.
51 Series of postage stamps, Poste magistrali, Sovrano Militare Ordine di Malta. The Grand Master receiving the standard of the Order from John the Baptist, gold coin, © Sovereign Military Order of Malta. Profile of Fra Andrew Bertie, *idem*. Baptism of Jesus, *idem*.
Lourdes Grotto and Basilica, *idem*.
52 Papal tiara, watercolor, coll. Luigi Ceccarelli. *Opening of the Holy Door*, engraving, in *L'Illustration*, cl. Gallimard.
52–3 Papal blessing, Piazza San Pietro, I. Caffi, oil on canvas, Museo di Roma © Scala.
53 *Julius II on the Sedia Gestatoria*, detail, Raphael, fresco, Stanza di Eliodoro, Musei di Vaticano © Scala.
54 Stages of restoration of the equestrian statue of Marcus Aurelius, bronze © C.R.
55 Stratigraphical section, cl. S. Pelizzoli. Erosion of the stone due to pollution, cl. E.

Scalfari/AGF.
Restoration of a statue *in situ*, cl. *idem*.
Adam, detail from *The Creation of Man*. Michelangelo, fresco before restoration, Sistine Chapel ceiling © Scala.
Idem, after restoration © Musei Vaticani/photo P. Zigrossi-A. Bracchetti.
56–7 Preparation of *carciofi alla romana*, cl. Gallimard, *La Cuisinère*, V. Campi, oil on canvas, Galleria Doria-Pamphili © Scala.
58 Chasuble, cl. N. Pacarel. Typical products, cl. Gallimard.
60 *Mime*, engraving in *La Vie des Grecs et des Romains*, all rights reserved.
Map of Rome, anon., oil on canvas, Palazzo Ducale, Mantua, 1538 © Scala.
Obelisk of San Giovanni in Laterano, engraving, all rights reserved.
65 *Basilica of Maxentius*, transversal section, P.-M. Gauthier, watercolor 1899 © ENSBA.
66 *Circus games in the Coliseum*, G. Lauro, engraving, all rights reserved
66–7 The Coliseum, after restoration. L.-J.Duc, 1830–1 © ENSBA.
67 Circus of Maxentius. A. Recoura, watercolor, 1899, *idem*.
Pompey's Theater, V. Baltard, watercolor, 1837, *idem*.
70 *The Trophies of Marius*, A.-M.Garnaud, wash, 1821, *idem*.
The Arch of Constantine, G. Lauro, engraving, all rights reserved.
70–1 *The Temple of Venus and Rome*, L. Vaudoyer, watercolor, 1830, *idem*.
83 *The Steps of the Pontifical Chapel*, G. B. Falda, engraving, all rights reserved.
84–5 Vault of St Ignazio A. Pozzo, fresco © Scala. Details, *idem*.
Façade of the Cancelleria, P. Letarouilly, engraving, all rights reserved, colored by Tony Cobb.
87 Façade of Palazzo Spada, overall view and detail, Pl Letarouilly, engraving, all rights reserved., colored by C. Quiec.
88–9 *Cortile del

Belvedere, Perin del Vaga, fresco, Castel Sant'Angelo © Scala.
90 Galleria Sciarra, fresco, cl. G. Berengo Gardin © TCI.
95 *Casino de Raphaël à Rome*, J. D. A. Ingres, oil on wood, cl. 1807 © Musée des arts décoratifs de la Ville-de-Paris/L. Sully-Jaulmes.
96 *Gallery of views of modern Rome, idem*. G. P. Pannini, oil on canvas, 1759, musée du Louvre, © RMN.
96–7 *Gallery of views of ancient Rome, idem*. Self-portrait of Pannini, drawing © British Museum, London.
98 *Goethe in the country*, J. H. Wilhelm Tischbein, 1787, Städelsches Kunstinstitut © AKG, Berlin.
98–9 *View of the French Academy in Rome*, G. Moreau, wash, musée Gustave Moreau © RMN.
100–1 *View of the Coliseum from the Farnese gardens*, J.-B. Corot, oil on canvas, cl. 1826, musée du Louvre © RMN.
Villa Borghese, G. Balla, oil on canvas, Galleria d'Arte Moderna © Scala.
101 Corot's signature, all rights reserved: Portrait of Corot by Nadar © Bibl. nat., Paris.
102–3 *View from the Pincio*, I. Caffi, coll. Noferi, Florence © Scala.
104 *View of Castel Sant'angelo*, V. Brayer, watercolor, private coll. © Giraudon/A. D. A. G P.
105 *Alaric takes Rome*, F. Chauneau, Engraving © Bibl. nat., Paris.
106 *Roman temple*, H. Robert, etching, *idem*.
107 *Mausoleum of Augustus*, details, G. B. Piranesi, engraving, *idem*. Mausoleum of Augustus, G. B. Piranesi, engraving, *idem*. Column of Phocas, Rossini, engraving, 1819, *idem*.
108–9 *Map of Rome*, engraving, 16th century, *idem*.
110–11 Detail of the frontispiece of *Monumenti antichi inediti*, Guattani, engraving by Mochetti, *idem*.
112 Leo XII in his

pontifical robes, watercolored litho, coll. L. Ceccarelli.
113 Portraits of popes, all rights reserved
The start of the barb horse race, Piazza del Popolo, B. Pinelli, litho © Bibl. Nat. Paris.
114 Trastevere personnage. coll. Ceccarius © Bibl. naz., Rome.
115 The Tiber, photo © ENIT.
116–17 *Forum Boarium*, engraving, P. Gall © Bibl. nat., Paris.
117 *Announcement of the gladiatorial games in Pompeii*, engraving in *La Vie des Grecs et des Romains*, all rights reserved. Horse race in Circus Maximus, postcard, private coll.
118 A. Curver, photo, all rights reserved. J. Gracq, photo © Lapi Viollet, Paris.
Nizon, cl. C. Seiler © Ed. J. Chambon.
118–19 *Fountain of the Four Rivers*, engraving Bibl. nat., Paris.
119 Study for the elephant in Piazza Minerva, Bernini, drawing, *idem*.
120 Biblioteca nazionale © ENIT.
121 *The Pincio Hill in the morning*, H. Caffi, oil on canvas, Ca'Pesaro © Scala.
122 View from the Janiculum © ENIT. Via della Conciliazione, cl. W. Louvet. The EUR, cl. N. Pascarel.
123 The Tiber, cl. *idem*. The Coliseum, cl. W. Louvet, Neptune Fountain, cl. S. Grandadan.
124 Trastevere café, cl. N. Pascarel.
Metro sign, cl. *idem*. Religious at the Vatican, cl. W. Louvet.
125 Market, cl. N. Pascarel. Flower seller in the Campo de' Fiori, cl. S. Grandadan. Roman policemen, cl. W. Louvet.
126 Via Appia Antica, cl. N. Pascarel. Façade of a house, cl. W. Louvet. Ecclesiastical clothes shop, cl. N. Pascarel.
127 Map of ancient Rome. A. Brambilla, engraving, 1582 © Bibl. nat., Paris.
128 Roman Forum, cl. W. Louvet. *Criminal flung from the Tarpeian Rock*,

◆ LIST OF ILLUSTRATIONS

R. Della Porta, *manuscript Romuleon* © Bibl. nat., Paris.
128–9 *Triumph*, G. Lauro, engraving, all rights reserved.
130 One of the Dioscuri on the Capitol Hill, cl. S. Bottani.
Statue of Marcus Aurelius, detail, G. P. Pannini, oil on canvas, 18th century, Galleria Nazionale dell'Arte Antica, Palazzo Corsini © Scala.
130–1 View of the Capitol, early 19th century photo © Brogi-Giraudon.
131 Piazza del Campidoglio by night © ENIT. Bas-relief of saints Peter and Paul, Mamertine Prison, cl. M. Marzot. Fragments of the colossus of Constantine, Cortile Palazzo dei Conservatori, cl. S. Grandadan and N. Pascarel. *Santo Bambino of the Aracoeli*, print, all rights reserved.
132 *Head of Constantine*, fragment of the colossus, 312–15, Musei Capitolini © Scala. *Young girl with a dove*, Greek stele, archaic period, *idem. Boy with a thorn*, bronze, 1st century BC, *idem.*
133 *Bust of Commodus as Hercules*, marble, *idem. Capitoline Brutus*, bronze head, *idem. Roman she-wolf*, Etruscan bronze, 5th century BC, *idem.*
134 *Triumph of Bacchus*, P. da Cortona, oil on canvas, *idem.*
134–135 *Dying Gaul*, marble, *idem. St John the Baptist*, Caravaggio, oil on canvas, Pinacoteca, *idem.*
135 *Capitoline Venus*, marble, *idem. Dove mosaic, idem.*
138 The Curia, photo © ICCD. *Roman senator*, sculpture, 3rd century BC © Nimatallah/Artephot, Paris.
139 Triumph, reconstruction from the arch of Septimius Severus, litho. all rights reserved. Effigy of Septimius Severus, coin © Bibl. nat., Paris. Arch of Septimius Severus, litho. all rights reserved.
140 *The Tabularium*, restored state, C. Moyaux, watercolor, 1865 © ENSBA. Column of the

Temple of Vespasian, photo © ENIT.
141 *The Tabularium*, present state, C. Moyaux, watercolor, 1865 © ENSBA. Statue on the Capitol, cl. W. Louvet. Temple of Concord, bronze coin of the time of Caligula © Bibl. nat., Paris.
142 Temple of the Dioscuri, cl. A. Idini. View of the Fountain of Juturna © Scala.
143 *Christ on the Cross*, fresco, Santa Maria Antiqua © Scala. *Saint, idem. San Teodoro*, A. Pinelli, watercolor, 1834, Museo di Roma, cl. B. Brizzi.
144 Statue of a Vestal cl. A. Idini. View of the temple of Antoninus and Faustina © Magnum, Paris. *Idem*, cl. W. Louvet.
144–145 *Basilica of Constantine*, J. J. Haffner, watercolor, 1921 © ENSBA.
145 *Capital and frieze of the Temple of Antoninus and Faustina*, Desgodetz, engraving, in *Les édifices de Rome* © Bibl. nat. Paris. View of the Temple of Antoninus and Faustina, cl. W. Louvet. Paving stones in the Forum, cl. M. Marzot.
146–147 Arch of Titus, photo, early 20th century © Alinari-Giraudon.
148 Funerary urn in the shape of an archaic hut, terracotta, Forum Antiquarium © Scala. Headless statue of Cybele, Palatine © Scala. *Io guarded by Argos, whom Mercury has just set free* and garlands, details of fresco, House of Livia © Scala.
149 *Apollo and Artemis*, decoration on a sacred pillar, terracotta from the Temple of Apollo, Palatine Antiquarium © Werner Forman Archive, London. Terracotta plaque, probably from the Temple of Apollo on the Palatine, today in the Palatine Antiquarium, 28 BC © TCI.
150 *Griffins*, from the House of Griffins, © Scala. *Septidozium*, S. Dupérac, engraving, all rights reserved.
150–151 *Palace of the Caesars*, J.-A. A. Deglane, watercolor, 1886 © ENSBA.
151 *Reconstruction*,

idem.
Ruins of the Basilica Flavia © Scala. Head of Heliogabalus, sculpture, 3rd century, Musei Capitoline © Scala.
152 Collection of S.P.Q.R. signs, cl. M. Marzot.
153 *View of the Coliseum*, A. Matveiev, oil on canvas, early 18th century, Tret'kov Gallery, Moscow © Scala.
154–155 Church of Santa Maria in Cosmedin and Temple of Vesta, postcard, all rights reserved.
155 Bocca della Verità, cl. M. Marzot.
156 Interior of St Giorgio in Velabro, *idem*. Casa dei Crescenzi and Money Changers' Arch, cl. A. Idini.
Mounted Amazon, detail of pediment of Temple of Apollo Sosiano © Barbara Malter.
156–157 *Rome scene in front of the Theater of Marcellus*, H.Bürkerl, oil on canvas © Kunstmuseum, Düsseldorf.
157 Section of Theater of Marcellus, A.L.T. Vaudoyer, watercolor, 1786 © ENSBA.
158 The three columns of the Temple of Apollo, cl. A. Idini.
The Portico of Octavia, photo, early 20th century © Alinari-Giraudon.
159 *Portico of Octavia*, reconstruction of façade, F. Duban, watercolor, 1827 © ENSBA.
Old houses by the Portico of Octavia, F. Roesler, oil on canvas, 19th century, Museo di Roma, cl. C. Bernoni.
Piazza Margana, cl. M. Marzot.
161 Jacket of Garibaldi's uniform, Museo Centrale del Risorgimento © Scala. Mussolini declares war on France from the balcony of the Palazzo di Venezia, photo © Roger-Viollet, Paris.
Horses of St Mark's in the courtyard of Palazzo di Venezia, coll Ceccarius © Bibl. naz., Rome.
162 Parade on Via dell'Impero, photo © Roger-Viollet, Paris.
Julius Caesar, engraving, all rights reserved.
162–163 *The Forum of Augustus*, reconstruction,

F.-J. T. Uchard, watercolor, 1869 © ENSBA.
163 Study for the base and the capitol of the Temple of Mars the Avenger, L. Noguet, Indian-ink drawing, 1869 © ENSBA.
164 *Augustus as pontiff*, marble, cl. Jean Mazenod, in *L'Art de l'ancienne Rome* © Editions Citadelles & Mazenod, Paris.
Temple of Minerva, photo © Siegert coll., Munich.
Forum of Nerva, detail, inscription, L. Noguet, 1869, watercolor © ENSBA.
164–165 *Trajan's Forum*, reconstruction, *idem.*
165 View of the Basilica Ulpia, Trajan's Forum © Scala.
Image of Trajan, coin © Bibl. nat., Paris.
166 *Section of Trajan's Column*, engraving © ICCD. Trajan's Column, A. Léon, colored photo, 1921 © musée Albert-Kahn-Dépt. des Hauts-de-Seine.
167 Details of Trajan's Column, bas-reliefs, cl. M. Marzot.
Main side of the pedestal of Trajan's Column, C. Percier, Indian ink and wash © ENSBA.
Statue of St Peter on Trajan's Column, engraving, all rights reserved.
View from the steps of Trajan's Market © Scala.
168 The Torre dei Conti Tower, Piazza Venezia, photo, Ceccarius coll. © Bibl. naz., Rome.
The Torre dei Milizie, cl. M. Marzot.
The campanile of Santa Francesca Romana, litho, all rights reserved.
168–169 Arch of Constantine and the Meta Sudans, photo, c. 1873, Piantanida-Sartori coll.
169 Vault of the apse, Santi Cosma e Damiano, mosaic © Scala.
The extension of Rome in the time of Trajan, geographical map © Scala.
170 *The interior of the Coliseum*, C. W. Eckersburg, oil on canvas, 19th century © Thorvaldsens Museum, Copenhagen.
170–171 The Coliseum, reconstruction, J. Duc, watercolor, 1830–1

472

© ENSBA.

171 *Golden Colossus of Nero*, reconstruction, detail, E.-G-Coquart, watercolor, 1863, *idem*. Underground passages beneath the Coliseum © Nimatallah/Artephot, Paris.

172 Gladiator's helmet, bronze, 1st century AD, Museo Archeologico, Naples © Dagli Orti, Paris.
Circus games, G. Lauro, engraving, all rights reserved.
Gladiators' combat, mosaic, musée de Nennig cl. Musée archéologique, Lattes.

172–173 *Amphitheater scene*, mosaic, 4th century AD, Archeological Museum, Madrid © Nimatallah/Artephot, Paris.

173 Gladiator's greave, gladiator's arm guard, and retiarius' shoulder guard, bronze, 1st century AD, musée du Louvre © RMN.
Ave Caesar, morituri te salutant, J.-L. Gérôme, oil on canvas, 19th century © Yale University Art Gallery, New Haven.
Base of an anemometer, marble, Vatican Museums © IGDA, Milan.

174 Compartment of coffered ceiling decorated with grotesques from the Domus Aurea, in *Dessins de peintures antiques*, S. Bartoli, 17th century, Bibl. nat., Paris.
Trajan's Baths, engraving, *idem*.

175 The Pyramid of Cestius, postcard, private coll.

177 View of the Aventine, cl. J.-L. Malroux.
The Sabine women interrupt the fighting between the Romans and the Sabine men, L. David, oil on canvas, musée du Louvre © RMN

178 *The Four Factiones of the Augurs*, mosaic, Museo Terme Diocleziano © Scala.

178–9 *Circus Maximus*, engraving, Bibl. nat., Paris © Giraudon.

179 Door of Santa Sabina, detail, wood © Scala.
Santa Sabina, A. Pinelli, watercolor, 19th century, Museo di Roma, cl. B. Brizzi.

180 *The Legend of St*

Alexis, fresco, San Clemente © Scala.
Alof de Wignacourt, Grand Master of the Order of Malta, Caravaggio, oil on canvas, musée du Louvre © RMN.

181 Emblem of the Order of Malta, detail of a stamp, all rights reserved. Drawing for stelae on the Piazza dei Cavalieri di Malta © Pierpont Morgan Library, New York.
Mithras sacrificing the bull, high relief, 1st–3rd century AD, musée du Louvre © Lauros-Giraudon.

182 Street on the Aventine, cl. J.-L. Malroux.
San Saba Church, F. Roesler, oil on canvas, Museo di Roma, cl. C. Bernoni.

182–3 *The Pyramid and the Protestant Cemetery*, *idem*.

183 Dedication on the Pyramid of Cestius, engraving all rights reserved.
The tomb of John Keats, cl. A. Idini.

184 Bull, on the door of the slaughterhouse, cl. A. Idini.
A slaughterhouse employee, photo, Primoli Foundation © O. Savio.
The Amphora Fountain, cl. M. Marzot.
View of Testaccio, cl. A. Idini.

185 Basilica of San Giovanni in Laterano, Charpentier, litho, all rights reserved.

186–7 *The Celio*, engraving © Bibl. nat., Paris.

187 Details of the façade of San Gregorio Magno, high reliefs, cl. M. Marzot.
Façade of San Gregorio Magno, cl. Gallimard.

188 Campanile of SS. Giovanni e Paolo, cl. Gallimard.
View of the apse of SS. Giovanni e Paolo © Scala.

189 Statue of Jupiter as Jupiter, Museo Pio-Celementino, Vatican © Scala.

190 Park of Villa Celimontana, cl. A. Idini.
The Dolabella Arch, *idem*.
Madonna and Child, apse mosaic, Santa Maria in Domnica © Scala.

190–1 *Interior of Santo Stefano Rotondo*, F.-M. Granet, oil on canvas, cl. B. Terlay © musée Granet,

Palais de Malte, Aix-en Provence.

191 Navicella Fountain, cl. M. Marzot. *Martyrs*, Pomarancio, fresco, Santo Stefano Rotondo, 16th century © A. de Luca.
Interior of Santo Stefano Rotondo, cl. A. Idini.

192 *Santi Quattro Coronati*, A. Pinelli, watercolor, Museo di Roma, cl. B. Brizzi.
Santi Quattro Coronati , cl. A. Idini.
Basin for ablutions, cloister of Santi Quattro Coronati, cl. M. Marzot.

193 *Triumph of the Cross*, apse mosaic of San Clemente © Scala.
St Catherine freed by angels, Masolino, fresco, *idem*.

194 Fragment of a fresco, probably a *Last Judgement*, nave of San Clemente © Scala.
Statue of Mithras, San Clemente © Scala.

195 Lambs, frieze of apse vault, mosaic, *idem*. © *idem*.

196 Altar of Mithra, *idem*. © *idem*.
Obelisk of San Giovanni in Laterano, engraving © Bibl. nat., Paris.

196–7 *Feast of St John*, J.-B. A. Thomas, watercolored litho © Bibl. nat., Paris.

197 Angels transporting the San Giovanni obelisk, detail *idem*.

198 Façade of San Giovanni in Laterano, photo © Alinari.
Interior of the Basilica of San Giovanni in Laterano, G.B. Piranesi, engraving © Bibl. nat., Paris.
Mussolini signing the Lateran Treaty, photo © Roger-Viollet, Paris.

199 Cosmatesque mosaics, cloister of San Giovanni in Laterano, litho, all rights reserved.
View of the cloister, San Giovanni in Laterano, *idem*.
Statue on the summit of San Giovanni in Laterano, cl. A. Idini.

200 The Castrense Amphitheater, cl. A. Idini.
Grenadiers' Barracks, *idem*.
Interior of Santa Croce in Gerusalemme, *idem*.
Façade of Santa Croce in Gerusalemme, © ENIT.

201 *Papal Blessing on Piazza San Pietro*, I. Caffi, Museo di Roma © Scala.

202 Swiss Guard, postcard, private coll.

203 *Porta Angelica*, F. Roesler, watercolor, Museo di Roma, cl. C. Bernoni.
The dome of St Peter's, cl. M. Marzot.

204 *L'Osservatore Romano*, newspaper name, all rights reserved. Passetto, cl. F. Marzi. Leonine Wall, cl. *idem*.

205 Latin Bible 614, folio 219 verso, ill. Ghirlandaio, Bibl. Vaticane, cl. F. Marzi. Tapestry, papal apartments, cl. F. Marzi.

206 St Peter's tomb, cl. F. Marzi. Statue of St Peter, Grotte Vaticane © Scala.

207 *The Creation of Man*, Michelangelo, fresco, Sistine Chapel © Musei Vaticani.

209 *Constantine's Basilica*, Tassoli, fresco, Grotte Vaticane, 16th century © Scala.
Mausoleum of Aelius Thyrannus, Necropoli del Vaticano, cl. Marzi-Morselli.

210 *Ponente*, marble paving stone, cl. Marci-Morselli.
Obelisk, Piazza San Pietro, engraving, © Bibl. nat., Paris.

210–11 *Project for the façade of St Peter's*, engraving © Electa, Milan.

211 Cardinals in St Peter's, cl. Marzi-Morselli. Nuns, Piazza San Pietro, cl. W. Louvet.
The Door of Death, cl. F. Marzi.
Holy water stoup in St Peter's, cl. Marzi-Morselli.

212 *Gloria*, Bernini, cl. Marezi-Morselli.
Pietà, Michelangelo, marble, St Peter's © Scala.

212–13 *Cardinal Melchior de Polignac visiting St Peter's Basilica in Rome*, G. P. Pannini, musée du Louvre © RMN.

213 View of the dome of St Peter's, cl. Marzi-Morselli.
St Longinus, Bernini, marble, cl. Marzi-Morselli. St Veronica, *idem*.

214 Spiral staircase to entrance of Vatican Museums, cl. A. de Luca. Pediment of Casina di Pius IV, bas-relief, cl. F. Marzi.
Domenico Fontana presenting his project for the Vatican library to

◆ LIST OF ILLUSTRATIONS

Sixtus V, P. Facchetti, fresco, Sistine Hall © Bibl. del Vaticano.

215 Palazzo del Governatorato, Vatican Station, Palazzo Apostolico, Vatican Gardens, corridor leading to the Sala Regia and interior of the Sala Regia, cl. Marzi-Morselli. Colossal head, Cortile della Pigna, sculpture © ENSBA.

216 Vatican Loggias, cl. F. Marzi.

217 The Chiaramonti Niobid, after a 4th-century Greek original, Museo Pio Clementino © Scala. *Geographical map*, fresco, Galleria delle Carte Geografiche, Musei Vaticani, cl. F. Marzi.

218 *The Delphic Sibyl*, Michelangelo, fresco, detail of the Sistine Chapel vault, photo A. Bracchetti © Musei Vaticani.

218–19 Overall view of the Sistine Chapel vault, Michelangelo, fresco, photo A. Bracchetti/P. Zigrossi © *idem.*

219 Adam, detail of *The Creation of Man*, *idem.* *Ignudo*, next to the scene of Noah's Flood, *idem.*

220 Scenes of the life of Moses, *Moses and Jethro's daughters*, S. Botticelli, fresco, late 15th century, Sistine Chapel, Vatican © Scala.

221 *The Last Judgement, the Damned and Christ Triumphant*, Michelangelo, 1537–41, *idem.*

222 *The Expulsion of Heliodorus from the Temple*, detail, Raphael and his pupils, fresco, Stanza d'Eliodoro, Vatican © Scala.

222–3 *The School of Athens*, Raphael, fresco, Stanza della Segnatura, *idem.*

223 *Erato, surrounded by Polyhymnia, Melpomene, Terpsichore and Urania*, Stanza della Segnatura, *idem.*

224 *Belvedere Apollo*, marble, Museo Pio Clementino, Vatican © Scala.

224–5 *The Laocoön*, *idem.*

225 *The Belvedere Torso*, *idem.* *Augustus of Prima Porta*, marble, Braccio Nuovo, Vatican © Scala. *The Sleeping Ariadne*,

marble, Museo Pio-Clementino, *idem.*

226 *Angel Musician*, M. da Forli, fragment of a fresco, c. 1480, cl. S. Grandadan. *Sixtus IV appointing Platina Prefect of the Vatican Library*, M. da Forli, c. 1475–7, fresco, Pinacoteca Vaticana © Scala.

226–7 *Madonna and Child*, Pinturicchio, fresco, Sala dei Santi, Appartamento Borgia, Vatican © Scala.

227 *St Lawrence ordained deacon by St Sixtus*, Fra Angelico, fresco, Capella di Niccolò V © Scala.

228 *Portrait of Raphael*, engraving, © Bibl. nat., Paris. *The Transfiguration*, Raphael, oil on canvas, Pinacoteca Vaticano © Scala. *The Expulsion of Adam and Eve from Paradise*, Raphael, fresco, Loggie di Raffaello © Scala. *Isaac blessing Jacob*, *idem.*

229 *The Madonna of Foligno*, Raphael, oil on canvas, Pinacoteca Vaticano © Scala. *The Crossing of the Red Sea*, Raphael © Scala. *The construction of Noah's Ark*, *idem.*

230 *Descent from the Cross*, Caravaggio, oil on canvas, 1604, Pinacoteca Vaticano © Scala.

231 *Pietà*, P. da Cortona, fresco, Cappella di Urbano VIII © Scala. *The Last Communion of St Jerome*, Domenichino, oil on canvas, 1614 Pinacoteca Vaticana © Scala. St Thomas, detail of *the Virgin between St Thomas and St Jerome*, G. Reni, oil on canvas, 1625–30, Pinacoteca Vaticana © Scala.

232 Piazza San Pietro, photo, early 20th century Alinari-Giraudon. Piazza San Pietro, cl. W. Louvet.

233 Shield with blazon and details of façades in the Borgo, cl. M. Marzot. Monk, Piazza San Pietro, cl. W. Louvet. *Via del Campanile* in the Borgo, F. Roesler, oil on canvas, 19th century, Museo di Roma, cl. C. Bernoni. *Reconstruction of*

Hadrian's Mausoleum, E. Vaudremer, watercolor, 1857 © ENSBA.

234 Firework display at the Castel Sant'Angelo, J. Wright of Derby, oil on canvas © Birmingham Art Gallery.

234–5 *Hadrian's Mausoleum, Castel Sant'Angelo*, E. Vaudremer, watercolor, 1857 © ENSBA.

235 *Idem*, longitudinal section. *Angel*, R. da Montelupo, marble, Cortile del Angelo © ENIT.

236 *Palazzo di Giustizia*, F. Roesler, oil on canvas, Museo di Roma, cl. C. Bernoni. View of Prati, photo © Primoli Foundation.

237 Ponte Sant'Angelo, photo © ENIT.

238 *The bridge and the Castel Sant'Angelo*, V. Brayer, watercolor © Giraudon/A.D.A.G.P.

239 Ponte Sant'Angelo, cl. A.Idini. Fragment of a double sacrifice to the god Mars, marble relief, musée du Louvre © RMN.

240 Ponte Sant'Angelo, cl. Malroux. Angel on the Ponte Sant'Angelo, Bernini, marble, cl. A. Idini.

241 *Tribune of the Church of San Giovanni dei Fiorentini*, G. cl. J.-L. Malroux.Van Wittle, oil on canvas, private coll. © Scala. Dome of San Giovanni dei Fiorentini, cl. A. Idini. Sculpture, San Giovanni dei Fiorentini, cl. J. L. Malroux. Via Giulia, cl. M. Marzot.

242 *The story of David*, F. Salviati, Palazzo Sacchetti © Scala. *Church of the Spirito Santo dei Napoletani*, A. Pinelli, watercolor, c. 1835 Museo di Roma, cl. B. Brizzi.

242–3 *Palazzo Sacchetti*, M. Corneille, wash on cardboard, T. Ashby coll. © Biblioteca Vaticana.

243 Window of Palazzo Sacchetti, cl. A. Idini. Façade of Santa Maria di Monserrato, cl. A. Idini. *The Last Communion of St Jerome*, Domenichino, oil on canvas, 1614 Pinacoteca Vaticana © Scala.

244 Fountain of the Mascherone, cl. M. Marzot.

Piazza Farnese, cl. *idem.*

244–5 *Triumph of Bacchus and Ariadne*, Annibale Carracci, fresco, Palazzo Farnese © Scala.

245 Palazzo Farnese, G. B. Piranesi, engraving © ENIT. Façade on the courtyard of Palazzo Farnese, cl. A. Idini. *Venus and Anchises*, detail, Annibale Carracci, fresco, Palazzo Farnese © Scala.

246 Façade of Palazzo Spada, cl. A. Idini. *Trompe l'oeil* gallery, Palazza Spada, F. Borromini © Scala. Monte di Pietà, fountain, cl. Gallimard.

247 *Portrait of St Charles Borromeo*, engraving © Bibl. nat., Paris. Via dei Giubbonari, cl. M. Marzot. *The Annunciation*, L. Lanfranco, oil on canvas, San Carlo ai Catinari © Scala.

248 Via di Grotta Pinta, cl. A. Idini. Campo de' Fiori, cl. *idem.* *Idem.*, cl. M. Marzot. *Idem.*, cl. J.-L. Malroux.

248–9 *Pompey's Theater*, V. Baltard, watercolor, 1837 © ENSBA. Model of Pompey's Theater © O. Greppi/Amis du plan de Rome, Université de Caen.

249 *Portrait of Giordano Bruno*, engraving © Bibl. nat., Paris. Head of Caesar or a priest, Museo Barracco © Scala.

250 Sant'Andrea della Valle, cl. J.-L. Malroux.

251 Temple A, Largo Argentina, cl. A. Idini. Temple B, *idem.* Temple C, *idem.*. Porticus Minucia Frumentaria, *idem.* *Music Festival in Teatro Argentina*, G. P. Pannini, oil on canvas, 1747, musée du Louvre J RMN.

252 *Roaring lion*, façade of Caio Manilio house, cl. M. Marzot. *Portico Ottavia and the fish market*, Charpentier, watercolored litho, all rights reserved.

253 Jewish shop, photo, Centro di Documentazione Ebraico Contemporaneo, Rome, all rights reserved. Via Botteghe Oscure, cl. M. Marzot. Ghetto street, cl. A. Idini.

LIST OF ILLUSTRATIONS ◆

Portrait of Alessandro Mattei, engraving © Bibl. nat., Paris.
254 Tortoise Fountain, cl. J.-L. Malroux.
Portrait of Beatrice Cenci, G. Reni, oil on canvas, Galleria Nazionale di Arte Antica © Scala.
The Synagogue, cl. A. Idini.
255 *The Pantheon*, I Caffi, oil on canvas, Ca Pesaro, Venice.
257 *St Ignatius of Loyola*, anon., oil on canvas, Duques del Infantino, Madrid © Artephot/Oronoz, Paris.
Urban VIII in the Gesù, A. Sacchi, oil on canvas, Galeria Nazionale d'Arte Antica © Scala.
258 Altar of St Ignatius of Loyola, Gesù © Scala.
Passage of the Camerette di Sant'Ignazio, A. Pozzo © Scala.
Palazzo Doria-Pamphili, cl. A. Idini.
259 *The Flight into Egypt*, Annibale Carracci, oil on canvas, Palazzo Doria-Pamphili © Scala.
Salome, Titian, *idem.*
Countryside with dancers, C. Lorrain, *idem.*
260 The marble foot, cl. A. Idini.
Marble plaque, Santa Maria sopra Minerva, cl. M. Marzot, *Christ*, Michelangelo, marble, Santa Maria sopra Minerva © Scala.
261 *Piazza della Minerva*, A. Pinelli, watercolor, c. 1835, Museo di Roma, cl. B. Brizzi.
Bernini's elephant bearing an obelisk, cl. M. Marzot.
The trompe l'oeil dome of Sant'Ignazio, A. Pozzo, fresco, 1685 © Scala.
262-3 Domes © G.-C. Gasponi.
264 *Dedication of the Pantheon*, engraving, all rights reserved.
264-5 *View of the Pantheon*, Marchi, oil on canvas, 1754, private coll., Rome © L. Pedicini, Naples.
265 Aerial view of the Pantheon © ICCD.
Dome of the Pantheon, view of the interior, cl. A. Idini.
Interior of the Pantheon, cl. W. Louvet.
266 *Pantheon*, G. C. Chédanne, watercolor, watercolor, 1891 © ENSBA.

Interior of the Pantheon © Scala.
267 *The Temple of Hadrian*, G. B. Piranesi, engraving © Bibl. Nat. Paris.
Bocconi Stores, early 20th century, postcard, private coll.
The top of Trajan's Column, cl. A. Idini.
The Column of Marcus Aurelius, Piazza Colonna, colored photograph, early 20th century, Museo di Storia della fotografia © Alinari.
268 *Reliefs on the Column of Marcus Aurelius*, G. Guerra, drawings, © Statens Museum for Kunst, Copenhagen.
Commemorative base of the Column of Antoninus Pius, Cortile delle Corazze, Vatican © Scala.
269 Views of the façades of Palazzo Montecitorio, cl. A. Idini.
Palazzo Chigi, cl. *idem.*
Galleria Colonna, cl. *idem.*
Palazzo Montecitorio © ENIT.
270 Piazza delle Coppelle, cl. A. Idini.
Santa Maria in Campo Marzio, cl. *idem.*
St Cecilia in Paradise, Domenichino, fresco, San Luigi dei Francesi © Scala.
270-1 *The Vocation of St Matthew*, Caravaggio, oil on canvas, 1599-1602, *idem.*
271 The salamander, emblem of Francis I, façade of San Luigi dei Francesi, cl. M. Marzot.
St Matthew and the Angel, detail, Caravaggio, oil on canvas, San Luigi dei Francesi © Scala.
Virgin, votive aedicule, Piazza San Luigi dei Francesi, cl. M. Marzot.
272 Palazzo Madama, A. Specchi, engraving, all rights reserved.
Cupola of Sant'Ivo, cl. M. Marzot.
273 Market on Piazza Navona, T. Cuccioni, photo, 1860 © Bibl. nat., Paris.
274 Via dei Coronari, cl. G. Peyrot.
Map of Rome, 1637 © Bibl. nat., Paris.
276 *Piazza Navona Flooded*, J.-B. A. Thomas, watercolored litho, in *Un an à Rome* © Bibl. nat., Paris.

276-7 *Piazza Navona*, G. Van Wittel, oil on canvas, private coll. © Ugo Bozzi Editore.
277 Fontana dei Quattro Fiumi, cl. G. Peyrot.
278 Nostra Signora al Sacro Cuore Church, cl. G. Peyrot.
Section of Sant'Agnese in Agone, engraving, Bibl. nat., Paris.
279 Palazzo Pamphili, cl. M. Marzot, *Portrait of Innocent X*, detail, D. Velázquez, oil on canvas, 17th century, Palazzo Doria Pamphili © Scala.
Palazzo Massimo, cl. G. Peyrot.
Via di Pasquino, street name, cl. *idem.*
Pasquino, talking statue, cl. G. Peyrot.
280 Façade of the Church of Santa Maria della Pace, cl. G. Peyrot.
Via di S. Maria dell'Anima, street name, cl. *idem.*
280-1 *Sibyls*, Raphael, fresco, Chigi Chapel, Santa Maria della Pace, early 16th century © Scala.
281 Cloister of Santa Maria dell'Anima, cl. G. Peyrot.
Piazza della Pace, cl. *idem.*
Terrina Fountain, cl. *idem.*
St Philip Neri, engraving © Bibl. nat., Paris.
282 Oratorio dei Filippini, cl. G. Peyrot.
Detail of San Salvatore in Lauro, bas-relief, cl. M. Marzot.
282-3 *Church and Oratory of Santa Maria in Vallicella*, G. B. Falda, engraving, all rights reserved.
283 Torre dell'Orologio, Chiesa Nuova, photo © ENIT.
Via dei Coronari, cl. G. Peyrot.
Façade of Palazzo Lancelotti, cl. *idem.*
284 Sign of the Albergo dell'Orso, J. H. Parker, photo, 1868 © Bibl. nat., Paris.
Torre della Scimmia, cl. G. Peyrot.
The Prophet Isaiah, Raphael, fresco, Sant'Agostino Church © Scala.
285 *Madonna of the Pilgrims*, Caravaggio, oil on canvas, Sant'Agostino © Scala.
Façade of Sant'Apollinare Church, cl. M. Marzot.
286 Views of façades 6

cl. J.-L.Malroux, 2 cl. M. Marzot, 1 cl. S. Bottani, 1 cl. W. Louvet.
287 *The Trevi Fountain*, G. Rohner, oil on canvas, Subes coll., Paris, 1966 © Scala.
289 *Montecavallo*, engraving, P. Bril, ink, Gabinetto degli Stampi, Florence © Scala.
290 Carriages parked on Piazza Barberini, photo, Ceccarius coll. © bibl. naz., Rome.
290-1 *The Triumph of Divine Providence*, P. da Cortona, fresco, Palazzo Barberini © Scala.
291 *Palazzo Barberini*, engravings, all rights reserved.
St Michael overcoming the Devil, G. Reni, oil on canvas, Church of the Cappuchins © G. Nimatallah/Ricciarini, Milan.
Church of Santa Maria della Concezione, crypt of the Cappuchins' Church, photo early 20th century © Alinari-Giraudon.
292 Emblem of the Barberini, stained-glass window in Santa Maria in Aracoeli, cl. J. L. Malroux.
La Fornarina, Raphael, oil on canvas, Galleria Nazionale dell'Arte Antica © Scala.
292-293 *Judith Beheading Holofernes*, Caravaggio, oil on canvas, *idem.*
293 *Madonna of Tarquinia*, F. Lippi, painting on wood, *idem.*
Portrait of Stefano Sciarra-Colonna, A. di Cosimo, *idem.*
294 *Piazza delle Quattro Fontane*, L. Cruyl, engraving, 17th century © The Cleveland Museum of Art.
Fountain representing the Nile, sculpture, cl. W. Louvet.
294-5 *Ecstasy of St Teresa*, Bernini, marble, Santa Maria della Vittoria © Scala.
295 Fountains representing the Tiber, Strength or Juno, Fidelity or Diana, sculptures, 1st century, cl. W. Louvet, 2nd and 3rd century, A. Idini.
Dome of San Bernardo, cl. A. Idini.
296 Façade of San Carlo alle Quattro Fontane, cl. A. Idini.
Façade of Sant'Andrea al Quirinale, cl. A. Idini.

◆ LIST OF ILLUSTRATIONS

Dome of San Carlo alle Quattro Fontane, cl. G. Berengo Gardin © TCI.
296–297 *Piazza del Quirinale,* G. Van Wittel, oil on canvas, Galleria Nazionale dell'Arte Antica © Scala.
297 Piazza del Quirinale, aerial view, photo © ENIT.
The Presidential Guard, State Room, Palazzo del Quirinale, © ENIT.
Spiral staircase, Palazzo del Quirinale, cl. G. Berengo Gardin © TCI.
298 Anita Ekberg in front of the Trevi Fountain, in *La Dolce Vita*, F. Fellini, private coll., Paris.
Virgin indicating the source of the spring to soldiers, bas-relief, Trevi Fountain, cl. A. Idini.
299 *Aurora,* G. Reni, fresco, Accademia di San Luca © Scala.
St Luke painting the Virgin Mary, Raphael, oil on canvas, *idem.* © Scala.
Trevi Fountain, cl. H. Simone Huber © SIE.
300 Galleria Colonna, cl. G. Berengo Gardin © TCI.
Peasant Eating Beans, Annibale Carracci, oil on canvas, Galleria Colonna © Scala.
Basilica dei Santi Apostoli, cl. A. Idini.
301 Galleria Sciarra, cl. G. Berengo Gardin © TCI.
Via della Pilotta, photo, early 20th century © Alinari-Giraudon.
Trasteverian figure, Ceccarius coll. © Bibl. naz., Rome.
302 Façade of San Silvestro in Capite, cl. *idem.*
Paparazzo in Via Veneto in *La Dolce Vita*, F. Fellini © P. Praturlon.
Via Veneto, postcard, private coll.
303 Trinità dei Monti, watercolor, Y. Brayer, private coll., Paris © Giraudon/A.D.A.G.P.
305 Via Peregrinorum, street name, cl. G. Peyrot.
View of the twin churches, cl. G. Peyrot.
306 Bust of G. Valadier, cl. G. Peyrot.
306–307 Piazza del Popolo looking onto the Pincio, photo 20th century © Alinari-Brogi-Giraudon.
307 Antique dealers, Via del Babuino, cl. G. Peyrot.
Caffè Canova cl. *idem.*
Piazza del Popolo © cl. *idem.*
The Prophet Daniel,

Bernini, marble, Santa Maria del Popolo © Scala.
308 Fountain of Silenus, cl. G. Peyrot.
Horse race down the Via del Corso, engraving, private coll.
309 Artists, Via Margutta, photos © ENIT.
Façades, Via del Corso, cl. W. Louvet.
Palazzo Bonaparte cl. G. Peyrot.
Façade of the Church of Santi Ambrogio e Carlo, cl. *idem.*
Kiosk on the Via del Corso, cl. *idem.*
310 *Res Gestae,* façade of the pavilion housing the Ara Pacis, cl. *idem.*
Mausoleum of Augustus, engraving, private coll., Paris.
Mausoleum of Augustus, cl. G. Peyrot.
Bas-relief, detail of the Ara Pacis, cl. *idem.*
310–311 Ara Pacis, overall view, cl. *idem.*
311 *Earth with her two children,* high relief, Ara Pacis, cl. *idem.*
Stands selling prints and engravings on Piazza Borghese, cl. *idem.*
Loggia of Palazzo Borghese, cl. *idem.*
312 *The Caffè Greco,* L. Passini, oil on canvas, 19th century, Hamburg Kunsthalle © AKG, Berlin.
312–13 Carriages for rent, Piazza di Spagna, cl. G. Peyrot.
313 Pediment, façade of the Collegio di Propaganda Fide, cl. G. Peyrot.
Piazza di Spagna, Collegio di Propaganda Fide, photo © Bibl. nat., Paris.
Casina Rossa, cl. G. Peyrot.
San Lorenzo in Lucina, cl. G. Peyrot.
314 Piazza di Spagna © ENIT.
Barcaccia Fountain, cl. G, Peyrot.
Church of the Trinità dei Monti, cl. *idem.*
314–15 *Church of Trinità dei Monti and Villa Medici,* F.-M. Granet, oil on canvas, musée du Louvre © RMN.
315 Doorway, Via Gregoriana, cl. M. Marzot.
Villa Medici, garden side, cl. W. Louvet.
Villa Medici, *idem.*
316 Front cover of the first edition of *Promenades dans Rome,*

Stendhal, Paris, 1829, Bibl. nat., Paris.
Casina Valadier, cl. G. Peyrot.
Henrico Toti Monument, cl. *idem..*
The Pincio, A. Léon, colored photo, 1921 © musée Albert-Kahn, Dépt. des Hauts-de-Seine.
317 Via Appia © V. Giannella.
318 Via Appia Antica, photo, early 20th century © Electa, Milan.
319 Via Appia Antica, cl. G. Peyrot.
320 *Mosaic of the athletes,* detail, Museo Gregoriano Profano, Vatican © Scala.
Caracalla, coin, 3rd C. AD © Bibl. nat., Paris.
Farnese Hercules, Museo Nazionale, Naples © Scala.
320–1 Baths of Caracalla, ground plan of its present state, J.-E. A. Duquesne, watercolor, 1901 © ENSBA.
321 Paving, colored mosaics of the Baths of Caracalla, cl. M. Marzot.
Mosaic of the athletes, detail, Museo Gregoriano Profano, Vatican © Scala.
House of Cardinal Bessarione, cl. G. Peyrot.
322 *Colombarium of Pomponius Hylas,* Campana, print, 1843 © Bibl. nat., Paris.
322–3 Stone sarcophagus of Scipio Barbatus, Museo Pio-Clementino, Vatican © Scala.
323 Brickwork of Aurelian Wall and Baths of Caracalla, cl. M. Marzot.
Porta Latina, cl. G. Peyrot.
324 Via di Porta San Sebastiano, street name, cl. G. Peyrot.
Porta di San Sebastiano, photo, Ceccarius coll. © Bibl. naz., Rome.
Milestone, cl. G. Peyrot.
324–5 *Quo Vadis* film poster, private coll. Paris.
325 Section of a catacomb, De Rossi, engraving, in *Roma sotterranea cristiana* © Bibl. nat., Paris.
The crypt of the popes, catacombs of San Callisto, *idem.*
326 Symbols in the catacombs, all rights reserved.
The Crypt of the Popes, Catacombs of San Callisto © Scala.

Symbols in the catacombs, all rights reserved.
327 *Felicitas,* inscription, Catacombs of Priscilla © Comissione di archeologia sacra.
Peacock, fresco, Catacombs of Priscilla, *idem.*
Miracle of the spring, Catacombs of Commodilla, *idem.*
Eel, Catacombs of Priscilla, *idem.*
The Good Shepherd, Giordani cemetery, *idem.*
Symbols of the catacombs, all rights reserved.
View of three tombs, Catacombs of San Sebastiano © Scala.
328 Church of Sant'Urbano alla Caffarella, cl. G. Peyrot.
Circus of Maxentius, present state, A. Recoura, watercolor, 1899 © ENSBA.
328–9 *Idem.,* reconstruction of main façade.
Idem., main façade as it was at the time.
329 Circus of Maxentius, cl. G. Peyrot.
330 Tomb of Cecilia Metella, details, cl. G. Peyrot.
Tomb of Cecilia Metella, photo, early 20th century © Alinari-Giraudon.
331 View of the interior of the Basilica of Santa Maria Maggiore, G. B. Piranesi, engraving, 18th century © Bibl. nat., Paris.
333 Piazza della Repubblica and details of the Fountain of the Naiads, cl. G. Peyrot.
Piazza Esedra with Termini Station and the Fountain of the Naiads © Alinari-Brogi-Giraudon.
334 *St Bruno,* A. Houdon, sculpture, Santa Maria degli Angeli, cl. *idem.*
The meridian of Santa Maria degli Angeli, cl. *idem.*
View of the *caldarium,* entrance of the Church of Santa Maria degli Angeli, cl. G .Peyrot.
334–5 *Reconstruction of the Baths of Diocletian,* E. Paulin, watercolor, 1880 © ENSBA.
335 Baths of the Ancient garden of the Diocletian, cl. M. Marzot.
336 *Young girl of Anzio,* statue, Museo delle Terme © Scala.

LIST OF ILLUSTRATIONS ◆

Battle of the Romans and the Germans, sarcophagus, *idem.*

336–7 *The Birth of Venus*, high relief, *idem.*

337 Maenads dancing before an urn for ashes, funerary stele, *idem.*
Niobid, marble, *idem.*

338 Termini Station, cl. G. Peyrot.
Obelisk of the Cinquecento, cl. *idem.*
Bernich's Aquarium, cl. G. Peyrot.

338–9 Termini Station, S. Bianchi, photo, early 20th century © Alinari-Giraudon.

339 The first Termini Station, P. V., photo 1866 © Bibl. Nat., Paris.
Ruins of the Temple of Minerva Medica in Rome, G. B. Busiri, oil on canvas, National Trust Photographic Library/Christopher Hurst © Felbrigg Hall, Norfolk.

340 Bas-relief of the Baker's Tomb, engraving, all rights reserved.
The Tomb of Eurysaces, cl. G. Peyrot.
Basilica of Porta Maggiore, stucco bas-relief © Scala.
Piazza Vittorio Emanuele II © Alinari-Giraudon.

341 *The water tower of the Aqua Giulia*, reconstruction, A. M. Garnaud, watercolor, 1821 © ENSBA.
Idem., actual state.
Trophies of Marius, idem.

342 Basilica of Santa Maria Maggiore, G.P. Pannini, oil on canvas, 18th century, Palazzo del Quirinale, © Giraudon.

343 The *Coronation of the Virgin*, J. Torriti, mosaic, Santa Maria Maggiore © Scala.
The Dormition of the Virgin, idem.
Jerusalem, idem.

344 *Christ teaching the Apostles*, mosaic, apse of Santa Pudenziana, cl. G. Peyrot.
Campanile and door of Santa Pudenziana, cl. G. Peyrot.
Architectural ornament, Santa Pudenziana, cl. M. Marzot.

345 *The heavenly Jerusalem*, mosaic on the triumphal arch of San Prassede © Scala.
Christ and saints, apse mosaic, *idem.*

Madonna and Child with St Praxedes and St Pudentiana, mosaic, St Zeno Chapel © Scala.

346 *Piazza San Pietro in Vincoli*, F. Roesler, 19th century, oil on canvas, Museo di Roma, cl. C. Bernoni.
The Salita di Borgia, cl. M. Marzot.

346–7 *Moses*, tomb of Julius II, Michelangelo, marble, Basilica of San Pietro in Vincoli © Scala.

347 Via Leonina, Via dei Ciancaleoni, Via Panisperna, cl. G. Peyrot.
Via degli Zingari, street name, cl. G. Peyrot.
Portrait of E. Majorana, photo © Roger-Viollet, Paris.

348 Statues of the Palazzo delle Esposizioni, cl. M. Marzot. San Paolo entro le Mura, cl. G. Peyrot.
Piccolo Eliseo, *idem.*
Interior of the Teatro dell'Opera, photo © ENIT.
Bottle of wine: *Est Est Est*, cl. Gallimard.

349 *Banks of the Tiber near the Regola*, F. Roesler, oil on canvas, 19th century, Museo di Roma, cl. C. Bernoni.

351 Danish artists in a Trastevere inn, D. C. Blunck, oil on canvas, © Thorsvaldsens Museum, Copenhagen.
Saltarello, F. D. Soiron, watercolored engraving, cabinet communal des Estampes.

352 San Bartolomeo, cl. A. Idini.
View of Isola Tiberina, cl. G. Rossi © The Image Bank, Milan.
The Tiber, cl. M. Marzot

353 The Ponte Rotto, cl. A. Idini.
Basilica of Santa Cecilia, cl. A. Idini.
Monumental gate to the basilica, *idem.*
Medieval houses in the Santa Cecilia neighborhood, F. Roesler, oil on canvas, Museo di Roma, cl. C. Bernoni.
St Cecilia, S. Maderno, marble, Santa Cecilia in Trastevere © Scala.

354 Madonna dell'Orto Church, cl. A. Idini.
Seraphim, details from *The Last Judgment*, P. Cavallini, fresco, Santa Cecilia © Scala.
The Blessed Lodovica Albertoni, Bernini, marble, Madonna dell'Orto

© Scala.

355 Porta Portese flea market, cl. M. Marzot.
Mamma Roma, P. P. Pasolini, still from the film © Archivio S.A.C.
Port of Ripagrande, postcard, private coll.
Façade of San Michele, cl. J.-L. Malroux.

356 Cloister of San Cosimato, Ceccarius coll. © Bibl. naz., Rome.
The Excubitorium, cl. A. Idini.
Medieval house in Via della Lungaretta, F. Roesler, oil on canvas, Museo di Roma, cl. C. Bernoni.

357 Trasteverian figures, Ceccarius coll. © Bibl naz., Rome.
Santa Maria in Trastevere, anon., oil on canvas, 19th century, Museo di Roma.

358 *The Dormition of the Virgin*, P. Cavallini, mosaic, Santa Maria in Trastevere © Scala.
Innocent II, apse mosaic, *idem* © Scala.

359 *Christ and the Virgin*, *idem*, Santa Maria della Scala, Pinelli, watercolor, 19th century, Museo di Roma, cl. B. Brizzi.

360 *Juno*, Raphael, fresco in the Loggia di Amore e Psiche, Palazzo della Farnesina, photo © ENIT.
Graffiti between two trompe l'oeil columns, B. Peruzzi, fresco in the Salone delle Prospettive, Palazzo della Farnesina © Accademia dei Lincei.

361 *Loggia della Farnesina*, F. Roesler, 19th century, oil on canvas, Museo di Roma, cl. C. Bernoni.
Salone delle Prospettive, B. Peruzzi, frescoes, Palazzo della Farnesina © Scala.
Triumph of Galatea, Raphael, *idem.*

362 Emblem of the Accademia dei Lincei, all rights reserved.
Venus and Adonis, detail, J. de Ribera, oil on canvas, 1637, Galleria Nazionale d'Arte Antica, Palazzo Corsini.

362–3 *St John the Baptist*, Caravaggio, oil on canvas, *idem.* © Scala.

363 The Orto Botanico, cl. A. Idini.
Trilussa, sculpture, Piazza Trilussa, *idem.*
Ponte Sisto Fountain, F. Roesler, oil on canvas,

19th century Museo di Roma, cl. C. Bernoni.

364 Aqua Paola Fountain, photo, early 20th century © Alinari-Giraudon.
Tempietto, Bramante, G. Berengo Gardin © TCI.

364–5 View from the Janiculum, cl. M. Marzot.

365 Tasso's oak, postcard, private coll.
Garibaldi Monument, postcard, private coll.

366 11 cl. M. Marzot, 3 cl. S. Grandadan, 2 cl. S. Bottani, 1 cl. J.-L. Malroux.

367 *Male Head*, Etruscan art, Villa Giulia © Scala.

368 *Portrait of J. J. Winckelmann*, engraving, all rights reserved.

368–9 Villa Doria-Pamphili, photo, early 20th century © Alinari-Giraudon.

370 Villa Giulia, aerial photograph, cl. G. Rossi © Image Bank, Milan.
Crater with figure of a hoplite, glazed terracotta, 460–70 BC, Villa Giulia © Scala.
Crater of Aurora, ceramic, *idem.*

370–1 *Apollo*, terracotta statue, late 6th century BC, *idem.*

371 Corner ornament, Etruscan art, *idem* © Scala.
Ficoroni Cista, marriage casket, Novius Plautius, bronze, 4th century BC, Villa Giulia © Scala.
Lid of cista, Etruscan art, bronze © Scala.
The Sarcophagus of the Bride and Bridegroom, terracotta, 6th century, Villa Giulia © Scala.

372 *View of the Villa Borghese*, J. W. Baur, oil on canvas, Galleria Borghese © Scala.
Pauline Borghese, A. Canova, marble, *idem* © Scala.

373 Statues of animals in the park of Villa Borghese, cl. M. Marzot.
Apollo and Daphne, Bernini, Galleria Borghese © Scala.
The Rape of Proserpina, *idem* © Scala.

374 *Sacred Love and Profane Love*, Titian, oil on canvas 1514, *idem.*
The Palefrenieri Madonna or *Madonna of the Serpent*, Caravaggio, oil on canvas, 1605, *idem.*

375 *The Deposition*, Raphael, oil on canvas,

◆ LIST OF ILLUSTRATIONS

idem..
Danaë, Correggio, oil on canvas, *idem.*
376–7 The statues of athletes at the Stadio di Marmo, cl. M. Marzot.
377 Fountain of the Sphere and the mosaic pavement, Ponte Milvio, cl. A. Idini.
Stadio dei Marmi cl. M. Marzot.
378 Accademia per l'educazione fisica, cl. A. Idini.
Loggia of the Villa Madama, G. Volpato, watercolor, private coll.
379 *The major churches of Rome*, engraving © Bibl. nat., Paris.
380 *St Agnes and Honorius I*, detail, apse mosaic of Sant' Agnese © Scala.
381 *Basilica of San Lorenzo fuori le Mure*, Vasi, engraving, all rights reserved.
381 Mausoleum of Santa Costanza, Villa Torlonia and the Peroni Brewery, cl. G. Peyrot.
382 *The Story of Adam and Eve*, miniature, Charles the Bald Bible, monastery library, San Paolo fuori le Mure, © Scala.
The Sarcophagus of the Grape Harvest, detail, San Lorenzo fuori le Mura, cl. G. Peyrot.
Views of the cloister of San Paolo fuori le Mure, cl. G. Peyrot.
383 *The Story of Adam and Eve*, detail, *op. cit.*
Façade of San Paolo fuori le Mura © ENIT.
384 Fascist propaganda poster © Cinecittà archives.
384–5 Laying the first stone of the Istituto Luce © Istituto Luce.
385 Filming Fellini's *Roma*, photo of the set © Franco Pinna.
Cleopatra, Mankiewicz, poster, private coll.
386 Mussolini, photo, 1937 © Roger-Viollet, Paris.
Palazzo della Civiltà del Lavoro, EUR., cl. W. Louvet.
387 Signature of Giorgio de Chirico, © Roger-Viollet, Paris.
The Melancholy of the Politician, G. de Chirico, oil on canvas, 1913, Basel Museum © Giraudon/ SPADEM.
Piazza Marconi, cl. G.

Peyrot.
388 Model of the Teatro di Marcello, Museo della Civiltà Romana © Scala.
The Ferris wheel at Luna Park, cl. M. Marzot.
Abbazia delle Tre Fontane, postcard private coll.
389 General view of the Cascatelle, Tivoli, photo © Alinari-Giraudon.
390 Medieval houses, cl. G. Peyrot.
391 Santa Maria Maggiore, cl. G. Peyrot.
The Temple of the Sibyl in Tivoli, C. Labruzzi, wash, late 18th century, Ashby coll. © Biblioteca Vaticana.
392 Villa d'Este, mosaic, cl. G. G. Peyrot.
Portrait of Ippolito d'Este, engraving © Bibl. nat., Paris.
The Water-Organ Fountain, cl. Gallimard.
Idem., cl. G. Peyrot.
Fountains, cl. Gallimard.
393 View of the Villa d'Este, cl. G. Peyrot.
Proserpina's Fountain, cl. G. Peyrot.
Frescoes, Villa d'Este, cl. G. Peyrot.
The Avenue of a Hundred Fountains, photo © ENIT.
394 Image of Hadrian, coin, 2nd century AD © Bibl. nat., Paris.
Title page of the book *Map of Hadrian's Villa*, Pirro Ligorio, all rights reserved.
Model of Hadrian's villa, Museo della Civiltà Romana © Scala.
395 Bust of Antinous, Museo Gregoriano Egizio, Vatican © Scala.
396 Cariatyd and crocodile on the Canopus, Villa Adriana, cl. G. Peyrot.
The cypress trees planted by Conte Fede, cl. G. Peyrot.
396–7 Colonnade of the Canopus, cl. G. Peyrot.
397 Cariatyds on the Canopus, photo © ENIT.
398 The right exedra of the Terrace of the Hemicycles, cl. G. Peyrot.
399 Cista from a princely tomb, Museo della Villa Giulia © Scala.
Palestrina, S. Pomardi, charcoal, late 17th century, Ashby coll. © Biblioteca Vaticana.
400–1 *The Nile in flood*, mosaic, 2nd century BC, Museo Archeologico di Palestrina © Scala.

402 Statue of G. Pier Luigi da Palestrina, Piazza Regina Margherita, and Sant'Agapito church cl. G. Peyrot.
G. Lollobrigida on her donkey, film: *Pane, amore e Fantasia*, L. Comencini, 1953, private coll. Paris.
403 Theatrical mask, Ostia cl. J.-L. Malroux.
404 *The carters' journey*, mosaic cl. A. de Luca.
405 Statue of Minerva as a winged Victory, Piazzale della Vittoria, cl. *idem.*
406 Inscription of the Firemen's Barracks, cl. *idem.*
406–407 Theater and Piazzale delle Corporazioni © ENIT.
407 *Roman ship with a cargo of wheat*, 3rd century, fresco, Bibl. Vaticana © Michael Dixon.
408 Mosaic showing the Ostia lighthouse, cl. A. de Luca.
408–409 General view and details of the Merchants' mosaics, cl. *idem.*
409 *Idem.*, details.
410 *Mithras killing the bull*, marble, Museo d'Ostia © Scala.
410–411 Model of an *insula*, Museo de la Civiltà Romana © Scala.
411 Bar decoration of the Thermopolium, 4th century AD, Museo di Ostia © Scala.
Via dei Molini, Casa di Diana and Forum, cl. A. de Luca.
412 Temple of Hercules, cl. A. di Luca.
Latrines, Temple of Rome and Augustus, pavement of colored marble in the Casa di Psiche e Amore and Casa degli Aurigi, cl. *idem.*
413 Terme dei Sette Sagi and the Serapeum, cl. A. de Luca.
Cupid and Psyche, statue, cl. *idem.*
Carnet d'Auguste © Bibl. nat., Paris.
414 Mithraeum of Felicissimus, cl. A. de Luca.
Fresco in the Insula degli Volte Dipinte, cl. A. de Luca.
Naval Combat, frieze of the Tomb of Cartilius Poplicola, bas-relief © Scala.
414–15 Horrea of Hortensius, cl. *idem.*
415 *Dyer's workshop*, engraving in *La Vie des*

Grecs et des Romains, 1894, all rights reserved.
Campo Magna Mater, postcard, all rights reserved.
Fish market, cl. A. de Luca.
416 Castello di Giulio © ENIT. *Una Domenica in Agosto*, L. Emmer, 1949, private coll., Paris.
Lido d'Ostia, cl. S. Grandadan.
Via Severiana crossing the Isola Sacra © Luisa Ricciarini, Milan.
419 Railtracks, cl. It Dagherrotipo/G. Rinaldi.
Freeway tollgate, cl. Marka/M. Martino.
421 Bus, DR.
Haorse and carriage, DR.
422 Eden Hotel.
424 Market in Porta Portese, DR.
425 San Giovanni in Laterano, cl. A. Idini.
Coliseum, DR.
426 Hostaria Farnese, via dei Baulari, cl. M. Marzot.
Ice cream and cold drink kiosk, cl. Gallimard.
427 Teatro Eliseo, cl. G. Peyrot.
Open-air play © ENIT.
430-445 We would like to thank the following establishments for providing photographs: Atlante Star, Sant'Anselmo, Bolivar, Sant'Anna, Holiday Inn Crowne Plaza Minerva, Raphael, Teatro di Pompeo, Art Deco, Locarno, Lord Byron, Hotel Cavalieri Hilton, Gigetto al Portico d'Ottavia, Cecchino dal 1887, Les Étoiles, Papà Giovanni, Agata e Romeo, Cicilardone, Sorella Lella, Al Ceppo, Alberto Ciarla, Fendi, Buccone.

List of illustrators:

Cover:
H. Dixon, J.-M. Guillou, R. Hutchins.
Nature:
16–17 : J. Chevallier, J.-M. Kacédan, P. Robin, F. Desbordes.
18–19 : F. Desbordes, J. Chevallier, C. Felloni.
20–1 : A. Bodin, J. Wilkinson, C. Felloni, J. Chevallier.
22–3 : F. Desbordes, J. Chevallier, C. Felloni.

adopted by Caesar known as C. Julius Caesar Octavianus, took the name of Augustus in 27 BC), born Rome 63 BC, first Roman emperor (27 BC–14 AD): *28, 138, 140, 149, 157, 163, 164, 309–311*

Aurelian (Lucius Domitius Aurelianus) born c. 214 AD, Roman emperor 270–5: *128, 323*

Caligula (popular name of C. Julius Caesar Germanicus), born 12 AD, son of Germanicus and Agrippina; Roman emperor 37–41: *28, 149*

Caracalla (Marcus Aurelius Antonius Bassianus), born in Lyon 188 AD, Roman emperor 211–17: *139, 141, 298, 320*

Claudius II Gothicus (Marcus Aurelius Valerius Claudius), born 219 AD, Roman emperor 268–70: *416*

Claudius (Tiberius Claudius Nero Germanicus), born in Lyons 10 BC, Roman emperor 41–54 AD: *189, 251, 339, 405*

Commodus (Lucius Aelius Aurelius Commodus Antoninus), born 161 AD, Roman emperor 180–92: *133, 330*

Constantius II (Flavius Julius Constantius), born 317, son of Constantine the Great, emperor of the East 337–50, sole Roman emperor 350–61: *156, 166, 178*

Constantine I, the Great (Flavius Valerius Claudius Constantinus), born c. 280 AD, Roman emperor 306–37, sole Roman emperor from 324: *130, 145, 169, 192, 196, 200, 206, 377, 381*

Diocletian (Caius Valerius Aurelius Diocletianus), born in Dalmatia 245 AD, Roman emperor 284–305: *29, 139*

Domitian (Titus Flavius Domitianus), born 51 AD, Roman emperor 81–96: *149, 150, 165, 239, 276*

Faustina, empress, wife of the emperor Antoninus Pius, died 141 AD: *145, 268, 329*

Flavians, dynasty of three Roman emperors: Vespasian and his two sons, Titus and Domitian (69–96): *146, 162*

Gallienus (Publius

Licinius Egnatius Gallienus), born c. 218 AD, Roman emperor 253–68: *29, 340*

Geta (Publius Septimius Geta), born 189 AD, Roman emperor 211–12. Shared Imperial power for a few months with his brother Caracalla who had him murdered: *139*

Hadrian (Publius Aelius Hadrianus), born 76 AD, Roman emperor 117–38: *29, 132, 146, 200, 233, 239, 264, 267, 394*

Heliogabalus or Elagabalus (Varius Avitus Bassianus), born 204, high priest from Emesa, Roman emperor 218–22: *151, 321*

Honorius (Flavius Honorius), Constantinople 384–Ravenna 423, emperor of the West 395–423: *234, 339, 380*

Julia Domna, wife of Septimius Severus: *139, 156*

Julian the Apostate (Flavius Claudius Julianus), born at Constantinople 331 AD, married to Helen, daughter of Constantine, Roman emperor 361–63, tried to restore paganism: *188*

Livia (Livia Drusilla), 58 BC–29 AD, wife of Augustus. Had two children from a previous marriage, Tiberius and Drusus: *311*

Marcus Aurelius (Marcus Annius Verus, then Marcus Aelius Aurelius Antonius), Rome 121, Roman emperor 161–80: *130, 267*

Maxentius (Marcus Valerius Aurelius Maxentius), son of Maximian, Roman emperor 306–12, beaten by Constantine at the Milvian Bridge (312): *145, 328*

Maximian (Marcus Aurelius Maximianus), born c. 250, Roman emperor 286–305 (with Domitian) and 307–8 (tetrarchy): *334*

Nero (Lucius Domitius Ahenobarbarus, then Claudius Nero), born 37 AD, Roman emperor 54–68: *165*

Nerva (Marcus Cocceius Nerva), born 26 AD, Roman emperor 96–8: *165*

Octavian (see Augustus)

Septimius Severus (Lucius Septimius Severus), born in Leptis Magna (Africa) 146 AD, Roman emperor 193–211: *139, 141, 156, 158, 164*

Theodosius (Flavius Theodosius), born 347 AD, Roman emperor 379–95, the last to rule the whole empire: *29, 206*

Tiberius (Tiberius Claudius Nero), born 42 BC, Roman emperor 14–37 AD: *28, 141, 149, 335*

Titus (Titus Flavius Vespasianus), born c. 40, Roman emperor 79–81: *146, 169, 170, 339*

Trajan (Marcus Ulpius Traianus), born 53 AD, Roman emperor 98–117: *29, 139, 165, 405*

Valerian (Publius Licinius Valerianus), Roman emperor 253–60: *29, 326*

Vespasian (Titus Flavius Vespasianus), born 9 AD, Roman emperor 69–79: *132, 164, 170, 339*

SAINTS

Adalbertus (saint), c. 956–97, Bishop of Prague, martyred in Prussia, stayed several times in the monastery of St Boniface on the Aventine: *180*

Agapitus (saint), young man martyred at Praeneste in the reign of Aurelian, 274 AD. Patron saint of the town: *402*

Agnes (saint), young girl martyred in the middle of the 3rd century. The details of her passion were already legendary in the 4th century: *278, 380*

Alexis (saint), his legend, which originated in the East spread to the West only in the 10th century: *180*

Ambrose (saint), Trier c. 330/40–97, Bishop of Milan. Father and Doctor of the Roman Church: *309*

Aurea (saint and martyr), 3rd century, from a great family, owned a villa in Ostia. Was thrown into the sea with a millstone tied to her neck: *416*

Benoît-Joseph Labre (saint), Amettes 1748–Rome 1783, French, penitant mystic, mendicant pilgrim,

traveled through Europe: *347*

Bibiana (saint), virgin venerated in Rome from the end of the 5th century. According to a late passion, she was tied to a column and whipped to death during the reign of Julian the Apostate (4th century). It is said in a popular tradition that powder from the column and the grass growing around her church provides a cure for epilepsy: *339*

Bridget of Sweden (saint), c. 1303–c. 1373, mystic. A Swedish lady of means, widow, foundress of the Order of the Blessed Sacrament (Bridgetines). Died in Rome.

Catherine of Sienna (saint), (Catherine Benincasa), 1347–80, member of the Dominican Third Order, mystic, played a decisive role in the return of the popes from Avignon. Doctor of the Church: *260*

Cecilia (saint and martyr), 3rd century, the church that is dedicated to her was founded by a certain Roman matron named Caecilia in the 4th century: *326, 354*

Charles Borromeo (saint), 1538–84, Cardinal-archbishop of Milan, key figure of the Italian Counter-Reformation: *247, 309, 345*

Chrysogonus (saint), not much is known about this person who was probably martyred under Diocletian. Often confused with St Chrysogonus of Aquileia (4th century): *356*

Constantinia, 4th century, daughter of the emperor Constantine, tradition gradually transformed her into a saint (St Constance): *380*

Cosmas and Damian (saints), brothers, Syrian doctors, probably martyred under Diocletian. The cult of these saints had a major iconographic impact: *168*

Dominic Guzman (saint), came from Castile, 1170–1221, founder of the Order of Friars Preachers (Dominicans): *179, 321*

Eligius (saint), born near Limoges c. 580, Bishop of Noyon 641–60 when he died.

King Dagobert's treasurer. Goldsmith and patron of goldsmiths: *243*

Four Crowned Saints (Santi Quattro Coronati), their legend: *192*

Francesca Romana (saint), Rome 1384–1440, Francesca Buzzi, widow of the noble Ponziani, foundress of the Oblates of Tor de'Specchi (Benedictine rule): *159, 169*

Francis of Assisi (Il Poverello), 1181–1226, founder of the Order of Franciscans: *354*

Francis of Paola (saint), Paola, Calabria 1416–1507, founder of the Order of Minims, died in France where he was summoned by Louis XI.

Gaetano di Thiene (saint), Vicenza 1480–1547, founder of the Theatine Fathers: *250*

Helen (saint), c. 255–338, mother of Emperor Constantine. According to tradition, she discovered the True Cross in Jerusalem and brought relics of Christ's passion back to Rome: *199*

Ignatius of Loyola (saint), born 1491, a Spanish gentleman, founder of the Society of Jesus (Jesuits), died in Rome 1556: *383*

Jerome (saint), c. 341–420, Doctor of the Church, translated the Bible into Latin (Vulgate). Was a hermit in Palestine, often portrayed in the company of a lion. Venerated in Rome where he spent many years: *231*

John and Paul (saints), venerated as martyrs since the 4th century, a church on the Coelian Hill is dedicated to them.There is no historical proof of their existence: *188*

Lawrence (saint), Deacon of the Church of Rome, martyred in 258. According to a late version of his passion he was burnt on a grid: *381*

Lodovica Albertoni (Blessed) 1474–1553, widow, Tertiary of St Francis, died in Rome: *354*

Monica (saint), Carthage c. 331–84, mother of St Augustine.

Died at Ostia as she was about to return to Africa with her son: *285*

Nereus and Achilleus (saints), according to one legend they were soldiers in charge of persecuting Christians, miraculously converted and themselves martyred, either under Nero (1st century) or under Diocletian (end of 3rd century). Legend of their church: *321*

Pantaleon (saint), doctor who treated patients free, apparently martyred in Nicomedia 305: *279*

Paul (saint), apostle, born at Tarsus, martyred in Rome c. 65 AD: *192, 247, 327, 328, 344, 382*

Peter (saint), apostle, martyred in Rome between 64 and 67 AD: *131, 181, 206, 209, 212, 321, 324, 327, 344*

Petronilla (saint), Roman virgin venerated as a martyr of the 1st century. According to her legend she was St Peter's daughter. Protectress of Frankish kings and the kings of France since the 8th century: *206*

Philip Neri (saint), Florence 1515–Rome 1595, popular saint, priest founder of the Congregation of the Oratory (Oratorians), sometimes referred to as the "Second Apostle of Rome": *190, 240, 279, 281*

Praxedes (saint), (1st–2nd century), Roman virgin, daughter of Pudens, sister of Pudentiana (see these names): *344*

Prisca (saint), founder of a church on the Aventine, honored as a 1st century martyr. Her legend: *181*

Pudens (saint), martyr (1st century), Roman senator converted by St Peter, father of Praxedes and Pudentiana (see these names). Possibly confused with another Pudens who founded a church in his house in the 3rd century: *344*

Pudentiana (saint), (1st–2nd century), virgin died aged 16. Daughter of Pudens, sister of Praxedes (see these names): *344*

Sabina (saint), founder of the basilica which bears her name, in the 5th century. A Sabina has been honored as a

2nd-century martyr since the 4th century. Her legend: *179*

Sebastian (saint), Roman martyr (end of 3rd century–beginning of 4th). The details of his legend were developed in the 5th century, officer of Diocletian, he was shot with arrows, survived and then beaten to death: *151, 180, 327*

Stanislaus Kostka (saint), 1550–68, Polish saint, died aged 18 in Rome while a novice with the Jesuits: *296*

Tarcisius (saint and deacon), 3rd century martyr. Known because of an inscription by Pope Damasus. Rather than surrender the Eucharist that he was taking to captive Christians he let himself be murdered. The legend often portrays him as a child: *326*

Teresa of Avila (saint), Avila, 1515–82, Spanish Carmelite nun, mystic, Doctor of the Church: *294*

POPES

Alexander III Bandinelli, Sienese, pope 1159–81: *358*

Alexander VI Borgia, Jativa (Spain), pope 1492–1503: *215, 243, 252, 343*

Alexander VII Chigi, Sienna, pope 1655–67: *210, 212, 213, 280, 307, 308, 382*

Anterus (saint), Greek, pope 235–6: *326*

Benedict III, Roman, pope 855–8: *343*

Benedict XIV Lambertini, Bologna 1675, pope 1740–58: *281, 342*

Boniface IX Tomacelli, Neapolitan, pope 1389–1404: *130*

Calixtus I (saint), Roman, pope 217–22, ex-slave became a deacon in charge of the cemetery which bears his name, then pope: *326, 358*

Celestine I (saint), Campania, pope 422–32: *179*

Clement I (saint), pope 91–101: *193, 194*

Clement XI Albani, Urbino 1649, pope 1700–21: *264*

Clement VIII Aldobrandini, Fano 1536, pope 1592–1605: *168, 343*

Clement X Altieri, Rome 1590, pope

1670–6: *344*

Clement XII Corsini, Florence 1652, pope 1730–40: *297*

Clement XIV Ganganelli, Sant'Arcangelo di Romagna 1705, pope 1769–74: *215, 301*

Clement VII Medici, Florence 1478, pope 1523–34: *234, 239, 274, 378*

Clement XIII Rezzonico, Venice 1693, pope 1758–69: *213*

Clement IX Rospigliosi, Pistoia 1600, pope 1667–9: *32, 240*

Cornelius (saint), Roman, pope 251–3: *326*

Eugenius III Paganelli, Montemagno, pope 1145–53: *214, 343*

Eugenius IV Condulmer, Venice 1383, pope 1431–47: *274*

Eusebius (saint), Greek, pope 309–10: *326*

Eutychian (saint), Luni (Tuscany), pope 275–83: *326*

Fabian (saint), Roman, pope 236–50: *326*

Felix IV (saint), Benevento, pope 526–30: *168, 191*

Gelasius I (saint), African, pope 492–6: *323*

Gregory I the Great (saint), Rome c. 540, pope 590–604, Doctor of the Church. Turned his family home on the Coelian Hill into a monastery: *182, 187, 235*

Gregory III (saint), Syrian, pope 731-41: *356*

Gregory IV, Roman, pope 827–44: *162, 358*

Gregory VI Graziano, Roman, pope 1045–6 (abdication): *323*

Gregory VII Hildebrand (saint), Sovana (Tuscany) c. 1015–20, pope 1073–85: *234, 323*

Gregory IX Segni, Anagni c. 1145, pope 1227–41: *353*

Gregory XI de Beaufort, French, Maumont 1329, pope 1370–8. Last of the Avignon popes, returned to Rome in 1377: *197, 342*

Gregory XIII Boncompagni, Bologna 1502, pope 1572–85: *191, 213, 281, 297, 342*

Gregory XVI Capellari, Belluno 1765, pope 1831–46: *391*

BIOGRAPHICAL INDEX ◆

Hadrian I, pope 772–95: *155, 358, 380, 382*

Hadrian VI Florenz, Utrecht 1459, pope 1522–3, last non-Italian pope before John-Paul II: *280*

Honorius I, Campania, pope 625–38: *380*

Honorius III Savelli, Roman, pope 1216–27: *179, 382*

Honorius II Scannabecchi, Bologna, pope 1124–30: *157*

Innocent XIII Conti, Rome 1655, pope 1721–4: *314*

Innocent VIII Cybo, Genoa 1432, pope 1484–92: *214*

Innocent X Pamphili, Rome 1574, pope 1644–55: *209, 240, 269, 276, 278, 279, 368*

Innocent II Papareschi, Roman, pope 1130–43: *358*

Innocent XII Pignatelli, Spinazzola (Basilicata) 1615, pope 1691–1700: *269*

Innocent III Segni, Gavignano 1160, pope 1198–1216: *168, 199, 214, 321*

John I (saint), pope 523-6: *191*

John VII, Greek, pope 705–7: *142*

John X, Ravenna c. 860, pope 914–28: *179*

John XXIII Roncalli, Sotto il Monte (near Bergamo) 1881, pope 1958–63: *211*

Julius III Ciocchi del Monte, Rome 1487, pope 1550-5: *370*

Julius II Della Rovere, Savona 1443, pope 1503–13: *209, 215, 235, 274, 240, 280, 346, 359, 360, 416*

Leo III (saint), Rome 750, pope 795–816: *197, 198, 321*

Leo IV (saint), Roman, pope 847-55: *192, 206, 234*

Leo XII Della Genga, Ancona 1760, pope 1823–9: *253*

Leo X Medici, Florence 1475, pope 1513-21: *161, 190, 197, 215, 241, 249, 274, 347, 360*

Leo XIII Pecci, Carpinetto Romano, pope 1878–1903: *253*

Liberius, Roman, pope 352–66: *342*

Lucius I (saint), Roman, pope 253–4: *326*

Mark (saint), Roman, pope January–October 366: *162*

Martin V Colonna, Genazzano 1368, pope 1417–31: *130, 197, 300, 416*

Miltiades (or Melchiades) (saint), African, pope 311–14: *196*

Nicholas IV Masci, Ascoli c. 1230, pope 1288–92: *343*

Nicholas III Orsini, Rome 1210/1220, pope 1277–80: *214, 234*

Nicholas V Parentucelli, Pisa 1398, pope 1447–55: *214, 234*

Paschal I (saint), Roman, pope 817–24: **190, 342, 343, 345**

Paschal II Raniero, Bieda (near Ravenna) c. 1050, pope 1099–1118: *192, 307, 312, 354*

Paul I (saint), Roman, pope 757–67: *143*

Paul II Barbo, Venice 1417, pope 1464–71: *161, 168, 274*

Paul V Borghese, Rome 1552, pope 1605–21: *32, 165, 209, 298, 311, 343, 357, 363, 364*

Paul IV Carafa, Naples 1476, pope 1555–9: *197, 252*

Paul III Farnese, Canino 1468, pope 1534–49: *31, 129, 215, 234, 244, 247, 257, 274*

Pelagius II, Rome 520, pope 579–90: *382*

Pius I (saint), Aquileia, pope 140–55: *344*

Pius VI Braschi, Cesena (Emilia) 1717, pope 1775–99: *318*

Pius VII Chiaramonti, Cesena (Emilia) 1742, pope 1800–23: *215*

Pius V Ghislieri (saint), Bosco Marengo (Lombardy) 1504, pope 1566–72: *343*

Pius IV Medici, Milan 1499, pope 1559–65: *161, 215, 247, 289, 294, 334*

Pius II Piccolomini, Corsignano, today Pienza 1405, pope 1458–64: *250, 391*

Pius IX Ratti, Desio (Lombardy) 1857, pope 1922–39: *198, 215*

Pius III Todeschini-Piccolomini, Sienna 1436, pope for 26 days, October–November 1503: *250*

Pontian (saint), Roman, pope 230-5, persecuted under Maximinus I, deported to Sardinia where he died: *326*

Sylvester I (saint), Roman, pope 314–35: *208, 346*

Simplicius (saint), Tivoli, pope 468–83: *191*

Sixtus II (saint), Greek, pope 257–8: *326*

Sixtus III (saint), Roman, pope 432–40: *179, 312, 342, 381*

Sixtus IV Della Rovere, Savona 1414, pope 1471–84: *214, 240, 274, 280, 306, 363*

Sixtus V Peretti, Grottamare 1520, pope 1585–90: *32, 131, 215, 253, 289, 295, 306, 332, 343*

Stephen II, Roman, pope 752–7: *206*

Stephen III, Sicilian, pope 768–72: *159*

Symmachus (saint), Sardinian, pope 498–514: *206, 214, 346*

Urban VIII Barberini, Florence 1568, pope 1623–44: *32, 131, 132, 212, 230, 265, 290, 291, 314, 339*

Urban V de Grimoard (Blessed), French, born near Mende 1310, died in Avignon, pope 1362–70

Zephyrinus (saint), Roman, pope 195–217: *326*

CARDINALS AND PRIESTS

Bessarione, Cardinal Giovanni, Trebizond c. 1402–72, Byzantine humanist and theologian living in Rome: *321*

Corsini, Neri, Florence 1685–Rome 1770, cardinal, actually governed the Church during the last years of Clement XII's pontificate: *362*

Della Rovere (see Julius II, pope)

Este (Cardinal Ippolito d'-), 1509–72, humanist and patron of the arts, belonged to the illustrious Este family from Ferrara. Died in his villa at Tivoli: *392*

Luther, Martin, Eisleben (Thuringen) 1483–1546, Church reformer: *260*

Mazzarino, Cardinal Giulio, 1602–61, French statesman of Italian origin: *298, 314*

Peter of Illyria, Roman priest of Illyrian origin, appointed by Pope Celestine I (422–32) to direct the construction of the Basilica of Santa Sabina on the Aventine: *179*

Ricci di Montepulciano, cardinal: *242, 315, 369*

KINGS AND QUEENS

Alaric I, king of the Visigoths 395–412, captured and sacked Rome (410): *177*

Alberico I, Marchese of Camerino, Duke of Spoleto, died c. 925 during an assault against Pope John X: *179*

Charlemagne, 742–814, king of the Francs in 768, crowned emperor of the Western Empire in 800 at Rome: *197, 206*

Charles V, born 1500, King of Spain in 1516, emperor of Germany in 1519. His troops captured and sacked Rome in 1527. He abdicated in 1556: *129*

Christina of Sweden, born 1626, queen of Sweden 1632–54, converted to Roman Catholicism, abdicated and opted for exile in Rome where she died in 1689: *214, 306, 362, 364*

Cleopatra VII, queen of Egypt 51–30 BC until her suicide after the Battle of Actium in 31: *143*

Henry IV, born 1050, German emperor 1056–1106. In his fight against the papacy he captured Rome in 1084: *234*

Louis XIV, born 1638, king of France 1643–1715: *316*

Napoleon I, Ajaccio St Helena 1769–1821, emperor of the French 1804–15: *40, 161, 315, 372*

Otto III, Paterno (near Viterbo) 980, German emperor 983–1002. Dreamed of reconstituting the Christian empire. Asserted his authority over Italy and settled in Rome from which he was finally expelled: *180, 352*

Phocas, Byzantine emperor 602–10: *141, 257, 262*

Theodoric the Great, c. 455–Ravenna 526, king of the Ostrogoths 474–526: *170*

Totila, king of the Ostrogoths 541–52, seized Rome in 546: *183, 234*

Umberto I, born in Turin 1844, second king of Italy 1878–1900, murdered by an anarchist: *302*

Victor Emmanuel II, Turin 1820, king of Piedmont-Sardinia 1849–61, first king of unified Italy from 1861–78: *160, 266*

Witigis, king of the Ostrogoths 526–40: *234*

GREAT FAMILIES

Aldobrandini, famous family, originally from Florence: 258, 372 (see Clement VIII, pope)

Anguillara, family name comes from their fiefdom on the Lake of Bracciano. Known in the 11th–12th centuries. Extinct by the 18th century: 351, 356, 357

Barberini, great Roman family originally from Barberino, near Florence: 265, 289–92, 398 (see Urban VIII, pope)

Bonaparte (family): 260, 309

Borghese, noble Roman family originally from Sienna; Cardinal Camillo elected pope in 1605 (see Paul V, pope); Cardinal Scipione: 188, 311, 372

Borgia, family originally from Aragon (12th century) moved to Rome when Alfonso became Pope Calixtus III in 1455. (See Alexander VI, pope)

Caetani, noble family originally from Gaeta, mentioned since the 12th century. Pope Boniface VIII 1294–1303. Still extinct: 168, 318, 330, 352

Capocci, noble Roman family in the Middle Ages, known since the 11th century: 346

Cenci, noble Roman family known especially because of the tragic story of Beatrice Cenci (16th century): 234, 254

Chigi, family of bankers originally from Sienna, which asserted itself in Rome in the 15th–16th centuries. Agostino: 307, 360, 363, 378 (see Alexander VIII, pope)

Colonna, Roman princely family mentioned as early as the 11th century. Very influential in Rome 13th–17th centuries: 298, 300, 310, 398

Cybo, family originally from Genoa, influential from the 15th century, now extinct: 307 (see Innocent VIII, pope)

Falconieri, great family originally from Tuscany which settled in Rome in the 16th century: 244

Farnese, noble family from upper Lazio, extinct by 1731; Cardinal Alexander (1468–1549) became Pope Paul III; Cardinal Alexander (1520–89), known as the Great Cardinal: 257, 360

Frangipani, noble Roman family played a major role in the Middle Ages, extinct by the 17th century: 146, 168, 284

Mattei, noble Roman family extinct by 1801: 190, 253, 351

Medici, merchants and bankers from Florence who became princes. Very influential 15th–18th centuries, especially in Tuscany. In Rome: 272, 347; Cardinal Ferdinand de' Medici (1548–1609): 315 (see Clement VII and Leo X, popes)

Odescalchi, family originally from Como, already mentioned in the 13th century. Settled in Rome when Benedetto Odescalchi was elected pope, taking the name of Innocent XI: 301

Orsini, powerful Roman family known since the 10th century, rivals of the Colonna, three of its members were made pope: 31 (see Nicholas III, pope)

Pamphili, noble Roman family originally from Gubbio whose direct lineage became extinct in 1760; title inherited by the Doria branch: 278 (see Innocent X, pope)

Papareschi, noble Roman family established in Trastevere, very powerful in the 12th–13th centuries, extinct by the 15th century: 351, 353 (see Innocent II, pope)

Pierleoni, noble Roman family settled on the Isola Tiberina: 352

Sacchetti, Florentine family, a branch of which settled in Rome in the 16th century: 242

Savelli, noble Roman family, powerful in the Middle Ages, became extinct in 1712. Two of its members became pope: 179 (see Honorius III, pope)

Spada, originally from Gubbio this family is now extinct: 243, 246

ARTISTS AND ARCHITECTS

Albani, Francesco, Bologna 1578–1660, painter: 259

Alberti, Leon Battista, Genoa 1404–72, architect: 233

Algardi, Alessandro, Bologna 1595–1654, sculptor, architect and painter: 133, 261, 368

Ameli, Paolo, active in Rome 1730–49, architect: 259

Ammanati, Bartolomeo, Settignano (Florence) 1511–92, sculptor and architect: 312, 370

Andrea del Sarto, Florence 1486–1531, painter: 292

Angelico (Fra) (Guido di Pietro, as a monk he was known as Fra Giovanni da Fiesole or Il Beato) Vicchio c. 1387–1455, painter: 214, 226, 260

Armanni, Osvaldo, Perugia 1855–1929, architect: 254

Arnolfo di Cambio, Colle Val d'Elsa, Sienna c. 1245–1302, architect and sculptor: 132, 354, 383

Baciccia or **Baciccio** (Giovanni Battista Gaulli), Genoa 1639–1709, painter: 258, 278, 301, 354

Baglione, Giovanni, Rome 1573–1644, painter

Bandinelli, Baccio, Florence 1493–1560, sculptor: 378

Baratta, Giovanni Maria, Massa Carrara, 17th century, architect: 285

Barocci, Federico, Urbino c. 1535–1612, painter: 281

Basile, Ernesto, Palermo 1857–1932, architect: 269

Bassano, Francesco (da Ponte) the Younger, Bassano del Grappa, 1549–92, painter: 257

Batoni, Pompeo, Lucca 1707–87, painter: 335

Bazzani, Cesare, Rome 1873–1939, architect: 215

Bernich, Ettore, Rome 1845 or 1848–1914, architect: 339

Bernini, Gian Lorenzo, Naples 1598–1680, architect, painter and sculptor: 133, 209, 210, 212, 213, 215, 260, 261, 265, 269, 276, 277, 285, 290, 291, 295–297, 301, 306, 307, 312, 313, 339, 356, 373, 393

Bernini, Pietro, (father of Gian Lorenzo), Sesto Fiorentino (Florence) 1562–1629, sculptor: 314

Bianchi, Salvatore, Rome 1821–84, architect: 338

Bigot, Paul, 1870–1942, French architect, Prix de Rome 1900, designed the model of Rome in the 4th century: 388

Borgognone, see: Courtois Guillaume

Borromini, Francesco, Bissone (Ticino) 1599–1667, architect: 198, 241, 244, 246, 272, 278, 282, 283, 291, 295, 299, 313, 323

Bracci, Filippo, Rome (?) 1727–after 1746, painter: 213

Bracci, Pietro, Rome 1700–73, sculptor: 298

Bramante (Donato di Pascuccio), Monte Asdruvaldo (near Urbino) 1444–1514, architect and painter: 145, 167, 209, 215, 235, 249, 263, 281, 364

Brandi, Giacinto, Poli (Rome) 1623–91, painter: 302, 309

Bregno, Andrea, Osteno (Como) 1418/1421–1503/1506architect and sculptor: 306

Bronzino, Agnolo di Cosimo, Florence 1503–72, painter: 259, 293, 299

Burne-Jones, Sir Edward Coley, Birmingham 1833–98, British painter: 348

Caffi, Ippolito, Belluno (Veneto) 1809–66, painter: 103, 279

Calandra, Davide, Turin 1856–1915, sculptor: 270

Calderini, Guglielmo, Perugia 1837–1916, architect: 236, 383

Canova, Antonio, Possagno (Treviso) 1757–1822, sculptor: 40, 213, 279, 284, 301

Caravaggio, Il (Michelangelo Merisi), Caravaggio (Bergamo) 1571/1572–1610, painter: 230, 259, 271, 285, 292, 293, 307, 359, 362, 369

Carimini, Luca, Rome 1830–90, architect: 333

Carracci, family of painters from Bologna; Annibale, 1560–1609: 244, 245, 259, 266, 300, 307; Agostino (his brother) 1557–1602: 245

Castelli, Domenico, known as Il Fontanino, Melide (Ticino), architect active in Rome 1619–58: 243

Cavaliere d'Arpino, (Giuseppe Cesari), Arpino (Frosinone) 1568–1640, painter: 198, 301, 322, 343, 365, 372

Cavallini, Pietro, painter and mosaic artist, active in Rome 1273–1321: 130, 354, 356, 358, 359

Cellini, Benvenuto, Florence 1500–71, sculptor and goldsmith: 234

church 391
Santa Maria Maggiore, dome of 263
Santa Maria Maggiore, mosaics of 343
Santa Maria Maggiore, Piazza 342
Santa Maria dei Miracoli 307
Santa Maria in Monserrato, church 243
Santa Maria di Montesanto, church 307
Santa Maria dell'Orazione e Morte, oratory 244
Santa Maria della Pace, church 280
Santa Maria della Pace, cloister 280
Santa Maria del Popolo, church 306
Santa Maria del Popolo, dome of 262
Santa Maria del Priorato, church 180
Santa Maria della Scala, church 359
Santa Maria Scala Coeli, church 388
Santa Maria dei Sette Dolori, church 364
Santa Maria sopra Minerva, church 260
Santa Maria del Suffragio, church 242
Santa Maria in Trastevere, basilica 357
Santa Maria in Trastevere, Piazza 357
Santa Maria in Vallicella, church 281
Santa Maria in Via, church 301
Santa Maria in Via Lata, church 260
Santa Maria della Vittoria, church 294
Santa Maria della Vittoria, dome of 263
Santa Prassede, church 344
Santa Prisca, church 181
Santa Pudenziana, church 344
Santa Sabina, church 179
Santa Susanna, church 294
Santi Ambrogio e Carlo al Corso, church 263, 309
Santi Andrea Claudio dei Borgognoni, church 302
Santi Apostoli, basilica 300
Santi Bonifacio e Alessio, church 180
Santi Cosma e Damiano, church 168
Santi Giovanni e Paolo, church 188
Santi Luca e Martina, church 131
Santi Nereo e Achilleo, church 321
Santi Quattro Coronati, church 192
Santi Vincenzo e

Anastasio, church 388
Santissmo Nome di Maria, church 167
Santissima Trinità dei Pellegrini, church of the 246
Santo Bambino, legend of the 131
Santo Stefano Rotondo, church 191
Sapienza, Palazzo alla 272
Sarcophagus of the Bride and Bridegroom 371
Saturn, Temple of 140
Scala Regia 215
Scala Santa 199
Sciarra, Galleria 301
Scienze, Palazzo delle 387
Scimia, Torre della 284
Scipio Barbatus, Sarcophagus of 322
Scipios, Tomb of the 322
Secular Games 158
Senate (Italian) 272
Septimius Severus, Arch of 139
Serapeum 413
Sette Sagi, Termi dei 413
Settimiana, Porta 359
Seven Churches 240
Sibilla, Tempio della 391
Sistina, Capella (Sistine Chapel) 218, 243
Sistine Chapel, restoration of 55
Sisto, Ponte 363
Small Baths (Villa Adriana) 396
Spada, Cappella 243
Spada, Palazzo 246
Spagna, Palazzo di 313
Spagna, Piazza di 313
Spanish Steps 313, 314
Sphere, Fountain of the 378
Spina 178
Spirito Santo dei Napoletani, church 242
Sport, Palazzo degli 388
S.P.Q.R. 152
Spring, Feast of 49
St Clement, miracle of 194
St Louis de France
Stadio dei Marmi 377
Stadio Olimpico 378
Stamperia, Via della 298
Statues, talking 46, 260, 279
Stazione Termini 338
Sublicius, Ponte 154
Synagogue 254

T

Tabularium 64, 128, 141
Tarpeian Rock 128
Tartarughe Fountain 254
Teatro Argentina 251
Teatro Eliseo 348
Teatro di Marcello 157
Tempe, Terrace of 394
Tempietto 364
Terme, Museo delle 335, 336
Terme, Palazzo delle 378

Terrina, Fontana della 281
Testaccio 184
Tetrarchy 29
Theater, Maritime 395
Theatines, Order of the 250
Tiberina, Isola 352
Tiberinus, Portus 154
Tibur 390
Tiburtina, Via 390
Titus, Arch of 146
Tivoli 390
Tobacco Factory 356
Tombs 319
Tor Sanguigna, Piazza 283
Torre di Roccabruna 397
Tosca 250
Trajan, Baths of 174
Trajan, Forum of 165
Trajan, Market of 167
Trajan's Column 166
Trappists 388
Trastevere 350
Trastevere, Viale 356
Tre Fontane, Abbazia delle 388
Treaty of Rome 33
Trent, Council of 31
Trevi Fountain 298, 299
Trevi Fountain, restoration of the 55
Trevi River 298
Tribunes of the people 27
Trilussa, Piazza 363
Trinità dei Monti, church 314
Trinità dei Monti, Obelisk of the 294
Trinità dei Monti, steps of the 314
Tritone Fountain 290
Triumph of the Cross 193
Tullianum Prison 131

U

Ulpia, basilica 165
University Campus 382
Urban VIII, Tomb of 213

V

Valadier, Casina 316
Vallicelliana, Biblioteca 282
Vandals 29
Varianus, Circus of 200
Vatican, The 202–36
Vatican Council II 33
Vatican Pinacoteca (Picture Gallery) 215
Velabro River 136
Veneto, Via 302
Venezia, Museo del Palazzo 161
Venezia, Piazza 160
Venus Cloacina, shrine of 138
Venus Genitrix, Temple of 163
Venus Victrix, Temple of 248
Vespasian and Titus, Temple of 141
Vestals, House of the 144
Via della Foce,

Republican Shrine of the 412
Via di Diana, Museo della 411
Via Ostiensis 404
Via Sacra 144
Vigiles, Barracks of the 406
Vigna 368
Villa Torlonia, gardens of the 381
Villino Ximenes 381
Vittoria, Piazzale della 405
Vittoriano 376
Vittorio Emanuele, Ponte di 122
Vittorio Emanuele, Biblioteca Nazionale 335
Vittorio Emanuele II, Piazza 340
Volte Dipinte, Via delle 414

W

Well of the Sortes 399

X

Ximines, Villano 381

Z

Zuccari, Palazzetto 314

MONUMENTS

Academies
–American Academy 365
–dell'Arcadia 364
–British School at Rome 376
–di Educazione Fisica 378
–di Finlandia 365
–di Francia 315
–dei Lincei 362
–di Spagna 364
–Nazionale di San Luca 299

Antiquarium
–of the Forum 146
–of the Palatine 151
Aqueducts
–Aqua Claudia 339
–Aqua Felice 289, 294
–Aqua Paola 363, 364
–Aqua Vergine 314
–Aqua Virgo 266, 277, 298

Ara Pacis Augustae 310
Area Sacra del Largo Argentina 250
Arches
–of Augustus
–of Constantine 169
–of Dolabella 190
–of Drusus 324
–of Gallienus 340
–of Janus 156

◆INDEX

–of the Money Changers 156
–of Septimius Severus 139
–of Titus 146

Auditorium of Maecenas 341
Aurelian Wall, the 306, 323

Basilicas (ancient)
–Aemilia 136
–Agrippa's 266
–of Maxentius and Constantine 145
–Ulpia 165

Basilicas (Christian)
see **Churches**

Baths, terme
–of Agrippa 266
–of Buticosus 413
–of Caracalla 319
–of Diocletian 288, 334
–of Neptune 406
–of the Seven Sages 413
–of Trajan 174

Bridges, ponte
–Cestius 353
–Fabricius 353
–Milvio 377
–Rotto 352
–Sant'Angelo 239
–Sisto 363
–Sublicius 154
–Vittorio Emanuele II 122
Canopus 397
Capitol (Campidoglio) 129
Capitolium of Ostia 411
Castra Praetoria 335

Catacombs
–of San Callisto 326
–of San Sebastiano 327

Cento Camerelle 396

Chapels
–Altemps 358
–Antamoro 243
–of the Blessed Sacrament 356
–Caetani 344
–Cenci 254
–Cerasi 307
–Chigi 280, 307
–Cornaro 294
–Cybo 307
–Fonseca 312
–Pauline 215, 343
–Ponzetti 281
–Raymondi 364
–of the Relics 200
–della Rovere 307
–St Silvester 192
–St Zeno 345
–Sistine 218, 343
–Spada 243

Churches and basilicas (Christian)
–Chiesa Nuova 281
–Domine Quo Vadis 324
–Il Gesù 257
–the Lateran 198
–della Madonna dell'Orto 354
–Nostra Signora al Sacro Cuore 278
–dei Re Magi 313
–San Bartolomeo 352
–San Benedetto in Piscinula 353
–San Bernardo alle Terme 295, 334
–San Bonaventura 151
–San Callisto 357
–San Carlo ai Catinari 247
–San Carlo alle Quattro Fontane 295, 296
–San Cesareo 322
–San Claudio de' Borgognoni 302
–San Clemente 193
–San Crisogono 356
–San Francesco a Ripa 354
–San Giacomo 309
–San Giorgio in Velabro 156
–San Giovanni Calibata 353
–San Giovanni dei Fiorentini 241
–San Giovanni Battista dei Genovesi 353
–San Giovanni in Laterano 198
–San Giovanni in Porta Latina 323
–San Girolamo della Carità 243
–San Giuseppe ai Falegnami 131
–San Gregorio Magno 187
–San Lorenzo in Damaso 249
–San Lorenzo fuori le Mura 381
–San Lorenzo in Lucina 312
–San Lorenzo in Miranda 145
–San Lorenzo in Panisperna 347
–San Luigi dei Francesi 271
–San Marcello al Corso 301
–San Marco 162
–San Martino ai Monti 346
–San Nicola 280
–San Nicola a Capo di Bove 330
–San Nicola in Carcere 156
–San Pantaleo 279
–San Paolo alla Regola 247
–San Paolo, cloister of 382
–San Paolo entro le Mura 348
–San Paolo fuori le Mura 382
–San Pietro 209–13
–San Pietro in Montorio 364
–San Pietro in Vincoli 346
–San Saba 182
–San Salvatore in Lauro 283
–San Sebastiano, church 151
–San Sebastiano, basilica 327
–San Silvestro al Quirinale 298, 392
–San Silvestro in Capite 302
–San Sisto Vecchio 321
–San Teodoro 142
–San Tommaso dei Cenci 254
–Sant'Agapito 402
–Sant'Agnese fuori le Mura 380
–Sant'Agnese in Agone 278
–Sant'Agostino 284
–Sant'Andrea delle Fratte 313
— Sant'Andrea al Quirinale 296
–Sant'Andrea della Valle 250
–Sant'Angelo in Pescheria 159
–Sant'Antonio dei Portoghesi 284
–Sant'Apollinare 285
–Sant'Eligio degli Orefici 243
–Sant'Ignazio 261
–Sant'Ivo 272
–Sant'Omobono 156
–Sant'Urbano alla Caffarella 328
–Santa Aurea 416
–Santa Bibiana 339
–Santa Caterina dei Funari 254
–Santa Cecilia 353
–Santa Croce in Gerusalemme 200
–Santa Dorotea 363
–Santa Francesca Romana 169
–Santa Francesca in Tor de' Specchi 159
–Santa Maria degli Angeli 334
–Santa Maria Antiqua 143
–Santa Maria dell'Anima 280
–Santa Maria in Aracoeli 130
–Santa Maria in Campitelli 159
–Santa Maria in Campo Marzio 270
–Santa Maria in Cappella 353
–Santa Maria della Concezione 290
–Santa Maria in Cosmedin 154, 155
–Santa Maria in Domnica 190
— Santa Maria di Loreto 167
–Santa Maria Maddalena 270
–Santa Maria Maggiore, basilica 342
–Santa Maria Maggiore, church 391
–Santa Maria di Monserrato 243
–Santa Maria di Montesanto 307
–Santa Maria della Pace 280
–Santa Maria della Pace, cloister of 281
–Santa Maria del Popolo 306
–Santa Maria del Priorato 180
–Santa Maria della Scala 359
–Santa Maria dei Sette Dolori 364
–Santa Maria sopra Minerva 260
–Santa Maria del Suffragio 242
–Santa Maria in Trastevere 357
–Santa Maria in Vallicella 281
–Santa Maria in Via 301
–Santa Maria della Vittoria 294
–Santa Prassede 344
–Santa Prisca 181
–Santa Sabina 179
–Santa Susanna 294
–Santi Ambrogio e Carlo al Corso 309
–Santi Apostoli 300
–Santi Bonifacio e Alessio 180
–Santi Cosma e Damiano 168
–Santi Giovanni e Paolo 188
–Santi Luca e Martina 131
–Santi Nereo e Achilleo 321
–Santi Quattro Coronati 192
–Santi Pietro e Paolo 388
–Santi Vincenzo e Anastasio 388
–Santissimo Nome di Maria 167
–Santo Stefano Rotondo 191
–Spirito Santo dei Napoletani 242
–Tre Fontane, Abbazia delle 388
–Trinità dei Monti 314
–Trinità dei Pellegrini 246

Circuses
–Flaminius 157
–Maxentius 328
–Maximus 177
–Varianus 200

Cloaca Maxima 156
Collegio di Propaganda Fide 313
Collegio Romano 258
Coliseum 123, 170
Columbarium of Pomponius Hylas 322

Columns, colonna
–of Antoninus Pius 268
–of Marcus Aurelius 267
–of Phocas 141
–of Trajan 166
Comitium 138

Convents
–of the Sacred Heart 315

omus
Augustana 150
Aurea 174
Flavia 150
Fulminata 414
Severiana 151
Tiberiana 149

orticos, porticus
degli Argonauti 266
dei Dei Consentes
40
Minucia Frumentaria
51
d'Ottavia 158
di Pompeio (and
eater) 248

xcubitorium 356

oro Italico 277

orums
of Augustus 163
Boarium 155
of Caesar 163
Holitorium 154
Imperial 162
of Nerva 165
of Ostia 411
Roman 136
of Trajan 165
Transitorium 165

ountains, fontana
delle Api (Bee Fountain
90
Aqua Felice 295
della Barcaccia (Boat
ountain) 314
del Bicchierone 393
dei Draghi (Fountain of
e Dragons) 393
del Facchino 393
di Nettuno 123, 278
di Juturna 142
del Mascherone 244
del Moro 278
delle Naiadi 334
della Navicella 190
dei Fiumi (Rivers)
77
Roman fountains 366
dell'Organo Idraulico
93
della Rometta 393
della Sfera (Fountain
f the Sphere) 378
della Terrina 281
delle Tartarughe
Tortoise Fountain)
54
di Trevi 298, 299
del Tritone (Triton
ountain) 290
Villa d'Este 393

alleria Sciarra 301

ates, porta
Appia (San
ebastiano) 318
Flaminia 306
Latina 323
Maggiore 339, 340
Marina 414
Ostiensis 182, 183
del Popolo 306
Portese 355
Romana 405
Santa (Holy Door) 211
Settimiana 359

Houses, casa
-of Augustus (Domus
Augustana) 148
-del Cardinale
Bessarione 321
-Caseggiato del Larario
412
-dei Crescenzi 156
-di Dante 357
-dei Grifi (Griffins) 150
-of Livia 148
-Romulus 148
-of the Vestals 144

Insula
-dei Dipinti 411
-di Giove e Ganimede
411
-delle Volte Dipinte 414

Isola Sacra 416
Lacus Curtius 141

Libraries, biblioteca
-Angelica 282
-of the Biblicum 299
-of Contemporary
History 254
-of the French School at
Rome 245
-Herziana 314
-Vallicelliana 282
-Vittorio Emanuele 335

**Mausoleums,
mausoleo**
-of Augustus 309
-of Hadrian 233, 235
-of Romulus 329
-of Santa Costanza 380

Mithraeum, mitreo
-of Felicissimus 414
-of San Clemente 196
-of Santa Prisca 181
-delle Sette Sfere (of
the Seven Spheres)

Monasteries
-of the Augustinians
284
-of Sant'Onofrio 365
-Tor de' Specchi 159

**Museums, museo;
galleries, galleria**
-del Alto Medioevo 387
-delle Anime in
Purgatorio 236
-Arte Moderna, Galleria
Nazionale d' 376
-delle Arti e Tradizioni
Popolari 387
-Astronomico e
Copernico 377
-delle Bandiere 161
-Barracco 249
-of the Baths 335
-della Calcografia
Nazionale 299
-del Campidoglio
(Pinacoteca) 133
-Capitolini 130, 132
-Centrale del
Risorgimento 161
-Chiaramonti 215
-della Civiltà Romana
388
-Colonna 268
-d'Arte Ebraica (Jewish)
254
-dei Conservatori 132

-Doria Pamphilj 259
-Etruscan 370
-del Folklore 359
-Geologico 302
-Hans Christian
Anderson museum 369
-Keats-Shelley
Memorial House 313
-Municipal Gallery of
Modern and
Contemporary Art 290
-Napoleonico 284
- Nazionale d'Arte
Antica, palazzo Corsini
292, 362
-Nazionale d'Arte
Moderna 376
-Nazionale Romano
delle Terme 335, 336
-Nuovo 133
-di Palazzo di Venezia,
161
-di Palestrina 402
-de la Porta Ostiensis
183
-Preistorico ed
Etnografico Pigorini 387
-di Roma 279
-Rossa (Casina) 313
-Spade 246
-delle Stampe
(Gabinetto) 360
-delle Terme 335
-del Vaticano
(Pinacoteca) 157, 215
-de la Via di Diana 411

Obelisks
-of Domitian 329
-of the Lateran 196
-of Piazza San Pietro
210
-of Ramses II 178
-of the Trinità dei Monti
294

Odeon 239

Oratories, oratorio
-dei Filippini 281
-dei Quaranta Martiri
142
-di San Giovanni in
Oleo 323
-di Santa Lucia del
Gonfalone 242

Palaces, palazzo
-Altemps 284
-Anguillara 356
-del Belvedere 214
-Bonaparte 309
-Borghese 311
-Braschi 279
-Caetani 253
-della Cancelleria 249
-Cenci Bolognetti 254,
258
-Chigi 268
-Cimarra 347
-della Civiltà del Lavoro
122, 387
-Colonna (palace and
gallery) 300
-dei Congressi 387
-dei Conservatori 130,
132
-de la Consulta 297
-Corsini 362

-Costaguti 254
-of Domitian 150
-Doria Pamphilj 258
-delle Esposizioni 348
-Falconieri 244
-Farnese 244
-Fiano 309
-di Giustizia 236
-del Governo Vecchio
281
-Lancelotti 283
-Madama 272
-Mancini 309
-Massimo alle Colonne
279
-Mattei di Giove 254
-Mattei di Paganica 253
-di Montecitorio 269
-Odescalchi 301
-Senatoriale 130
-Pamphilj 278
-dei Penitenzieri 232
-Piombino 302
-del Quirinale 297
-Ricci 243
-Rondini 309
-Rospigliosi-Pallavicini
298
-Ruspoli 312
-Sacchetti 242
-di San Callisto 357
-della Sapienza 272
-delle Scienze 387
-Serristori 232
-Spada 246
-di Spagna 313
-degli Sport 388
-Taverna 283
-delle Terme 378
-Torlonia 232
-di Venezia 161
-Zuccaro 314

Portus Tiberinus 154
Pyramid of Cestius
182

Rostra, Imperial 140

Square, piazza
-Barberini 290
-Bocca della Verità, 155
-Borghese 311
-del Campidoglio 129
-Campo de' Fiori 125,
241, 247–249
-dei Cavalieri di Malta
180
-Colonna 267
-dei Cinquecento 338
-delle Coppelle 270
-delle Corporazione 407
-Esedra 333
-dell'Esquilino 342, 344
-Farnese 244
-de la Magna Mater 415
-Marconi 387
-Margana 159
-Mattei 254
-della Minerva 260, 261
-di Montecitorio 269
-Navona 3, 239, 276
-delle Nazioni Unite
387
-d'Oro 395
-dell'Orologio 282
-della Pace 281
-in Piscinula 353
-del Popolo 306
-di Porta Portese 355
-delle Quattro Fontane
294
-de la Quercia 246

◆ INDEX

–del Quirinale 297
–Regina Margherita 402
–della Repubblica 333
–della Rotonda 264
–San Cosimato 356
–di San Martino ai Monti 346
–San Pietro 210
–San Pietro in Vincoli 346
–San Silvestro 301
–Sant'Egidio 359
–Sant'Ignazio 261
–Santa Maria Liberatrice 184
–Santa Maria Maggiore 342
–Santa Maria in Trastevere 357
–di Spagna 313
–Tor Sanguigna 283
–Trilussa 363
–Venezia 160
–della Vittoria 405
–Vittorio Emanuele II 340

Stadium of Domitian 276

Tabularium 64, 128

Temples, tempio, shrines
–of Antoninus and Faustina 144, 145
–of Apollo 149, 156

–of Apollo Sosianus 158
–of Bellona 158
–of Concord 141
–of the Dioscuri 142
–of the Divine Claudius 189
–of the Divine Julius 143
–of the Fabri Navales 414
–of Fortuna 1 (Rome) 56
–of Fortuna (Praeneste) 398
–of Hadrian 267
–of Heliogabalus or Elagalabalus 151
–of Hercules Victor (Tivoli) 390
–of the Janiculum (shrine) 355
–of Janus 138
–of the Magna Mater 148
–of Mars Ultor 163
–of Mater Matuta 156
–of Matidia 267
–of Minerva Medica 339
–of Peace 164
–Pantheon 264
–of Portunus 155
–of Quirinus 288
–of Rome and Augustus 412
–of Romulus 144
–of Saturn 140
–Serapeum 413

–of the Sybil 391
–of Venus Cloacina 138
–of Venus Genitrix 163
–of Venus Victrix 248
–of Vespasian and Titus 141
–of Vesta 144, 155
–of Via della Foce (shrine) 412

Theaters, teatro
–Argentina 251
–of Balbus 253
–of the Corporations (Ostia) 406
–Eliseo 348
–di Marcello 157
–di Pompeo 248
–dei Pupi Siciliani dei

Tombs, tombe
–of Cartilius Poplicola (Ostia) 414
–of Cecilia Metella 330
–of Eurysaces 339
–of the Horatii and the Curiatii 330
–Meta Remi 182
–of the Scipios 322

Towers, torre
–Anguillara 356
–dei Conti 168
–dei Margani 159
–delle Milizie 168
–Millina 279
–di Roccabruna 397
–della Scimmia 284

Trajan's market 167
Triopius of Heriodias Atticus 329
Trophies of Marius 130 341
Tullianum Prison 131

Villas
–Adriana 394
–Albani 368
–Barberini 369
–Borghese 372, 374
–Celimontana 190, 369
–Colonna 298
–Doria Pamphilj 20, 368, 369
–d'Este 88, 89, 392
–Farnese 369
–Farnesina 88, 360
–Giulia 370
–Gregoriana 391
–Lante 365
–Madama 378
–Mattei 369
–Medici 89, 315, 369
–Torlonia 368, 381

Casilina (via) **G** C 3-4

Casinò Algardi (viale) **D** C-D 3

Castelfidardo (via) **B** D 4

Castellini Gualtiero (via) **B** A-B 3

Castello (lungotevere) **D** A 4

Castel Sant'Angelo **D** A 4

Castro Pretorio Rione **B** D 4

Castro Pretorio (stazione metropolitana) **G** A 1

Castro Pretorio (via) **G** A 1

Catanzaro (via) **C** D 2-3

Cava Aurelia (via della) **D** B 2

Cavalieri di Vittorio Veneto (viale dei) **A** B-C 2

Cavazzi (via) **I** C 1

Cavour (piazza) **D** A 4

Cavour (ponte) **E** A 1

Cavour (stazione metropolitana) **E** B 3

Cavour (via) **E** B 3

Celano Tommaso da (via) **I** B 4

Celimontana (piazza) **E** C-D 3-4

Celio Rione **E** D 3

Celio Vibenna (via) **E** C 3

Celsco Cornelio (via) **C** D 2

Cenci (lungotevere dei) **E** C 1

Ceneda (via) **I** A 3-4

Cerbara Giuseppe (via) **I** D 2-3

Cernaia (via) **E** A 4

Cerveteri (via) **G** D 2

Cesi Federico (via) **A** D 4

Cestari (via dei) **E** B 1

Cestio (ponte) **E** C 1

Chelini Domenico (via) **B** B 2

Chiabrera Gabriele (via) **H** D 3

Chiana (via) **C** B 1

Chiarini Giovanni (largo) **I** A 1

Chiavari (via dei) **E** B 1

Chiesa Nuova (piazza della) **E** B 1

Chigi (largo) **F** B 3

Chini Eusebio (via) **I** C 2

Cialdi Alessandro (via) **H** C 3-4

Ciappi Anselmo (via) **H** C 1

Cicerone (via) **A** D 4

Cilicia (via) **I** B 2-3

Cinque Vicolo del **E** C 1

Cinquecento (piazza dei) **E** A 4

Cinque Giornate (piazza delle) **A** C 4

Cipro (via) **A** D 1-2

Circo Massimo (stazione metropolitana) **E** D 3

Circo Massimo (via del) **E** C-D 2

Citerni Carlo (via) **I** B 1

Città del Vaticano **D** A 2

Civinini Filippo (via) **B** B 2

Claudia (via) **E** C 3

Clementino (via del) **F** B 1-2

Clitunno (via) **C** B-C 1

Clivio Rutario (via) **D** D 2

Clodia (circonvallazione) **A** B-C 2-3

Clodio (piazzale) **A** C 3

Cloro Costanzo (via) **H** D 4

Cola di Rienzo (piazza) **A** D 4

Cola di Rienzo (via) **A** D 4

Col di Lana (via) **A** C 4

Collazia (via) **I** A 3

Collegio (via) **F** B-C 2

Collegio Romano (piazza) **E** B 2

Collina (via) **B** D 4

Colombo Cristoforo (via) **I** B-D 1-2

Colonna (piazza) **E** A 2

Colonna (via) **E** A 1

Colonna Marcantonio (via) **A** D 4

Colonna Antonina (via) **F** C 2

Colosseo (piazza del) **E** C 3

Colosseo (stazione metropolitana) **E** C 3

Colosseo (via del) **E** C 3

Colossi (via) **H** D 3

Commercio (via del) **H** B 3

Como (via) **C** D 2

Conciliazione (via della) **D** A 3-4

Condotti (via) **E** A 2

Condottieri (piazza dei) **G** C 4

Consolazione (via della) **E** C 2

Conte Carmagnola (via del) **G** C 4

Conti Rossini Carlo (via) **I** C 2

Coppelle (via delle) **F** B 1-2

Corallo (via del) **E** B 1

Cordonata (via della) **F** D 4

Coronari (via dei) **D** A 4

Coronelli (via) **G** D 4

Corridoni Filippo (via) **A** B 3

Corsica (via) **C** C 2

Corso (via del) **E** A-B 2

Cossa Pietro (via) **F** A 1

Costantino (via) **H** D 4

Cottolengo (via del) **D** B 2

Crati (piazza) **C** A 2

Crescenzio (via) **D** A 3-4

Crispi Francesco (via) **F** A-B 4

Croce (via della) **B** D 2

Croce Rossa (piazza) della **C** D 1

Crociate (piazzale delle) **C** D 4

Crugnola Gaetano (via) **H** D 1

Cubertin Pietro de (via) **B** A 1

Cuccagna (vicolo della) **F** C 1

D

Dalla Chiesa Carlo Alberto (via) **A** D 3

Dall'Ongaro Francesco (via) **D** D 4

Dalmazia (piazza) **C** C 1

Dalmazia (via) **C** C 1

Dandini Girolamo (via) **I** A-B 1

Dandolo (via) **D** D 4

Dante (lungotevere) **H** D 1-2

Dante (piazza) **G** C 1

Dardanelli (via) **A** C 3

Dataria (via della) **F** C 4

D'Avanzo Nicola (via) **G** A-B 4

De Agostini Giovanni (via) **G** D 4

De Carolis Ugo (via) **A** C 1

De Jacobis (via) **I** C 1

De Mattias Beata Maria (via) **I** A 2-3

De Nicola Enrico (viale) **E** A 4

De Nobili Roberto (via) **I** C 1

De Notaris Giuseppe (via) **B** B 2

Denza Francesco (via) **B** A-B 2

De' Renzi (piazza) **E** C 1

De Rossi Giovanni Battista (via) **C** C 2-3

De Vecchi Pieralice Giacinto (via) **A** D 1

Dionigi (via) **F** A 1

Di Pietro Angelo (via) **D** B 1

Di Tullio (via) **A** D 1

Dogana Vecchia (via) **F** C 1

Dolci Carlo (via) **B** B 1

Domizia Lucilla (via) **A** D 1

Donatello (via) **A** B 4

Donizetti Gaetano (via) **B** C 4

Don Minzoni Giovanni (piazzale) **B** B 2

Donna Olimpia (via di) **H** A 1

Don Orione (largo) **I** A 4

Doria Andrea (via) **A** D 2

Druso (via) **E** D 4

Duca d'Aosta (ponte) **A** A 3

Due Macelli (via) **E** A 2

Dunant Enrico (piazzale) **H** B 1

Durante Alfredo (via) **A** A 1

Durazzo (via) **A** B 3

Duse Eleonora (via) **B** A 3

E

Edison Tommaso (piazzale) **H** D 2

Efeso (via) **H** D 3

Einstein Alberto (via) **H** B 2

Eleliana (via) **G** C 2

Emanuele Filiberto (via) **G** C 1

Emo Angelo (via) **D** A 1-2

Empoli Giovanni da (via) **H** B 3

Emporio (piazza dell') **E** D 1

Epiro (piazza) **I** A 3

Equi (via degli) **G** B 2

Eritrea (viale) **C** A-B 2

Eroi (piazzale degli) **A** D 2

Esquilino (piazza dell') **E** B 4

Esquilino Rione **E** C 4

Esquilino (via dell') **E** C 4

Etiopia (viale) **C** A 3

Etruria (via) **I** A 3-4

Etruschi (via degli) **G** B 2

Euclide (piazza) **B** A 2

Ezio (via) **A** D 4

F

Fabio Massimo (via) **A** D 3

Fabriano Gentile da (piazza) **A** A 3

Fabricio (ponte) **E** C 2

Fabrizi Nicola (via) **D** C-D 4

Falegnami (via dei) **E** B 1

Farini (via) **E** B 4

Farnese (piazza) **E** B 1

Farnese Alessandro (via) **A** D 4

Farnesina (lungotevere della) **D** B 4

Faro (piazza del) **D** B 3

Fauro Ruggero (via) **B** A 3

Fea Carlo (via) **C** C 2

Febo (largo) **F** C 1

Fedro (via) **A** C 2

Feltre Bernardino da (piazza) **D** D 4

Fermi Enrico (piazza) **H** C 2

Fermi Enrico (via) **H** C 2-3

Ferraris Galileo (via) **E** D 4

Ferratella (via della) **E** D 4

Fienili (via dei) **E** C 2

Filippi (via) **H** D 3

Filzi Fabio (via) **A** B 3

Finanza (piazza della) **E** A 4

Fiori Mario de' (via) **F** A 3

Fioritto Enzo (largo) **I** A 1

Flaminio (lungotevere) **A** B 4

Flaminio (quartiere) **A** A 4

Flaminio (stazione metropolitana) **B** C 1-2

Flavia (via) **B** D 4

Fochetti Angelo (largo) **I** C 2

Foligno (via) **G** D 3

Fontana di Borghese (largo) di **F** B 2

Fontanella di Borghese (via) **F** A 2

Fonteiana (via) **D** D 2

Fori Imperiali (via) **E** B-C 2-3

Forlì (via) **C** D 2

Forlì Melozzo da (piazza) **A** A-B 4

Fornaci (via delle) **D** B-C 3

Fornetto (via del) **H** B 1-2

Fornovo (via) **A** C 4

◆ STREET INDEX

Foro Italico (quartiere)
A A 3
Foscolo (via) **G** C 1
Fracassini Cesare (via)
B B 1
Fra' Mauro (via) **G** D 4
Franchetti Raimondo (via)
I C-D 2
Francia (corso) di **B** A 1
Frangipane (via)
E B-C 3
Fratelli Bonnet (via)
D D 3
Frattina (via) **E** A 2
Fregene (via) **G** D 2
Frentani (via) **G** A 2
Frescobaldi Gerolamo (via)
B C 3
Frezza (via della)
B D 1-2
Friggeri Attilio (via)
A B 1

G

Gaeta (via) **E** A 4
Galamini Cardinal Agostino
(largo) **D** B 1
Galeria (piazza) **I** A-B 3
Galilei Galileo (via)
G C 1
Gallia (via) **E** D 4
Galvaligi (largo) **I** C 2
Galvani (via) **H** A 3
Garbatella (stazione
metropolitana) **H** C 4
Garbatella (via della)
H C 4
Garibaldi (ponte) **E** C 1
Garibaldi (via) **D** C 4
Garigliano (via) **C** B 1
Gastaldi Bartolomeo
(piazza) **B** B 2
Gelsomini Manlio (largo)
H A 3-4
Generale Bengivenga
Roberto (via) **C** A 4
Genocchi Giovanni (via)
I D 1-2
Genovesi (via dei) **E** C 1
Germanico (via) **A** D 3
Gesù (via del) **E** B 2
Gesù e Maria (via di)
B D 2
Gherzi Luigi (via) **A** A 1
Gianicolense
(circonvallazione) **H** B 1
Gianicolense (lungotevere)
D B 3-4
Gianicolense (quartiere)
H B 1
Gianicolo (passeggiata del)
D B-C 3
Gianicolo (via del) **D** B 3
Giardino maresciallo
(piazza) **A** B 3
Gigli Beniamino (piazza)
E A-B 3
Gioberti (via) **E** B 4
Giolitti Giovanni (via)
G B 1
Giorgi (via) **E** B-C 3
Giotto (viale) **I** A 1
Giovane Italia (piazza)
A C 3
Giovannelli Ruggero (via) **B**
C 4
Giovannipoli (via)
H C-D 4
Giubbonari (via dei)
E B 1
Giulia (via) **D** B 4

Giuliana (via della)
A C-D 2-3
Giuliani padre Reginaldo
(via) **I** C 1
Giulio Cesare (viale)
A D 3-4
Giustiniani (via) **F** C 1-2
Giustiniano Imperatore (via)
H D 4
Gladiatori (viale dei)
A A 3
Glorioso (viale) **D** D 4
Gobetti Piero (viale)
G A 2
Goito (via) **E** A 4
Goldoni (largo) **F** A 2
Gomenizza (via) **A** B 3
Gorizia (viale) **C** B-C 2
Governale (piazza)
A C 1
Governo Vecchio (via del) **D**
B 4
Gozzi Gaspare (via)
H D 3
Gracchi (via dei) **A** D 4
Gradisca (via) **C** B 2
Gramsci Antonio (via)
B B-C 2
Grazioli Lante (via)
A C 3
Gregorio VII (viale)
D B 1-2
Gregorovius (largo) **I** B 4
Grillo (piazza) del **F** D 4
Grimaldi Francesco (via)
H C 2
Grogoriana (via) **F** A 3-4
Grotta Pinta (via di)
F D 1
Guarnieri-Carducci Rosa
(via) **I** D 1
Gubbio Oderisi da (via)
H B-C 2
Guglia (via di) **F** C 2
Guidi Ignazio (via) **I** C 2
Guido d'Arezzo (via)
C B 3
Guidotti Obizzo (via)
I C 1
Guinizelli Guido (via)
H A 1

I

Iberia (via) **I** A 3
Imera (via) **I** A 3
IIndipendenza (piazza) **E** A 4
Industria (ponte dell') **H** B 2
Innocenzo III (via) **D** B 2
Inventori (lungotevere degli)
H C 2
Ippocrate (viale) **C** D 2-3
Ipponio (piazzale) **E** D 4
Ipponio (via) **E** D 4
Isola Tiberina **E** C 1
Isonzo (via) **B** C-D 3-4
Istria (piazza) **C** B 2
Italia (corso d') **B** D 3-4
Ivrea (via) **I** A 4

J

Jacopo d'Ancona (via)
H C 3-4
Josè de San Martin
(piazzale) **B** C 2

L

Labicana (via) **E** C 4
Lago di Lesina (via)
C A-B 2

La Goletta (via) **A** D 2
La Guardia Fiorello (viale) **B**
C 2
La Malfa Ugo (piazzale)
E D 2
Lanciani Rodolfo (via)
C B 3
Lancisi (via) **C** D 2
Lando Michele di (via)
C C 3
Lanza Giovanni (via)
E B 3-4
Lariana (via) **C** B 1
La Spezia (via) **G** D 2
Latina (via) **I** A 3
Latini (via dei) **G** B 2
Lattanzio (via) **A** C-D 1
Lavatore (via del) **F** B 3
Lazzerini (largo) **I** A 1
Lecce (piazza) **C** D 2
Lega Lombarda (via della) **C**
D 3
Leone IV (via) **A** D 3
Leone XIII (via) **D** C-D 1
Leopardi (largo) **E** B 4
Lepanto (stazione
metropolitana) **A** D 4
Lepanto (via) **A** C-D 4
Levi Civita Tullio (via)
H D 3
Libertà (piazza della)
B D 1
Libia (viale) **C** A 3
Licia (via) **I** A 3
Licinio Calvo (via)
A A-B 1-2
Lidia (via) **I** B 3
Liegi (viale) **B** B-C 4
Lima (via) **B** B 4
Lisbona (via) **B** B 4
Livorno (via) **C** C 3
Lodi (piazza) **G** C-D 3
Lombardi (largo dei)
F A 2
Lombardia (via) **B** D 3
Longobardi (piazza)
I C 1
Lorenzo il Magnifico (via)
C D 3-4
Loria Lamberto (largo)
I C 2
Lovanio (via) **B** B 4
Lucchesi (via dei) **F** C 3
Luce (via della) **E** C 1
Lucilio (via) **A** A-B 1-2
Lucio Fabio Cilone (via)
I A 1
Ludovico di Savoia (via)
G C 1-2
Ludovisi (rione) **B** D 3
Ludovisi (via) **B** D 3
Lungara (via della)
D B 4
Lungaretta (via della)
E C 1
Lupa (via della) **F** B 2
Lusitania (via) **I** A 3

M

Macedonia (via) **I** B 4
Machiavelli Nicolò (via)
G C 1
Macinghi Strozzi Alessandro
(via) **I** D 1
Macrobio Teodosio (via)
A B 1
Magliana (via della)
H D 1
Magliana Antica (via)
H C 1-2
Maglio (via del) **D** C 2

Magnaghi Giovan Battista
(via) **I** C 1
Magna Grecia (via)
G D 1
Magnanapoli (largo)
F D 4
Magni Cornelio (via)
I C 2
Magnifico Lorenzo il (via) **C**
D 3-4
Magnolie (viale delle)
B D 2
Majorana Quirino (via)
H B-C 1-2
Makalle (via) **C** A 3
Malfante (via) **I** C 2
Mameli Goffredo (via)
D C 4
Manara Luciano (via)
D C 4
Manfredi Eustachio (via)
B B 2
Mangili Giuseppe (via)
B B-C 2
Mantellini Giuseppe (via)
I B 4
Mantova (via) **B** D 4
Manunzio Aldo (via)
H A 3
Manzoni (stazione
metropolitana) **G** C 1
Manzoni Alessandro (viale)
G C 1
Marco Aurelio (via)
E C 3-4
Marco e Marcelliano (via) **I**
D 2
Marconi Guglielmo (ponte)
H D 2
Marconi Guglielmo (viale) **H**
B-C 2
Maresciallo Cadorna
(lungotevere) **A** A-B 3
Maresciallo Giardino
(piazza) **A** B 3
Maresciallo Pilsudski (viale)
B A 1-2
Margana (piazza) **F** D 2
Margutta (via) **B** D 2
Mario Alberto (via)
D D 3
Mario de' fiori (via) **F** A 3
Marmorata (via) **H** A 3
Marsala (via) **G** A-B 1
Marsi (via dei) **G** B 2
Martini Placido (via)
A C 1
Marzi Giovanni Battista
(largo) **H** A 2
Marzio (lungotevere)
E A 1
Masaccio (via) **A** A 4
Massaia Guglielmo (viale) **I**
C 1
Massi Francesco (via)
H A-B 1
Massimi (via) **A** A 1
Mastai (piazza) **E** C 1
Matera (via) **G** D 2-3
Mattei (piazza) **E** C 2
Matteotti Giacomo (ponte)
B C 1
Matteucci Pellegrino (via) **H**
B 4
Mazzarino (via) **F** D 4
Mazzini Giuseppe (piazza) **A**
C 4
Mazzini Giuseppe (ponte) **D**
B 4
Mazzini Giuseppe (viale)
A C 3-4
Mecenate (via) **E** C 4

Medaglie d'Oro (piazzale)
A B 2
Medaglie d'Oro
(viale delle) **A** B 1-2
Medici Giacomo (via)
D C 3
Mellini (lungotevere dei)
B D 1
Meloria (via della)
A D 1-2
Mengarini Guglielmo (via)
H C 1
Menotti Ciro (via) **A** C 4
Mercadante Saverio (via)
B C 3
Mercalli Giuseppe (via)
B B 2-3
Mercati Michele (via)
B B-C 2
Mercede (via della)
F B 3
Meropia (via) **I** D 3
Merulana (via) **E** B-C 4
Messina (via) **B** D 4
Metauro (via) **B** C 4
Metronio (viale) **I** A 2-3
Meucci Antonio (piazza)
H C 1-2
Michelangelo (lungotevere)
B D 1
Michele di Lando (via)
C C 3
Micheli Pietro Antonio (via)
B B 2
Michelini Tocci Franco (via)
A B 2
Mignanelli (piazza) **E** A 2
Milano (via) **E** B 3
Milizie (viale delle)
A C-D 3-4
Minerva (piazza di)
F C 2
Minghetti (via) **F** C 3
Mirandola (via) **G** D 3
Moletta (via della)
H B 4
Monserrato (via) **D** B 4
Montecitorio (piazza di)
E A 2
Monte del Gallo (via di)
D B 2
Monte della Farina
(via del) **F** D 1
Monte Grappa (piazza)
A C 4
Monte Oppio (viale del)
E C 3-4
Monterone (via) **E** B 1
Monte Santo (via) **A** C 3
Monte Testaccio (via)
H C 3
Monte Zebio (via)
A B-C 4
Monti **E** B 4
Monti Vincenzo (via)
H A 1
Monti di Pietralata
(via dei) **C** C-D 4
Monti Parioli (via dei)
B B 1-2
Monti Tiburtini (via dei)
C B 4
Mordini Antonio (via)
A C 4
Morgagni Gian Battista (via)
C D 2
Moro Aldo (piazzale)
G A 2
Moroni (via) **C** C 3
Moschea (viale della)
B A 3
Muggia (via) **A** C 3

Mura Aurelie (viale delle)
D B 3
Mura Gianicolensi
(viale delle) **D** C-D 3
Mura Latine (viale delle)
I A-B 3
Muratte (via delle) **F** C 3
Muro Torto (viale del)
B D 2-3
Musa Antonio (via)
C D 2
Museo Borghese
(viale del) **B** C-D 3

N

Napoleone I (piazzale)
B D 2
Napoli (via) **E** A 3-4
Navi (lungotevere delle)
B C 1
Navicella (via della)
E D 4
Navigatori (piazzale dei)
I C-D 2
Navona (piazza) **E** B 1
Nazareno (via) **F** B 3
Nazionale (via) **E** A-B 3
Negri Francesco (via)
H B 3-4
Nemorense (via) **C** A 2
Nenni Pietro (ponte)
B D 1
Nerazzini Cesare (piazza)
I C 2
Nibby Antonio (via)
C C 2
Nicolai Filippo (via)
A C 1
Nicosia (piazza) **F** B 1
Nicotera Giovanni (via)
A C 4
Nievo Ippolito (piazza)
D D 4
Nisco Nicola (via) **I** B 4
Nizza (via) **B** C-D 4
Nomentana
(circonvallazione)
C B-C 4
Nomentana (via)
C B-D 1-2
Nomentano (quartiere)
C C 3
Novella (via di) **C** A 2
Numa Pompilio (piazzale)
I A 2

O

Oberdan (lungotevere)
A B 4
Oderico da Pordenone
(piazza) **I** D 1-2
Odescalchi Carlo Tommaso
(viale) **I** D 2
Olimpiadi (viale delle)
A A 3
Omboni Tito (via) **I** C 2
Ombrone (via) **C** C 1
Oriani Barnaba (via)
B A-B 2-3
Oristano (via) **G** D 3
Orso (via dell') **F** B 1
Orti d'Alibert (via degli)
D B 3
Oslavia (via) **A** C 3
Ostiense (circonvallazione)
H B-C 4
Ostiense (piazzale)
H A 4
Ostiense (quartiere)
H D 4

Ostiense (via) **H** B-C 3
Ostilia (via) **E** C 3
Ottaviano (stazione
metropolitana) **A** D 3
Ottaviano (via) **A** D 3
Ottavilla (piazza)
D D 2
Otto Marzo (viale)
D C-D 1
Ovidio (via) **A** D 4
Oxilia Nino (via) **B** B 3

P

Pace (piazza della)
F D 4
Pace (via della) **D** D 4
Pacini Giovanni (via)
B C 4
Pacinotti Antonio (via)
H B 2
Padova (via) **C** D 3
Padre Semeria (via)
I C 2
Paisiello Giovanni (via)
B B-C 3
Paladini Ettore (via)
H C 1
Palatino (ponte) **E** C 2
Palestro (via) **B** B 4
Pallaro (largo del) **F** D 1
Panama (via) **B** B 4
Panaro (via) **C** B 2
Pancaldo Leon (via)
I C-D 2
Panetteria (via della)
F B 2
Panisperna (via) **E** B 3
Pannonia (via) **I** A 2
Pantera (piazza) **H** C 4
Paoli (piazza) **D** A 4
Paolo Emilio (via)
A D 3-4
Papa Achille (via) **A** B 4
Papareschi (lungotevere dei)
H B-C 3
Papi Lazzaro (piazza)
I B 4
Parini Giuseppe (via)
H A-B 2
Parioli (quartiere) **B** A 2-3
Parioli (viale dei) **B** B 3
Parione Rione **E** B 1
Parlamento (piazza del)
E A 1-2
Partigiani (piazzale dei)
H B 4
Passino Francesco (via)
H C 4
Pasubio (via) **A** C 4
Paulucci de' Calboli Fulcieri
(via) **A** C 3
Pavia (via) **C** C 2
Pellegrino (via)
D B 4
Pellico Silvio (via)
A C 3
Penna (via della) **B** D 1
Percoto (via) **C** C 1
Pereira Romano Rodriguez
(via) **A** B-C 1
Persico Ignazio (via)
I C 1
Petrolini Ettore (via)
B A 3-4
Pettinari (via dei)
E B-C 1
Pezzana Giacinta (via)
B A 3-4
Piave (via) **B** D 4
Euclide Stazione (piazza)
B A 2

Piccolomini (via)
G C 3
Piccolomini Nicolò (via)
D C 1
Piè di Marmo (via) **F** C 2
Piemonte (via) **B** D 3
Pietra (piazza di) **F** C 2
Pietralata (via di) **C** A 4
Pietra Papa (lungotevere di)
H C 2-3
Pietri Dorando (via)
B A 1
Pietro de Cubertin (via)
B A 1
Pigafetta Antonio (via)
H B 4
Pigna Rione **E** B 2
Pigneto (via del)
G C-D 4
Pilo Rosolino (piazza)
D D 3
Pilotta (piazza della)
E B 2
Pilotta (via della) **F** C 3
Pilsudski maresciallo (viale)
B A 1-2
Pinciana (via) **B** D 3
Pinciano (quartiere)
B B 2-3
Pinturicchio (viale) **A** A 4
Pio Borgo **D** A 3
Pio IV (via) **D** B 1
Pio XII (piazza) **D** A 3
Piramide (stazione
metropolitana) **H** A 3-4
Piramide Cestia (viale della)
H A 4
Pisa (via) **C** C 3
Piscinula (piazza in)
E C 1
Pittore O. F. (via) **A** C 1
Platone (viale) **A** C 2
Plebiscito (via del) **E** B 2
Po (via) **B** C 4
Poerio Alessandro (via)
H A 1-2
Poggio Catino (via)
C A 2
Policlinico (stazione
metropolitana) **E** A 4
Policlinico (viale del)
C D 1-2
Pollio Alberto (via) **G** B 4
Polo Marco (viale)
H A-B 4
Pomezia (via) **I** A 3-4
Pompei (piazza) **I** A 3
Pompeo Magno (via)
A D 4
(ponte) Rione **D** A 4
(ponte) Lungo (piazza di)
I A 4
Ponte Lungo (stazione
metropolitana)
I A 4
Ponte Umberto I (piazza)
E A 1
Ponziani (piazza dei)
E C 1-2
Ponzio (via) **H** A 4
Popolo (piazza del)
B D 1
Populonia (via) **I** A 3
Porcari Stefano (via)
D A 3
Porro Gian Giacomo (via) **B**
A 3
Porta Ardeatina **I** B 2
Porta Ardeatina (viale di)
I B 2
Porta Asinara **G** D 2
Porta Capena **E** D 3

505

◆ STREET INDEX

Porta Capena (piazza di)
E D 3
Porta Cavalleggeri
D A 3
Porta Cavalleggeri (via)
D A 2-3
Porta del Popolo
B D 1
Porta Latina I A 2
Porta Latina (via di)
I A 2
Porta Maggiore G C 2
Porta Maggiore (piazza)
G C 2
Porta Maggiore (via di)
G C 2
Porta Metronia E D 4
Porta Metronia (piazza di)
E D 4
Porta Pia B D 4
Porta Pinciana B D 2-3
Porta Pinciana (via di)
B D 2-3
Porta Portese E D 1
Porta Portese (via di)
E D 1
Porta Portuense
(piazza di) E D 1
Porta San Giovanni
G D 1
Porta San Giovanni (piazza
di) G D 1
Porta San Lorenzo
G B 2
Porta San Paolo H A 4
Porta San Paolo (piazza di)
H A 4
Porta San Sebastiano
I B 2
Porta San Sebastiano
(via di) I A 2
Porta Tiburtina G B 2
Portico d'Ottavia (via)
E C 1-2
Porto di Ripetta
(piazza del) F A 1
Porto Fluviale (via del)
H B 3
Portuense (lungotevere)
E D 1
Portuense (quartiere)
H C 1-2
Portuense (via) H B 2
Prati (lungotevere) E A 1
Prati Rione A D 4
Prati degli Strozzi (piazza
dei) A C 3
Prefetti (via dei) F B 2
Premuda (via) A C 2
Prenestina (via) G C 3-4
Prenestino-Labicano
(quartiere) G C 4
Prestinari Marcello (via)
A B-C 4
Pretoriano (viale) G A-B 1
Principe Amedeo (via)
G B 1
Principe Amedeo Savoia
Aosta (ponte)
D B 3-4
Principe Umberto (via)
G B 1-2
Prisciano (via) A A-B 2
Priscilla (via) C A 2
Procida Giovanni da (via)
C C-D 3
Provincie (piazzale) delle
C D 3
Provincie (viale) delle
C D 3
Pullino Giacomo (via)
H C 4

Q

Quattro Cantoni (via)
E B 4
Quattro Fontane (via delle)
E A 3
Quattro Novembre (via)
F D 3-4
Quattro Venti (piazzale dei)
H A 1
Quattro Venti (viale dei)
H A 1
Quirinale (piazza del)
E B 3
Quirinale (via del) F C 4
Quiriti (piazza) dei A D 4

R

Radio (piazza) della
H B 2
Raimondi Pietro (via)
B C 3
Raimondi Garibaldi Rosa
(via) I D 1
Rammi (via dei) G B 2
Rasella (via) F B 4
Ravenna (via) C C-D 2-3
Recina Elvia (via) I A 3
Re di Roma (piazza dei)
G D 2
Re di Roma (stazione
metropolitana) G D 2
Regina Elena (viale)
G A 2-3
Regina Margherita (piazza)
C C 1
Regina Margherita (ponte) B
D 1
Regina Margherita (viale) C
C-D 1
Regola Rione D B 4
Reni Guido (via) A A 4
Repubblica (piazza della) E
A 4
Repubblica (stazione
metropolitana) E A 3-4
Reti (via delle) G B 2-3
Riari (via dei) D B 3-4
Riccardi Placido (largo)
H D 3
Ricciotti Nicola (via)
A C 4
Righi Augusto (piazza)
H C 2
Rinascimento (corso del) E
A-B 1
Ripa (lungotevere)
E C-D 1-2
Ripa Rione E D 2
Ripetta (passeggiata di)
B D 1
Ripetta (via di) B D 1
Risorgimento (piazza del)
A D 3
Risorgimento (ponte del)
A C 4
Rizzo Luigi (via) A D 1-2
Robbia Leonardo della (via)
H A 3
Rodi (via) A C 2
Roiti Antonio (via) H C 2
Rolli Ettore (via) H A-B 2
Roma-Lido di Ostia
(stazione) H A 4
Romania (via) B B 3
Roma-Ostiense (stazione)
H B 4
Roma Termini (stazione
centrale) G B 1
Roma-Tiburtina (stazione)
C D 4

Romei Romeo (via)
A B-C 2
Romolo e Remo (largo)
E B 3
Rosa Ercole (via) I A 1
Roselle (piazza) I B 3
Rosetta (via della) F B 2
Rosini (via) F B 2
Rossetti Gabriele (via)
D D 3
Rossini Gioacchino (viale) B
B-C 3
Rotonda (piazza della)
E B 1
Rotonda (via) F C 2
Rotto (ponte) E C 2
Rovere (piazza della)
D A-B 3
Rozat Bartolomeo (viale)
D C 2
Rubens Pietro Paolo (via) B
B 1
Rubicone (via) C B-C 1
Rubino Antonio (via)
I C 1
Rufina Valeria (via) I D 2

S

Sabelli (via dei) G B 2
Sabotino (via) A C 3
Sacchi Andrea (via)
D C-D 4
Sacconi Giuseppe (via)
A A 4
Saffi Aurelio (viale)
D D 4
Sagrestia D A 2
Salaria (circonvallazione)
C A 3-4
Salaria (via) B C-D 4
Salario (quartiere) C C 1
Salentini (via dei) G B 2
Salento (via) C C 3
Sallustiana (via) B D 3-4
Sallustiano (rione)
B D 3-4
Sallustio (piazza) B D 4
Salvini Tommaso (via)
B A 3
San Bernardo (piazza)
E A 3-4
San Calisto (piazza)
E C 1
San Cipriano (via) A C 1
San Claudio (piazza)
F B 3
San Cosimato (piazza)
D C 4
San Filippo Martire (via)
B A 3-4
San Francesco a Ripa (via) D
C-D 4
San Francesco di Sales
(vicolo di) D B 3-4
San Giovanni (porta)
G D 2
San Giovanni (stazione
metropolitana) G D 2
San Giovanni in Laterano
(via di) E C 4
San Gregorio (via di)
E C-D 3
Sanità Militare (largo della)
E D 3-4
San Lorenzo (piazzale)
G A 3
San Lorenzo in Lucina
(piazza) F B 2
San Lucio (via) D B 1
San Marco (piazza)
F D 3

San Marco (via) F D 3
San Nicola da Tolentino (via)
E A 3
Sannio (via) G D 1
Sanniti (piazza dei)
G B 2
San Pancrazio (via di)
D C 3
San Paolo (lungotevere di)
H C-D 3
San Paolo (stazione
metropolitana) H D 3
San Paolo (viale di)
H D 3
San Paolo del Brasile (viale)
B D 2-3
San Pietro (basilica di)
D A 2
San Pietro (piazza)
D A 3
San Pietro (stazione)
D B 2
San Quintino (via)
G C 1-2
San Roberto Bellarmino (via)
B B 3
San Silvestro (piazza)
E A 2
Santa Balbina (piazza di) E
D 3
Santa Costanza (piazza di)
C B 2
Santa Croce in
Gerusalemme (via)
G C 2
Santa Galla (via di) I B 1
Sant'Alessio (via di) E D 2
Santa Maria alle Fornaci
(piazza) D B 3
Santa Maria dell'Anima
(via di) E A-B 1
Santa Maria delle Grazie
(piazza di) A D 2
Santa Maria in Trastevere
(piazza)
D C 4
Santa Maria Maggiore
(piazza) E B 4
Santa Maria Maggiore (via)
E B 3-4
Santa Maria Mediatrice
(via di) D A-B 1
Sant'Angela Merici (via di)
C B 3
Sant'Angelo (borgo)
F D 2
Sant'Angelo (ponte)
D A 4
Sant'Angelo (rione)
E B 2
Sant'Anselmo (piazza)
E D 2
Sant'Anselmo (via di)
E D 2
Santa Petronilla (via)
I D 2
Santa Prisca (via di)
E D 2
Santa Sabina (via di)
E D 2
Sant'Emerenziana (piazza
di) C A 2
San Teodoro (via)
E C 2
Sant'Eufemia (via) F D 3
Santiago del Cile (piazza)
B A-B 3
Sant'Ignazio (piazza)
F C 2
Sant'Ignazio (via) F C 2
Sant'Ippolito (via di)
C D 3